# JUSTICE SOCIETY OF AMERICA

# MONUMENT POINT

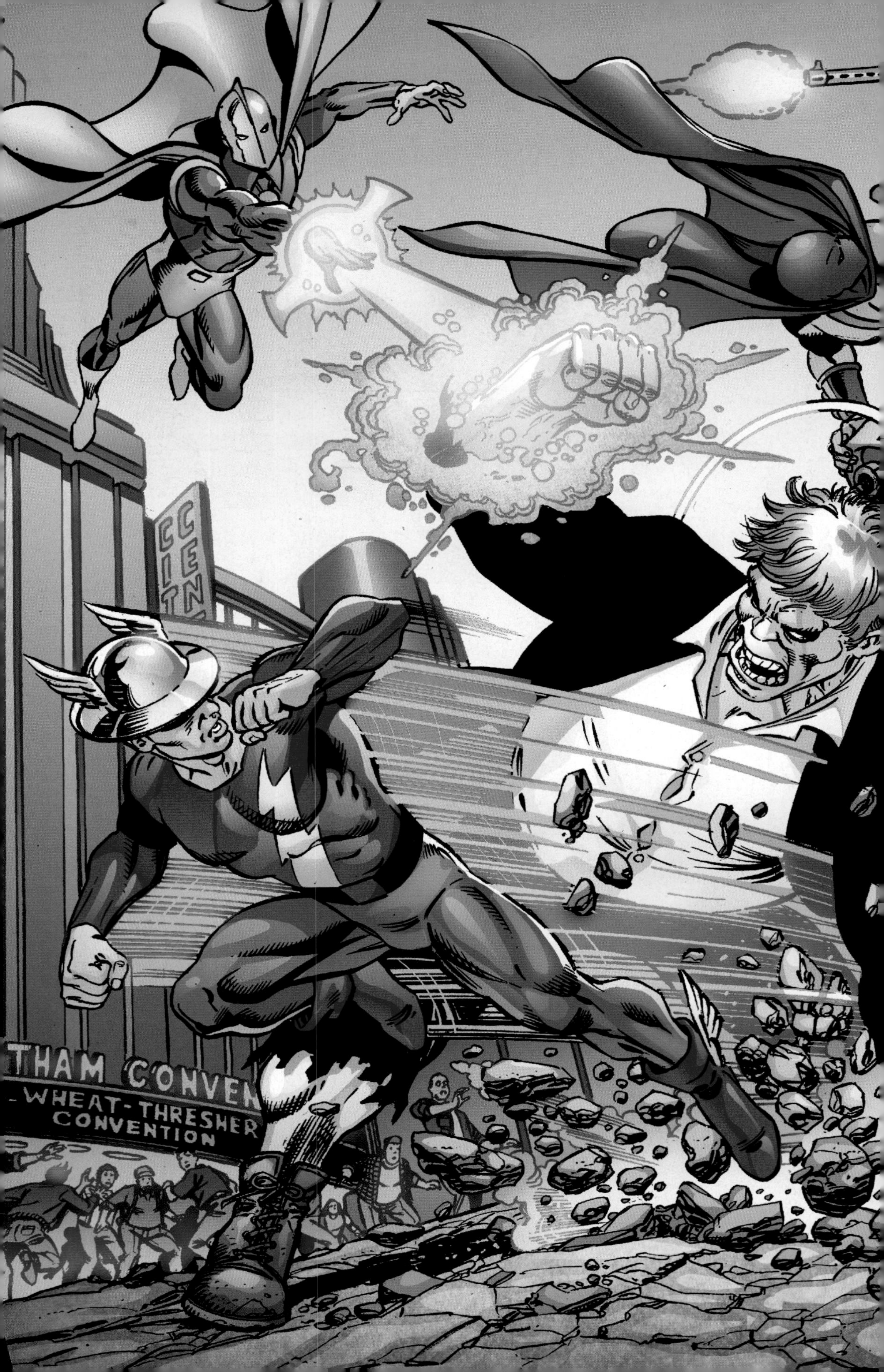

THAM CONVEN
-WHEAT-THRESHER
CONVENTION

# JUSTICE SOCIETY of AMERICA

# MONUMENT POINT

**MARC GUGGENHEIM**
WRITER

**TOM DERENICK**
**JERRY ORDWAY**
SEAN PARSONS
BOB McLEOD
GEORGE PÉREZ
SCOTT KOBLISH
HOWARD CHAYKIN
FREDDIE WILLIAMS II
ARTISTS

**MIKE ATIYEH**
**HI-FI**
**JESUS ABURTOV**
**RICHARD & TANYA HORIE**
COLORISTS

**ROB LEIGH**
LETTERER

**FELIPE MASSAFERA**
COVER

JUSTICE SOCIETY OF AMERICA: MONUMENT POINT

Published by DC Comics. Cover and compilation
Copyright © 2012 DC Comics. All Rights Reserved.

Originally published in single magazine form in
JUSTICE SOCIETY OF AMERICA 50-54 Copyright © 2011
DC Comics. All Rights Reserved. All characters, their
distinctive likenesses and related elements featured in
this publication are trademarks of DC Comics. The
stories, characters and incidents featured in this
publication are entirely fictional. DC Comics does
not read or accept unsolicited ideas, stories or artwork.

DC Comics, 1700 Broadway, New York, NY 10019
A Warner Bros. Entertainment Company
Printed by RR Donnelley, Salem, VA, USA. 1/13/12.
First Printing.
ISBN: 978-1-4012-3368-6

Cover by FELIPE MASSAFERA

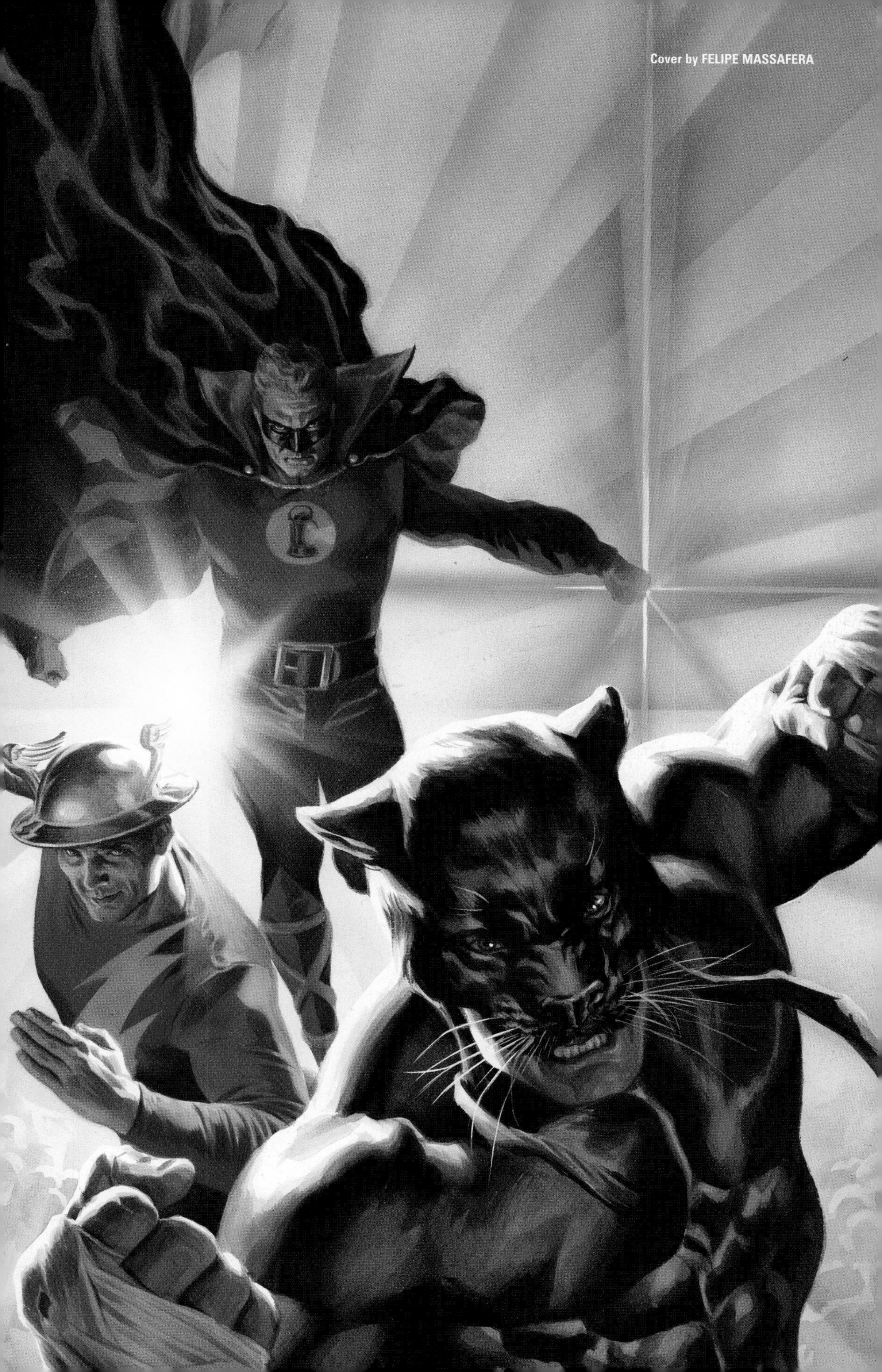

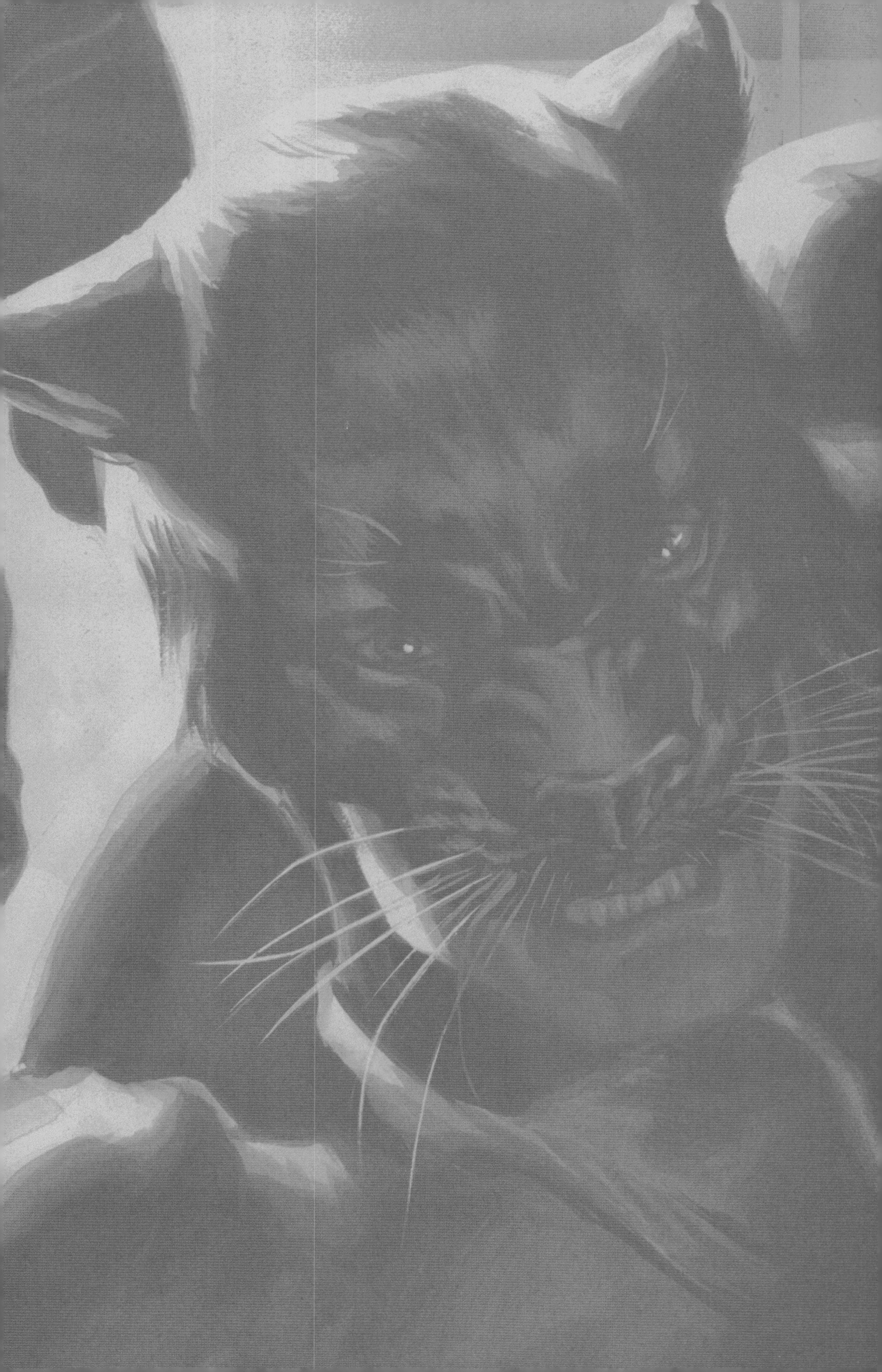

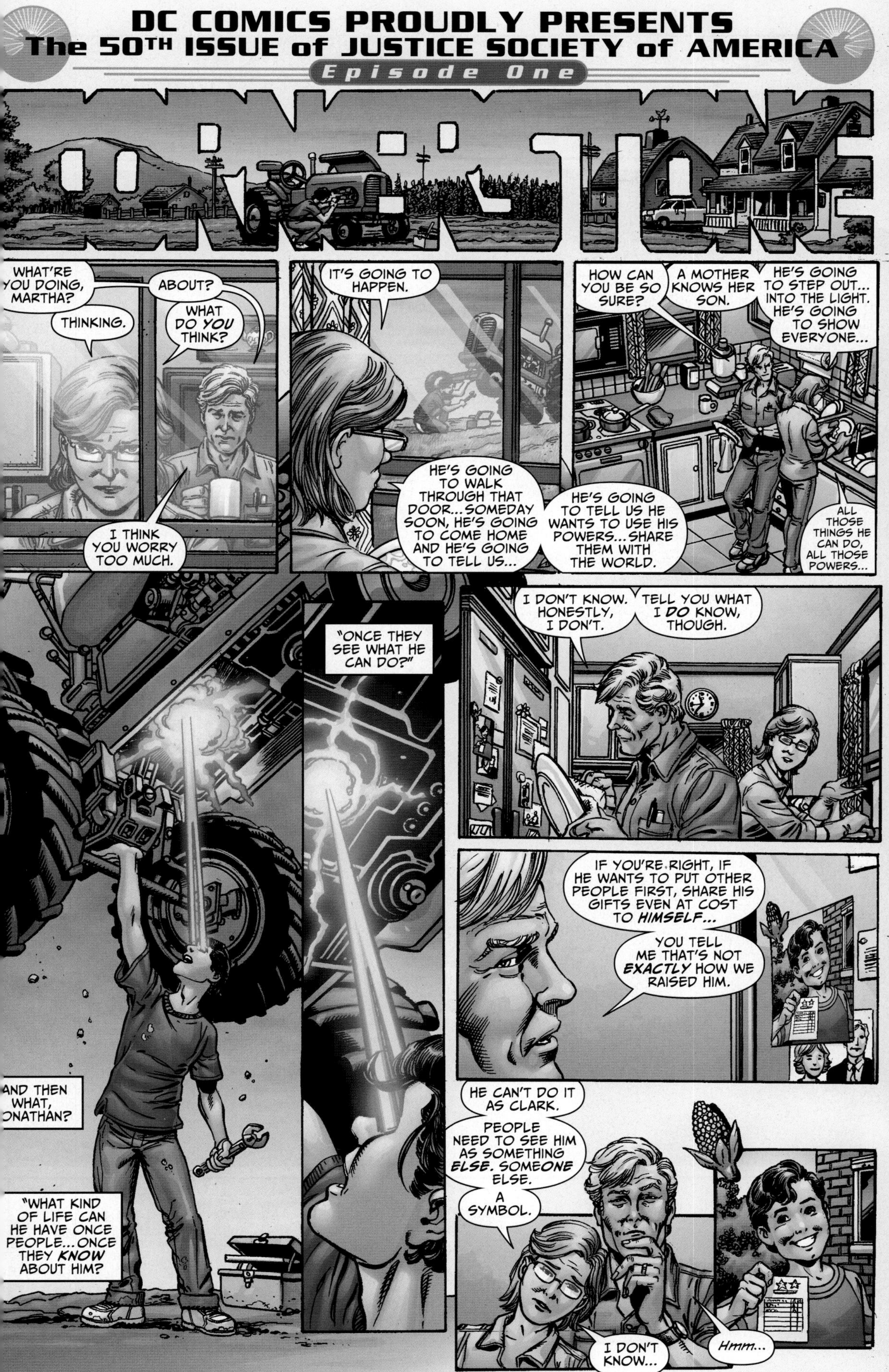
DC COMICS PROUDLY PRESENTS
The 50TH ISSUE of JUSTICE SOCIETY of AMERICA
Episode One
WHAT'RE YOU DOING, MARTHA?
THINKING.
ABOUT?
WHAT DO YOU THINK?
I THINK YOU WORRY TOO MUCH.
IT'S GOING TO HAPPEN.
HE'S GOING TO WALK THROUGH THAT DOOR... SOMEDAY SOON, HE'S GOING TO COME HOME AND HE'S GOING TO TELL US...
HE'S GOING TO TELL US HE WANTS TO USE HIS POWERS... SHARE THEM WITH THE WORLD.
HOW CAN YOU BE SO SURE?
A MOTHER KNOWS HER SON.
HE'S GOING TO STEP OUT... INTO THE LIGHT. HE'S GOING TO SHOW EVERYONE...
ALL THOSE THINGS HE CAN DO, ALL THOSE POWERS...
AND THEN WHAT, JONATHAN?
"WHAT KIND OF LIFE CAN HE HAVE ONCE PEOPLE... ONCE THEY KNOW ABOUT HIM?
"ONCE THEY SEE WHAT HE CAN DO?"
I DON'T KNOW. HONESTLY, I DON'T.
TELL YOU WHAT I DO KNOW, THOUGH.
IF YOU'RE RIGHT, IF HE WANTS TO PUT OTHER PEOPLE FIRST, SHARE HIS GIFTS EVEN AT COST TO HIMSELF...
YOU TELL ME THAT'S NOT EXACTLY HOW WE RAISED HIM.
HE CAN'T DO IT AS CLARK.
PEOPLE NEED TO SEE HIM AS SOMETHING ELSE. SOMEONE ELSE.
A SYMBOL.
I DON'T KNOW...
Hmm...

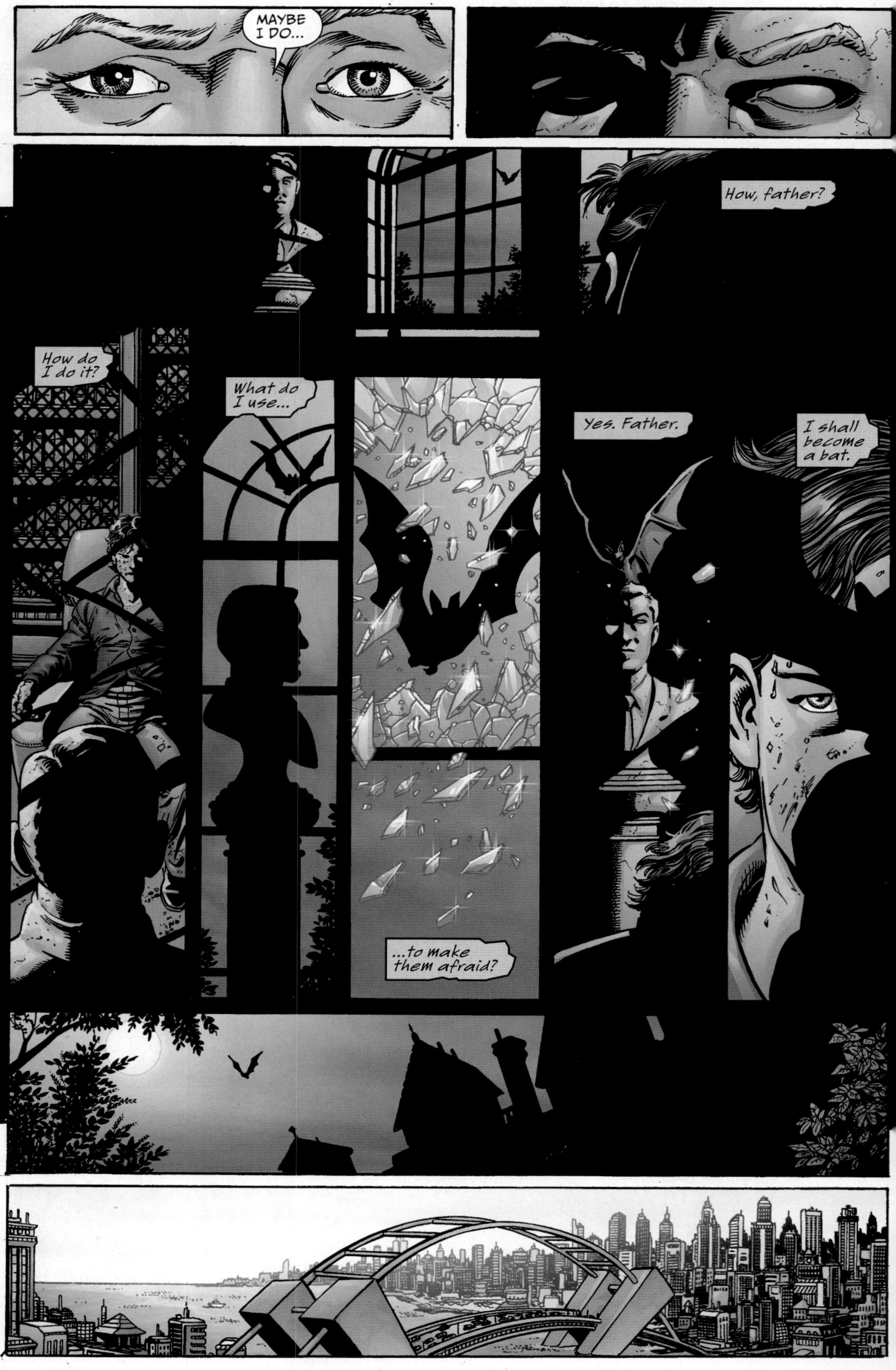
MAYBE I DO...
How, father?
How do I do it?
What do I use...
...to make them afraid?
Yes. Father.
I shall become a bat.

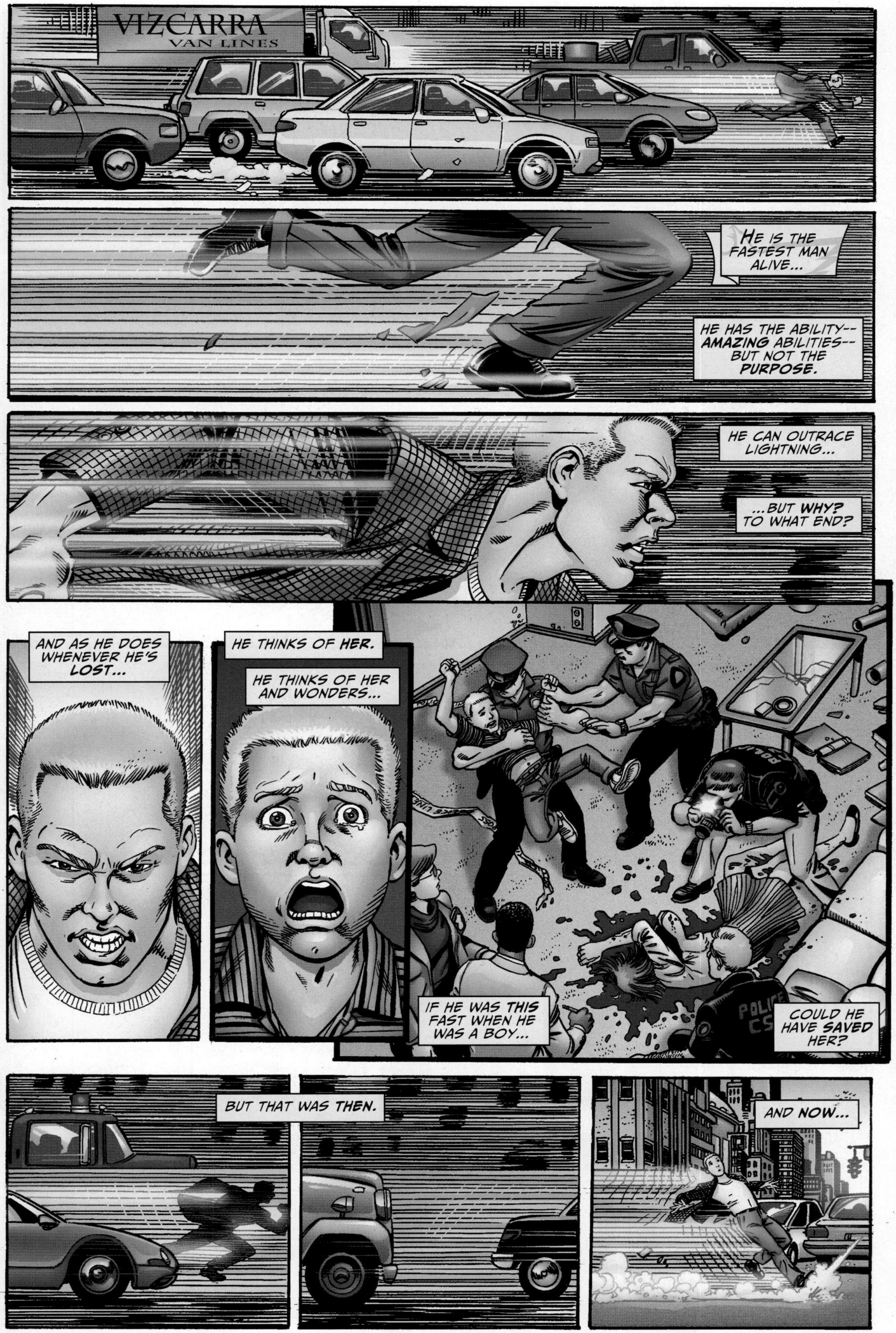
VIZCARRA
VAN LINES
HE IS THE FASTEST MAN ALIVE...
HE HAS THE ABILITY-- **AMAZING** ABILITIES-- BUT NOT THE **PURPOSE.**
HE CAN OUTRACE LIGHTNING...
...BUT **WHY?** TO WHAT END?
AND AS HE DOES WHENEVER HE'S **LOST...**
HE THINKS OF **HER.**
HE THINKS OF HER AND WONDERS...
IF HE WAS **THIS** FAST WHEN HE WAS A BOY...
COULD HE HAVE **SAVED** HER?
BUT THAT WAS **THEN.**
AND **NOW...**

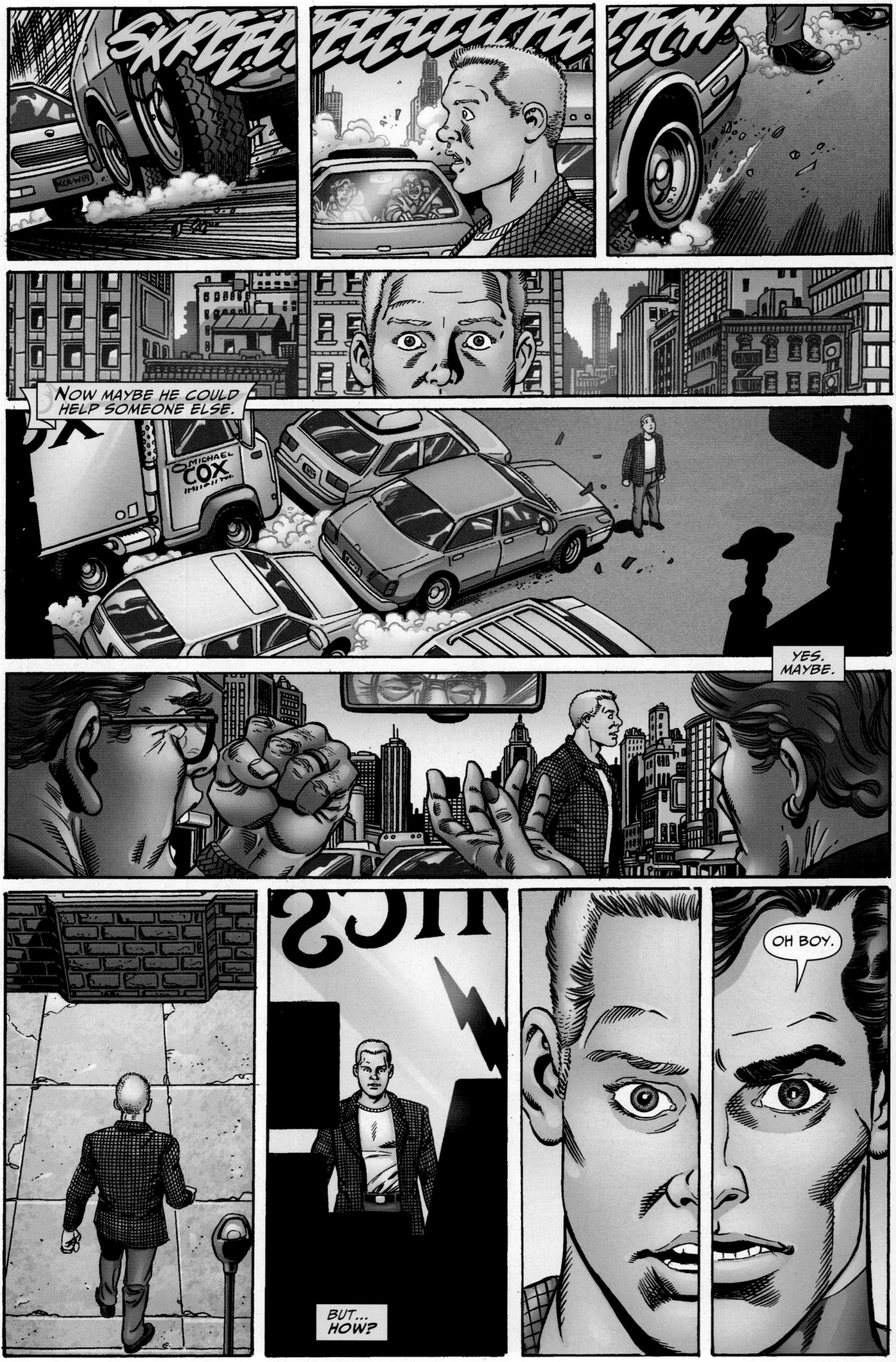
SKREEEEEEEEEEEEEEEEEEECH
NOW MAYBE HE COULD HELP SOMEONE ELSE.
MICHAEL COX
YES. MAYBE.
BUT... HOW?
OH BOY.

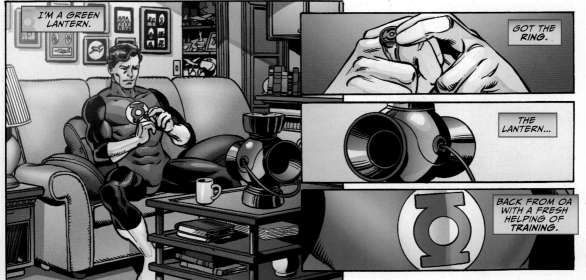

I'M A GREEN LANTERN.

GOT THE RING.

THE LANTERN...

BACK FROM OA WITH A FRESH HELPING OF TRAINING.

I'M A GREEN LANTERN.

I'M GREEN LANTERN.

THE WORLD IS SO TOTALLY SCREWED.

GIVE IT BACK.

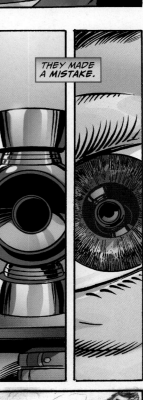

THEY MADE A MISTAKE.

HUGE MISTAKE.

GO BACK UP THERE AND TELL THEM.

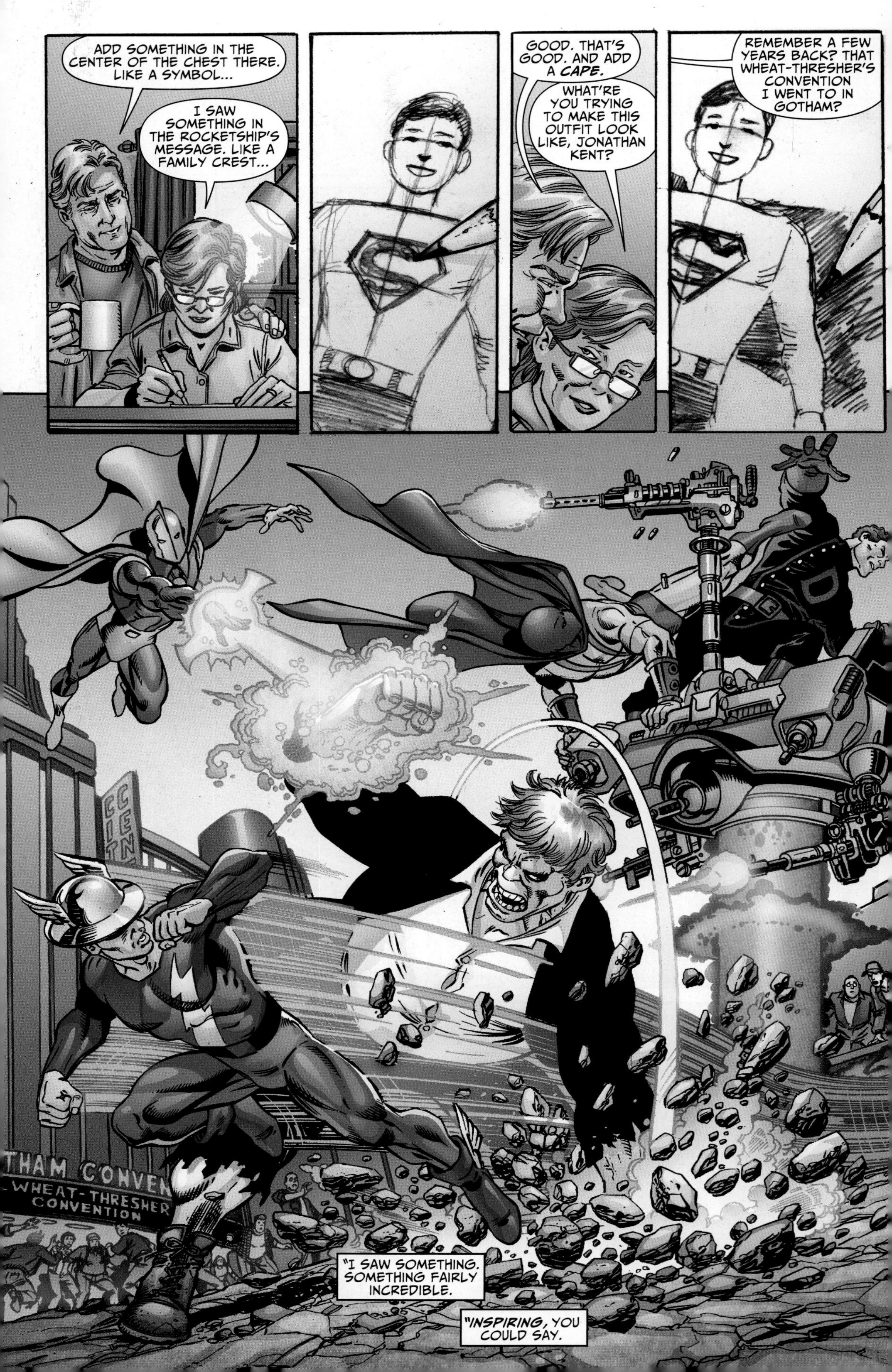
ADD SOMETHING IN THE CENTER OF THE CHEST THERE. LIKE A SYMBOL...
I SAW SOMETHING IN THE ROCKETSHIP'S MESSAGE. LIKE A FAMILY CREST...
GOOD. THAT'S GOOD. AND ADD A *CAPE.*
WHAT'RE YOU TRYING TO MAKE THIS OUTFIT LOOK LIKE, JONATHAN KENT?
REMEMBER A FEW YEARS BACK? THAT WHEAT-THRESHER'S CONVENTION I WENT TO IN GOTHAM?
THAM CONVEN
WHEAT-THRESHER CONVENTION
"I SAW SOMETHING. SOMETHING FAIRLY INCREDIBLE.
"*INSPIRING,* YOU COULD SAY.

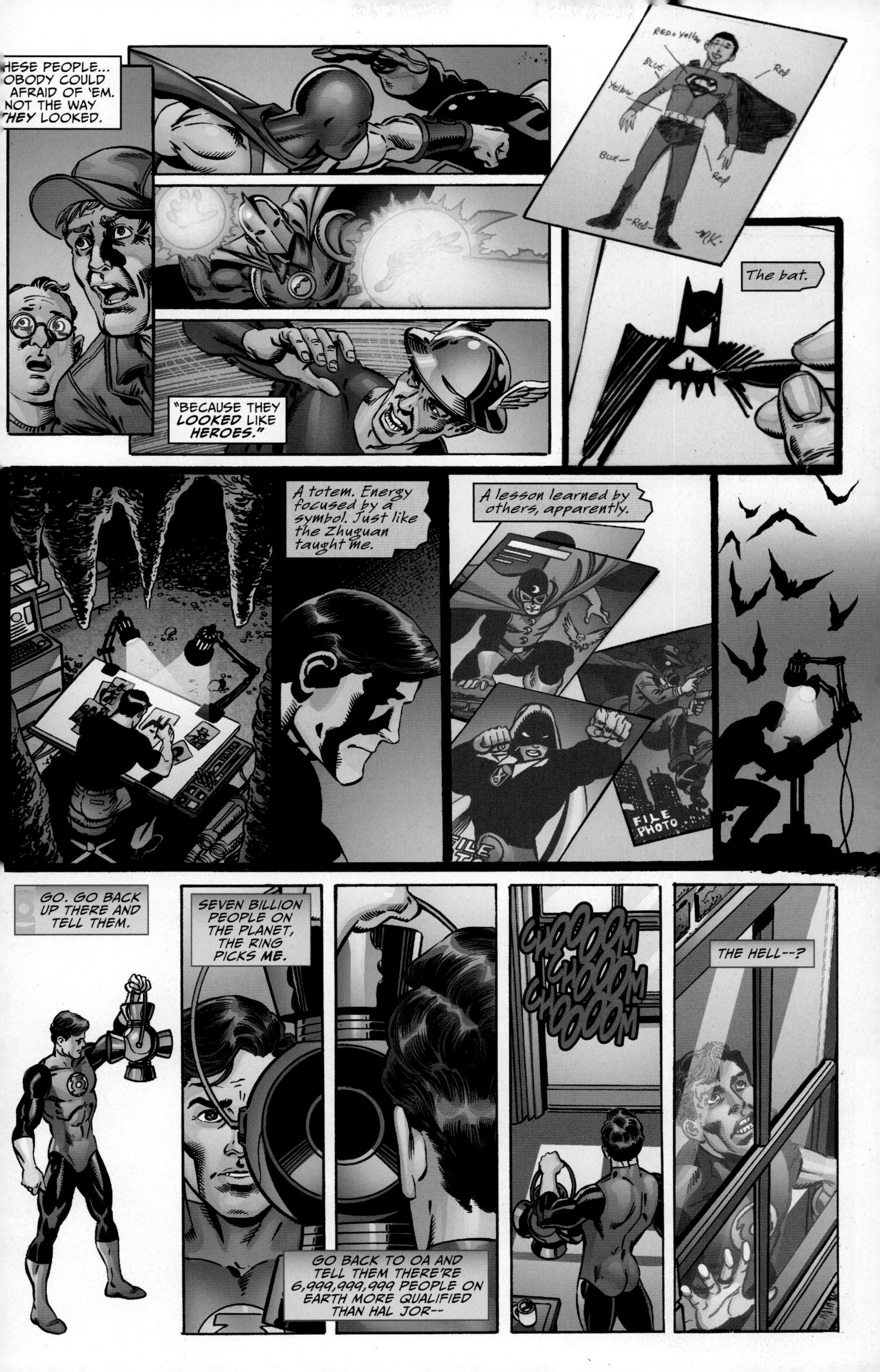

HESE PEOPLE... OBODY COULD AFRAID OF 'EM. NOT THE WAY THEY LOOKED.
"BECAUSE THEY LOOKED LIKE HEROES."
RED + Yellow
BLUE
Red
Yellow
BLUE
Red
Red
The bat.
A totem. Energy focused by a symbol. Just like the Zhuguan taught me.
A lesson learned by others, apparently.
FILE PHOTO
GO. GO BACK UP THERE AND TELL THEM.
SEVEN BILLION PEOPLE ON THE PLANET, THE RING PICKS ME.
GO BACK TO OA AND TELL THEM THERE'RE 6,999,999,999 PEOPLE ON EARTH MORE QUALIFIED THAN HAL JOR--
CHOOOOM CHOOOOM CHOOOOM
THE HELL--?

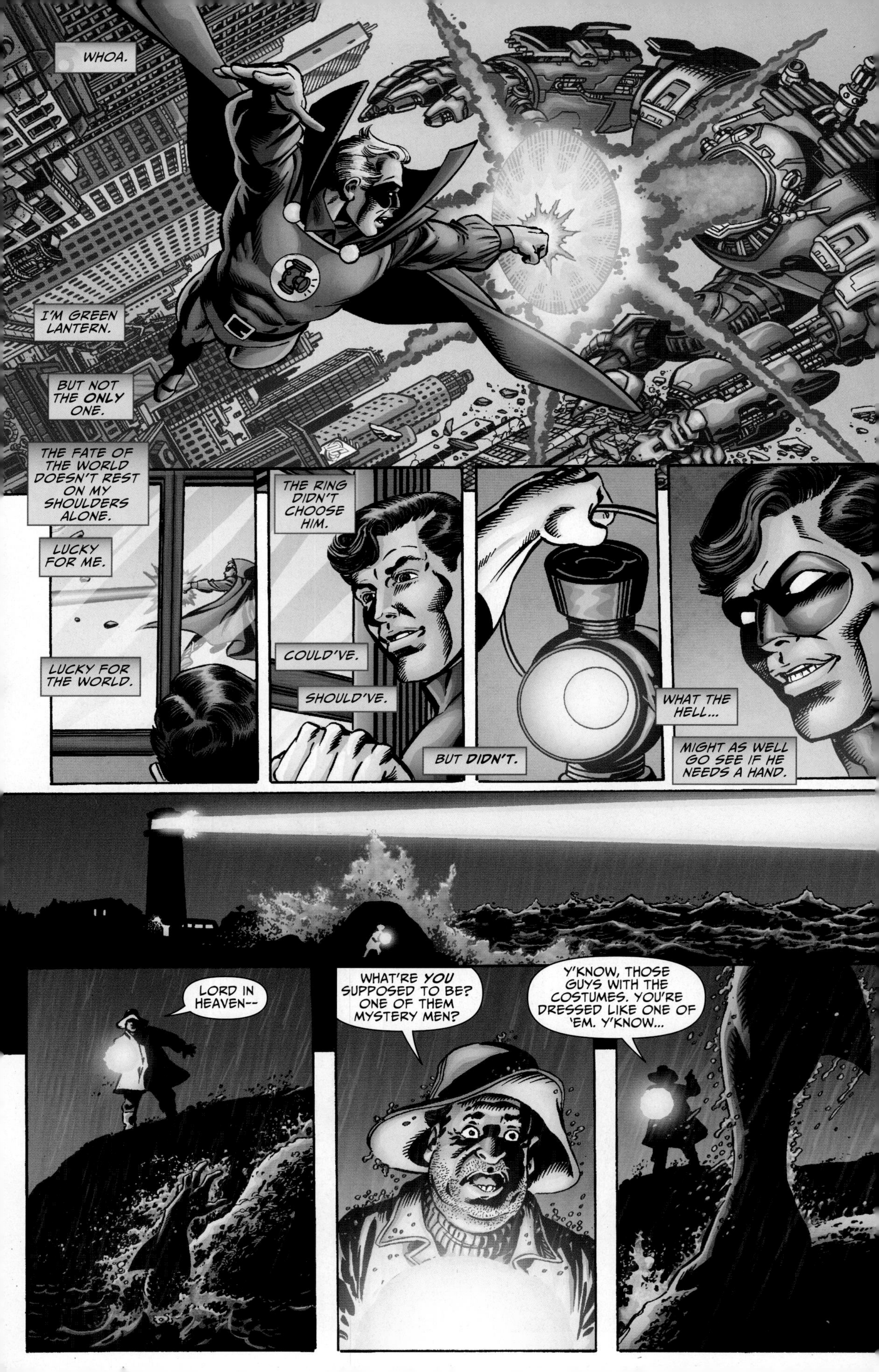
WHOA.
I'M GREEN LANTERN.
BUT NOT THE ONLY ONE.
THE FATE OF THE WORLD DOESN'T REST ON MY SHOULDERS ALONE.
LUCKY FOR ME.
LUCKY FOR THE WORLD.
THE RING DIDN'T CHOOSE HIM.
COULD'VE.
SHOULD'VE.
BUT DIDN'T.
WHAT THE HELL...
MIGHT AS WELL GO SEE IF HE NEEDS A HAND.
LORD IN HEAVEN--
WHAT'RE YOU SUPPOSED TO BE? ONE OF THEM MYSTERY MEN?
Y'KNOW, THOSE GUYS WITH THE COSTUMES. YOU'RE DRESSED LIKE ONE OF 'EM. Y'KNOW...

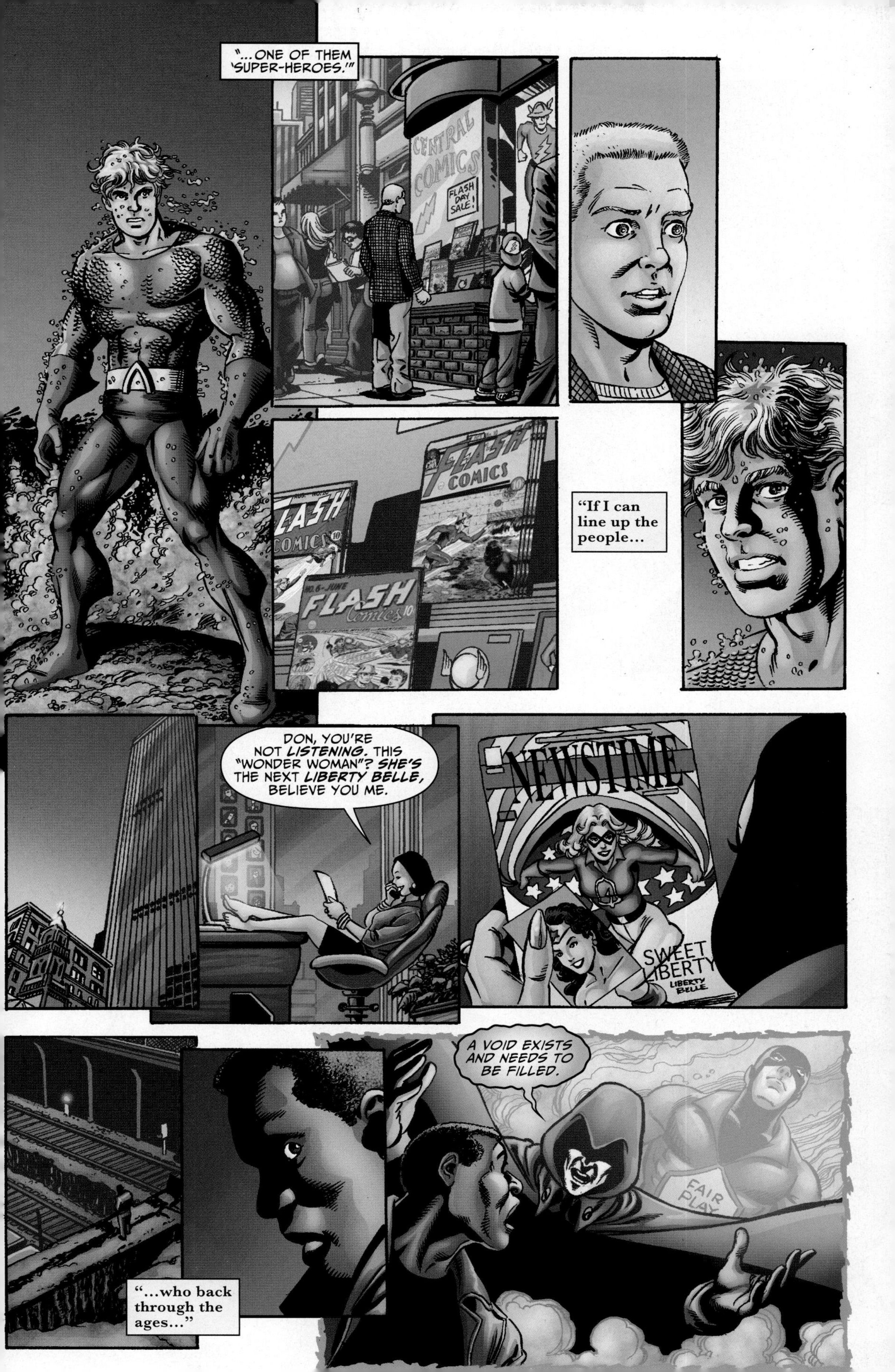
"...ONE OF THEM 'SUPER-HEROES.'"
CENTRAL COMICS
FLASH DAY SALE!
FLASH COMICS
FLASH COMICS
FLASH Comics
"If I can line up the people...
DON, YOU'RE NOT LISTENING. THIS "WONDER WOMAN"? SHE'S THE NEXT LIBERTY BELLE, BELIEVE YOU ME.
NEWSTIME
SWEET LIBERTY
LIBERTY BELLE
A VOID EXISTS AND NEEDS TO BE FILLED.
FAIR PLAY
"...who back through the ages..."

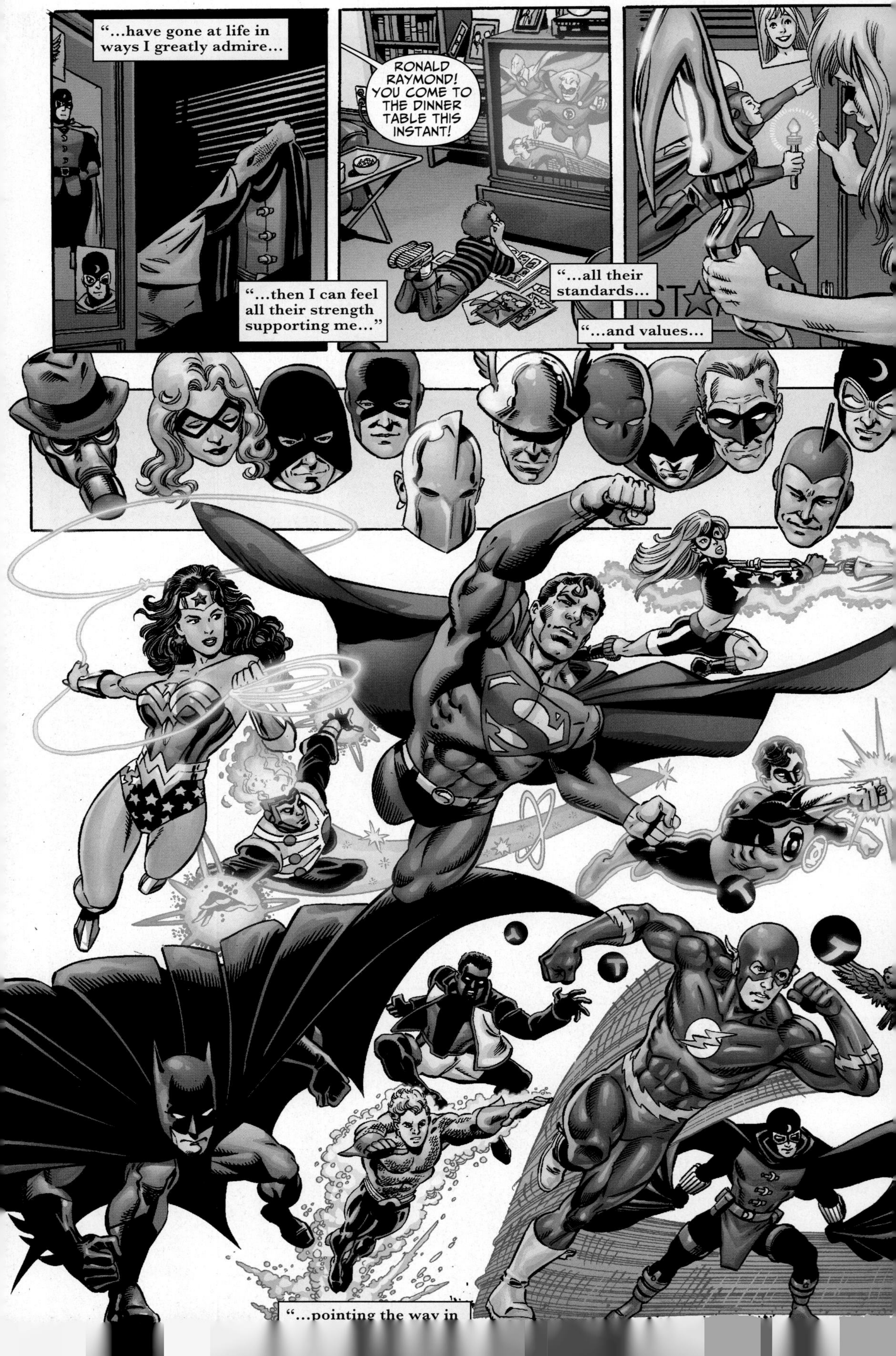
"...have gone at life in ways I greatly admire...
"...then I can feel all their strength supporting me..."
RONALD RAYMOND! YOU COME TO THE DINNER TABLE THIS INSTANT!
"...all their standards...
"...and values...
"...pointing the way in

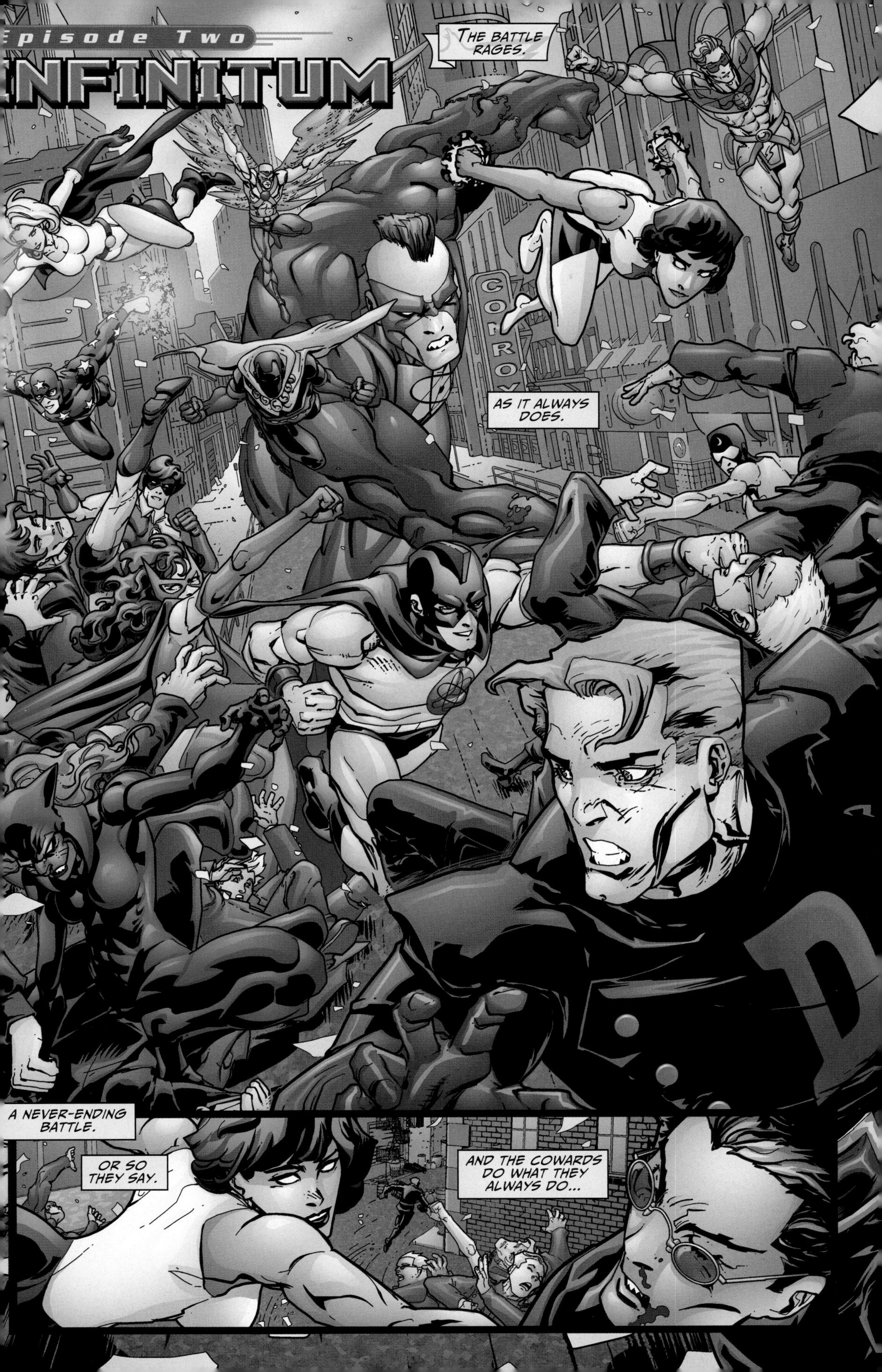
pisode Two
NFINITUM
THE BATTLE RAGES.
AS IT ALWAYS DOES.
A NEVER-ENDING BATTLE.
OR SO THEY SAY.
AND THE COWARDS DO WHAT THEY ALWAYS DO...

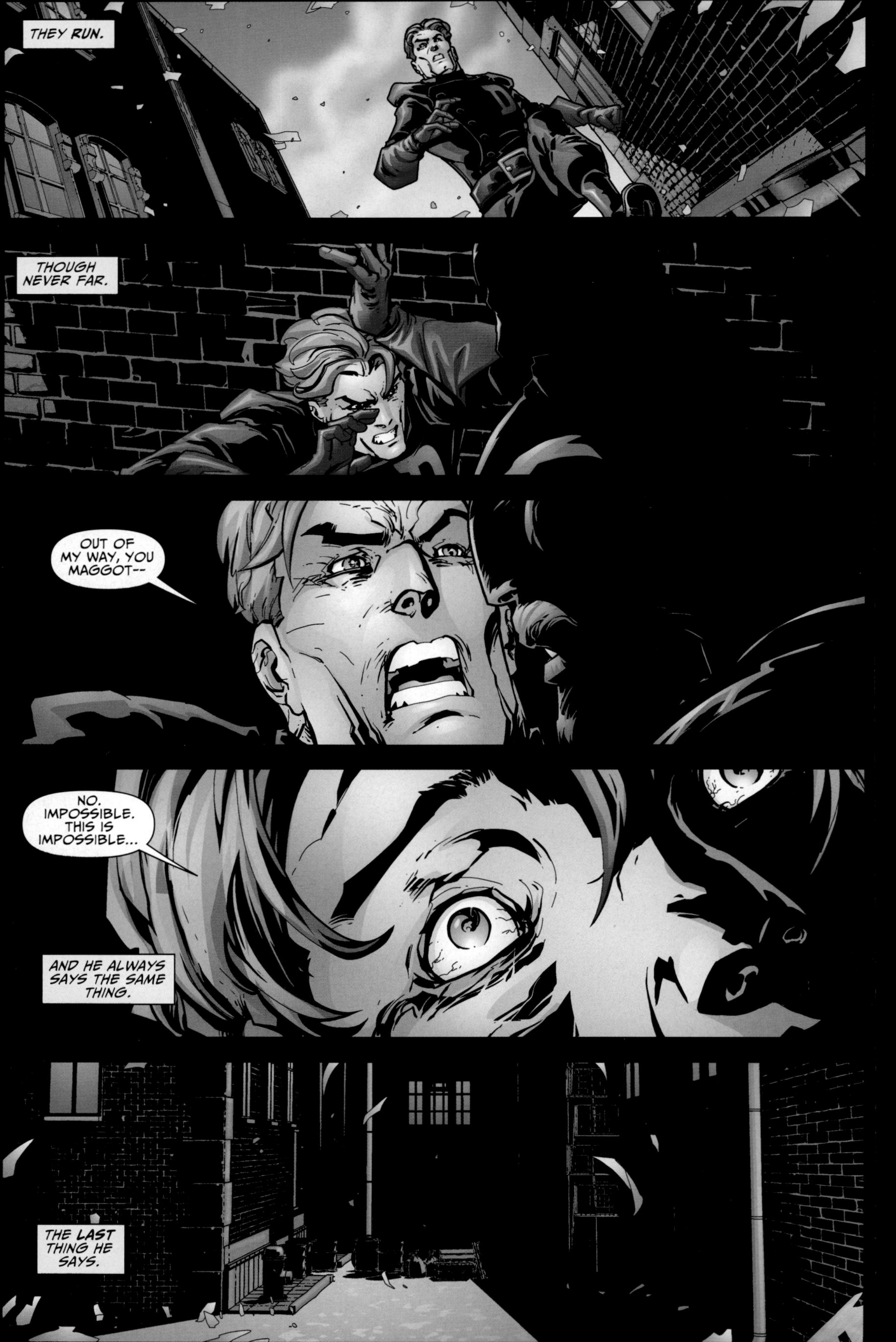
THEY RUN.
THOUGH NEVER FAR.
OUT OF MY WAY, YOU MAGGOT--
NO. IMPOSSIBLE. THIS IS IMPOSSIBLE...
AND HE ALWAYS SAYS THE SAME THING.
THE LAST THING HE SAYS.

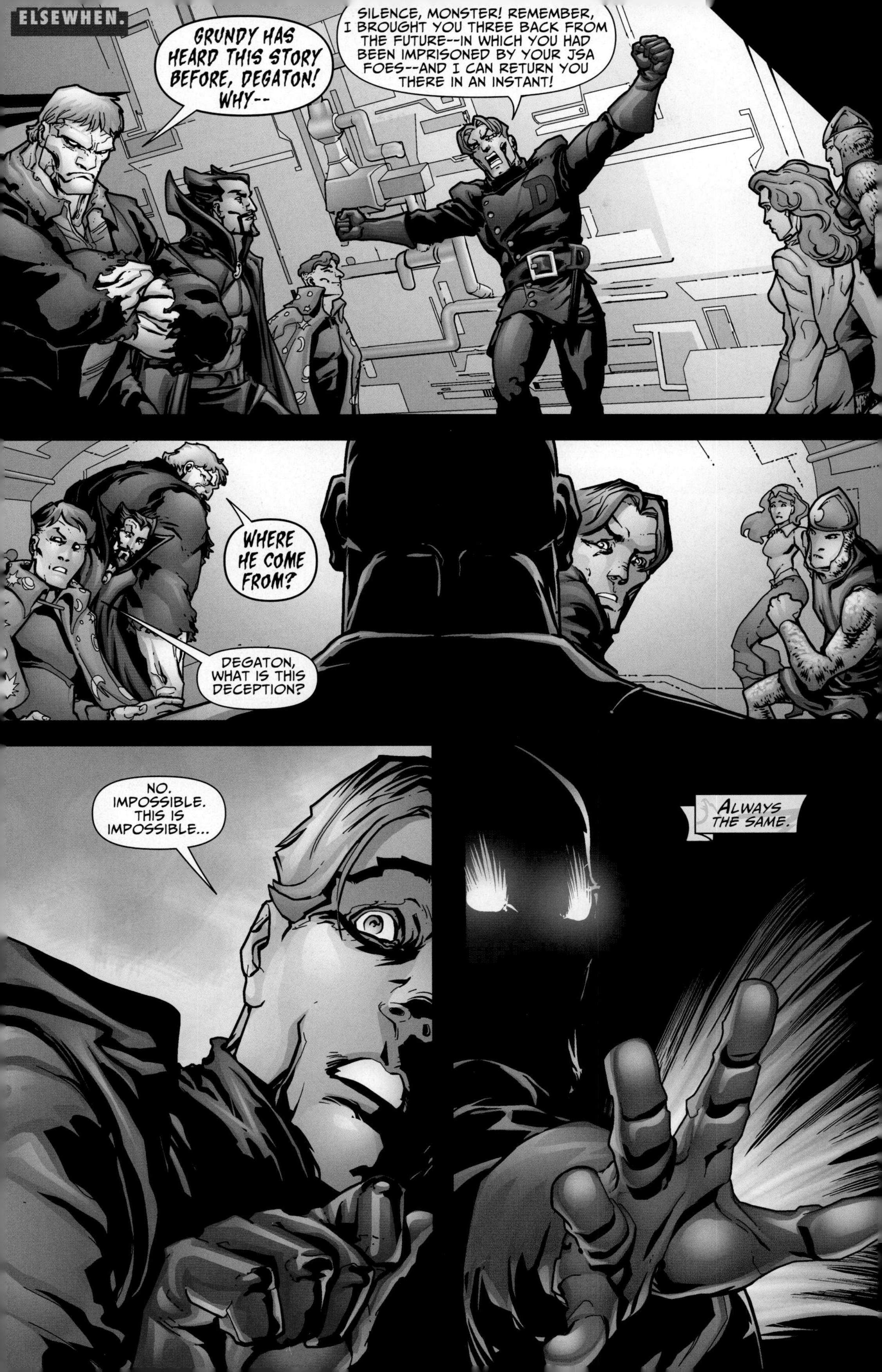
ELSEWHEN.
GRUNDY HAS HEARD THIS STORY BEFORE, DEGATON! WHY--
SILENCE, MONSTER! REMEMBER, I BROUGHT YOU THREE BACK FROM THE FUTURE--IN WHICH YOU HAD BEEN IMPRISONED BY YOUR JSA FOES--AND I CAN RETURN YOU THERE IN AN INSTANT!
WHERE HE COME FROM?
DEGATON, WHAT IS THIS DECEPTION?
NO. IMPOSSIBLE. THIS IS IMPOSSIBLE...
ALWAYS THE SAME.

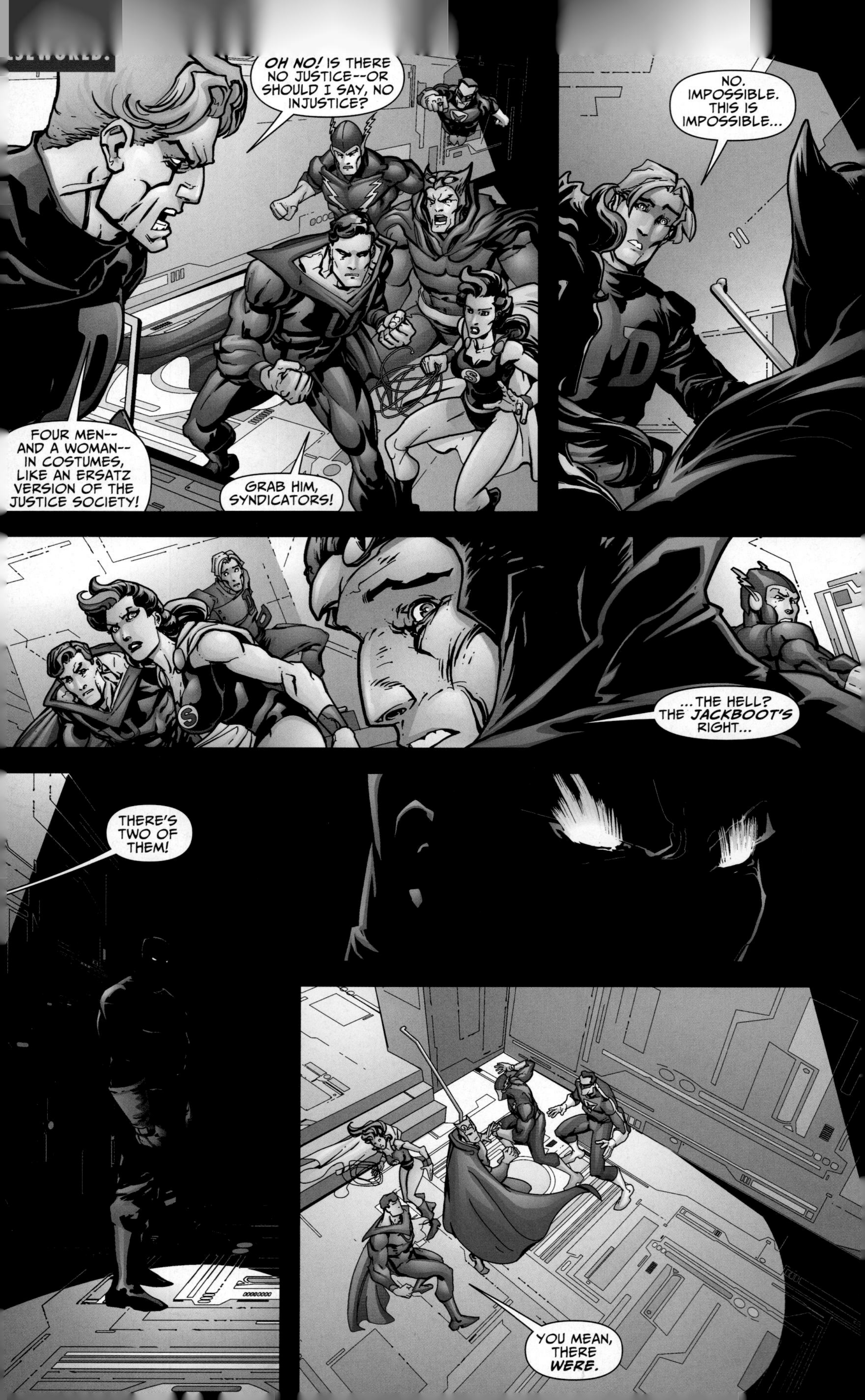
ELSEWORLDS
OH NO! IS THERE NO JUSTICE--OR SHOULD I SAY, NO INJUSTICE?
FOUR MEN--AND A WOMAN--IN COSTUMES, LIKE AN ERSATZ VERSION OF THE JUSTICE SOCIETY!
GRAB HIM, SYNDICATORS!
NO. IMPOSSIBLE. THIS IS IMPOSSIBLE...
...THE HELL? THE JACKBOOT'S RIGHT...
THERE'S TWO OF THEM!
YOU MEAN, THERE WERE.

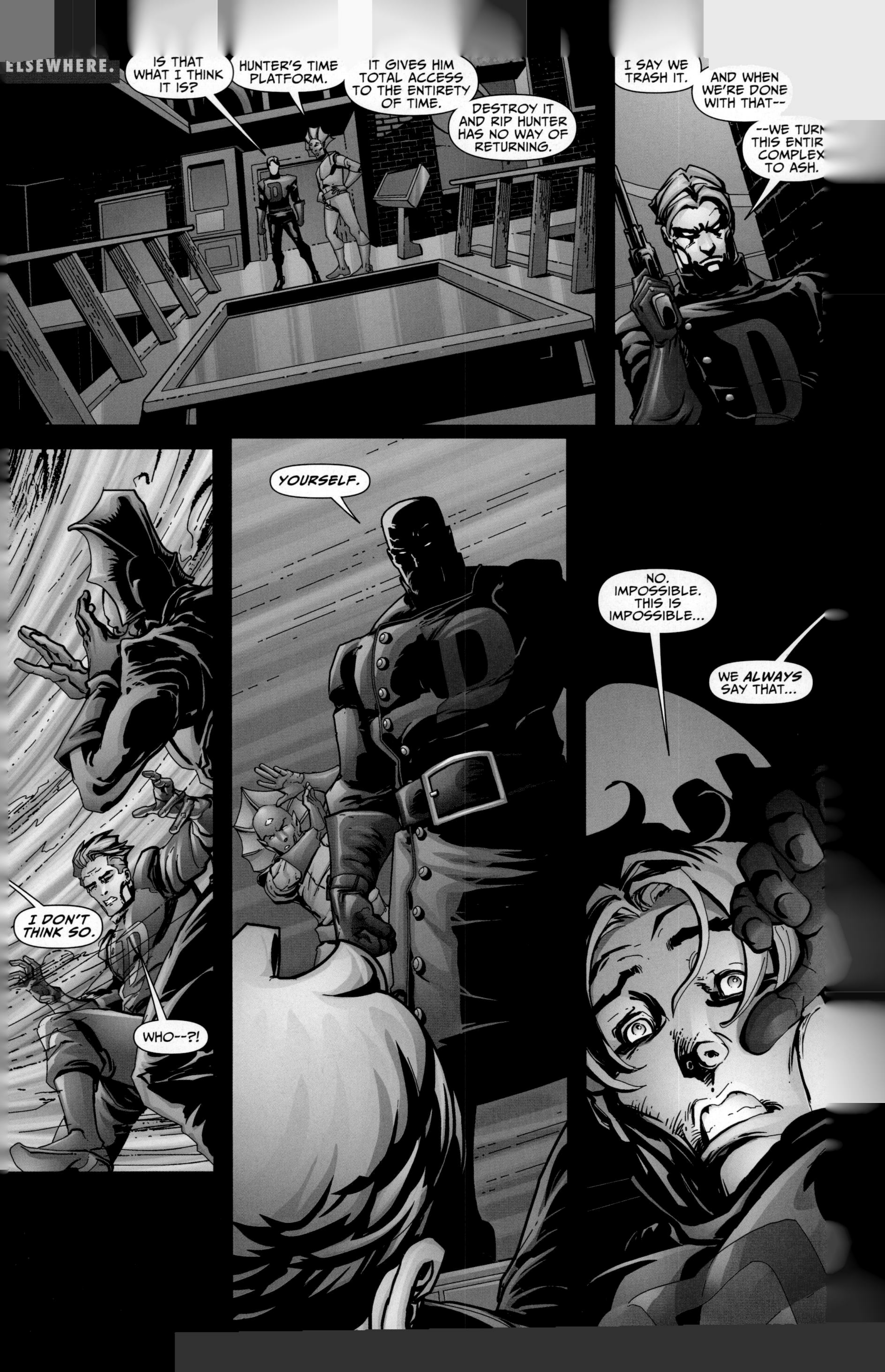
ELSEWHERE.
IS THAT WHAT I THINK IT IS?
HUNTER'S TIME PLATFORM.
IT GIVES HIM TOTAL ACCESS TO THE ENTIRETY OF TIME.
DESTROY IT AND RIP HUNTER HAS NO WAY OF RETURNING.
I SAY WE TRASH IT.
AND WHEN WE'RE DONE WITH THAT--
--WE TURN THIS ENTIR COMPLEX TO ASH.
I DON'T THINK SO.
WHO--?!
YOURSELF.
NO. IMPOSSIBLE. THIS IS IMPOSSIBLE...
WE ALWAYS SAY THAT...

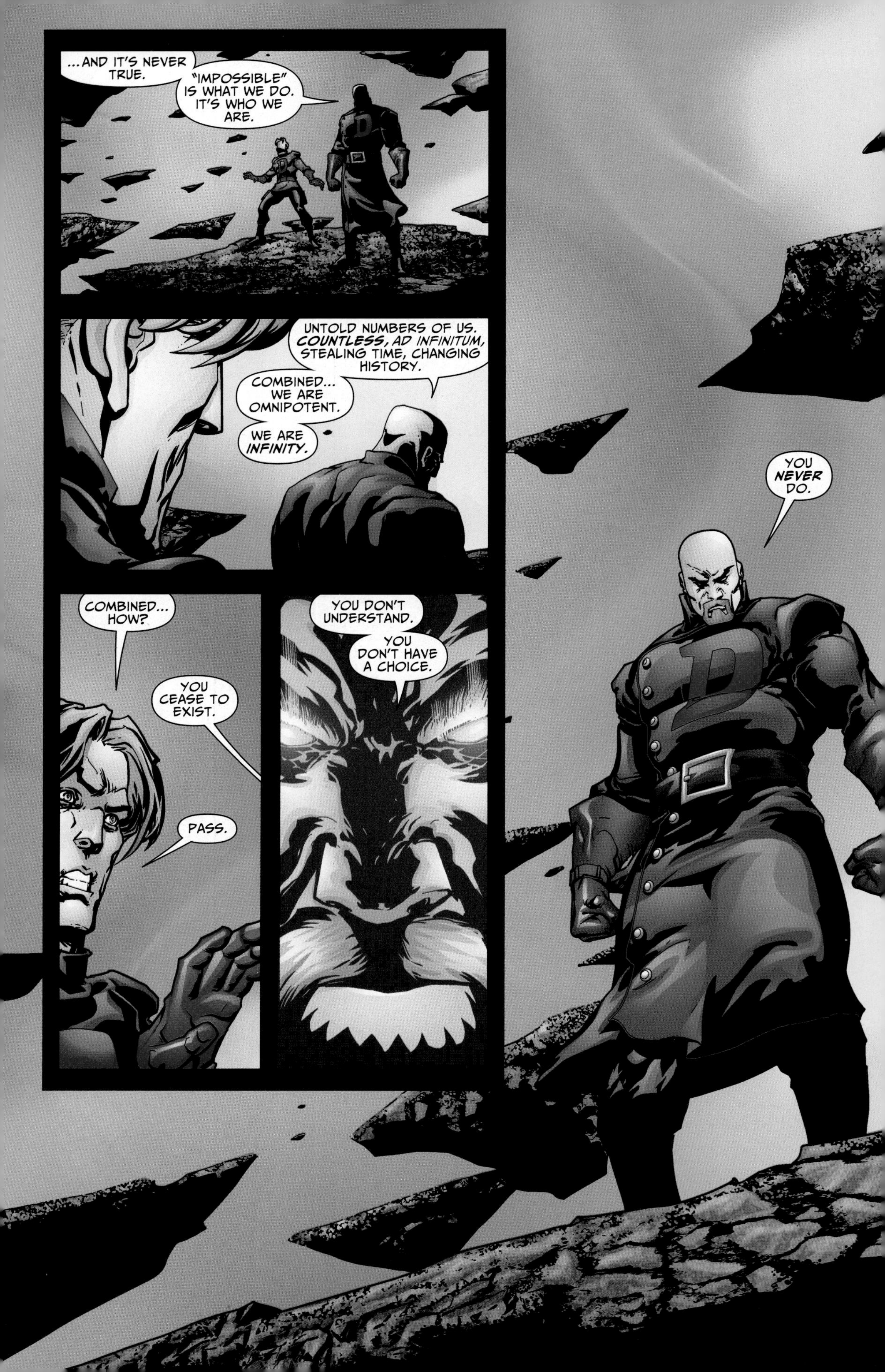
...AND IT'S NEVER TRUE.
"IMPOSSIBLE" IS WHAT WE DO. IT'S WHO WE ARE.
UNTOLD NUMBERS OF US. COUNTLESS, AD INFINITUM, STEALING TIME, CHANGING HISTORY.
COMBINED... WE ARE OMNIPOTENT.
WE ARE INFINITY.
COMBINED... HOW?
YOU CEASE TO EXIST.
PASS.
YOU DON'T UNDERSTAND.
YOU DON'T HAVE A CHOICE.
YOU NEVER DO.

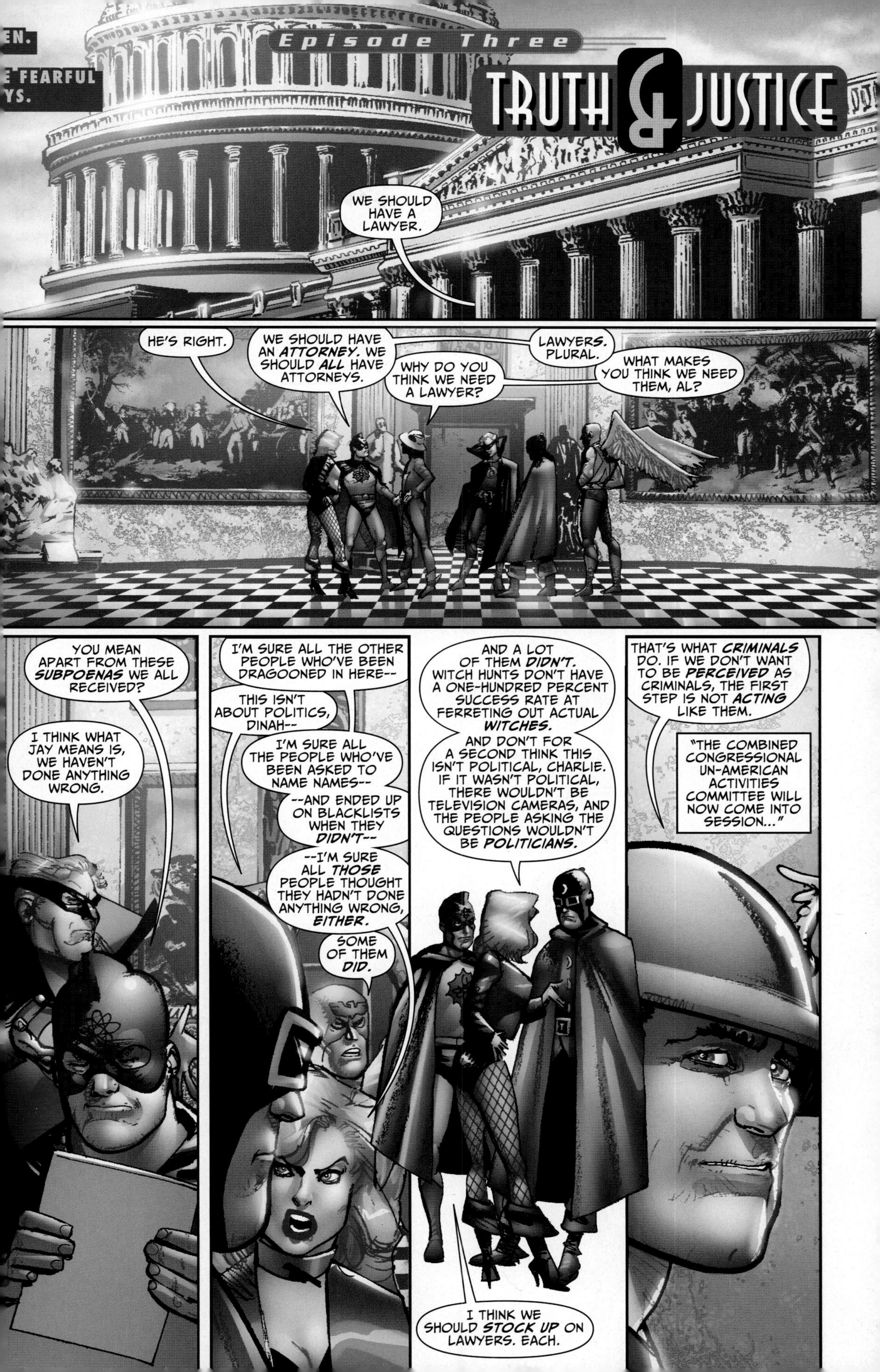
EN.
E FEARFUL
YS.
Episode Three
TRUTH & JUSTICE
WE SHOULD HAVE A LAWYER.
HE'S RIGHT.
WE SHOULD HAVE AN ATTORNEY. WE SHOULD ALL HAVE ATTORNEYS.
LAWYERS. PLURAL.
WHY DO YOU THINK WE NEED A LAWYER?
WHAT MAKES YOU THINK WE NEED THEM, AL?
YOU MEAN APART FROM THESE SUBPOENAS WE ALL RECEIVED?
I THINK WHAT JAY MEANS IS, WE HAVEN'T DONE ANYTHING WRONG.
I'M SURE ALL THE OTHER PEOPLE WHO'VE BEEN DRAGOONED IN HERE--
THIS ISN'T ABOUT POLITICS, DINAH--
I'M SURE ALL THE PEOPLE WHO'VE BEEN ASKED TO NAME NAMES--
--AND ENDED UP ON BLACKLISTS WHEN THEY DIDN'T--
--I'M SURE ALL THOSE PEOPLE THOUGHT THEY HADN'T DONE ANYTHING WRONG, EITHER.
SOME OF THEM DID.
AND A LOT OF THEM DIDN'T. WITCH HUNTS DON'T HAVE A ONE-HUNDRED PERCENT SUCCESS RATE AT FERRETING OUT ACTUAL WITCHES.
AND DON'T FOR A SECOND THINK THIS ISN'T POLITICAL, CHARLIE. IF IT WASN'T POLITICAL, THERE WOULDN'T BE TELEVISION CAMERAS, AND THE PEOPLE ASKING THE QUESTIONS WOULDN'T BE POLITICIANS.
I THINK WE SHOULD STOCK UP ON LAWYERS. EACH.
THAT'S WHAT CRIMINALS DO. IF WE DON'T WANT TO BE PERCEIVED AS CRIMINALS, THE FIRST STEP IS NOT ACTING LIKE THEM.
"THE COMBINED CONGRESSIONAL UN-AMERICAN ACTIVITIES COMMITTEE WILL NOW COME INTO SESSION..."

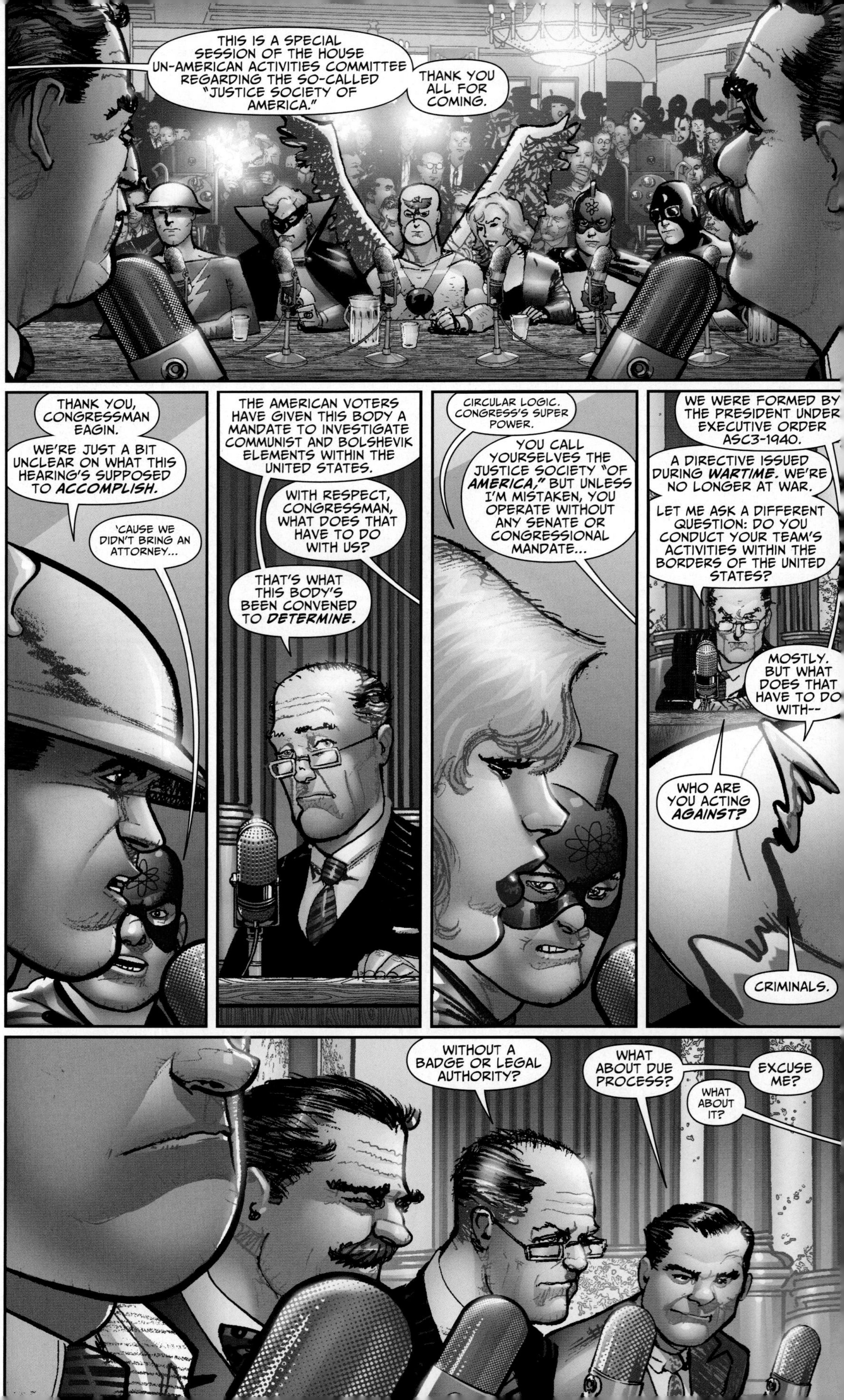
THIS IS A SPECIAL SESSION OF THE HOUSE UN-AMERICAN ACTIVITIES COMMITTEE REGARDING THE SO-CALLED "JUSTICE SOCIETY OF AMERICA."
THANK YOU ALL FOR COMING.
THANK YOU, CONGRESSMAN EAGIN.
WE'RE JUST A BIT UNCLEAR ON WHAT THIS HEARING'S SUPPOSED TO ACCOMPLISH.
'CAUSE WE DIDN'T BRING AN ATTORNEY...
THE AMERICAN VOTERS HAVE GIVEN THIS BODY A MANDATE TO INVESTIGATE COMMUNIST AND BOLSHEVIK ELEMENTS WITHIN THE UNITED STATES.
WITH RESPECT, CONGRESSMAN, WHAT DOES THAT HAVE TO DO WITH US?
THAT'S WHAT THIS BODY'S BEEN CONVENED TO DETERMINE.
CIRCULAR LOGIC. CONGRESS'S SUPER POWER.
YOU CALL YOURSELVES THE JUSTICE SOCIETY "OF AMERICA," BUT UNLESS I'M MISTAKEN, YOU OPERATE WITHOUT ANY SENATE OR CONGRESSIONAL MANDATE...
WE WERE FORMED BY THE PRESIDENT UNDER EXECUTIVE ORDER ASC3-1940.
A DIRECTIVE ISSUED DURING WARTIME. WE'RE NO LONGER AT WAR.
LET ME ASK A DIFFERENT QUESTION: DO YOU CONDUCT YOUR TEAM'S ACTIVITIES WITHIN THE BORDERS OF THE UNITED STATES?
MOSTLY. BUT WHAT DOES THAT HAVE TO DO WITH--
WHO ARE YOU ACTING AGAINST?
CRIMINALS.
WITHOUT A BADGE OR LEGAL AUTHORITY?
WHAT ABOUT DUE PROCESS?
EXCUSE ME?
WHAT ABOUT IT?

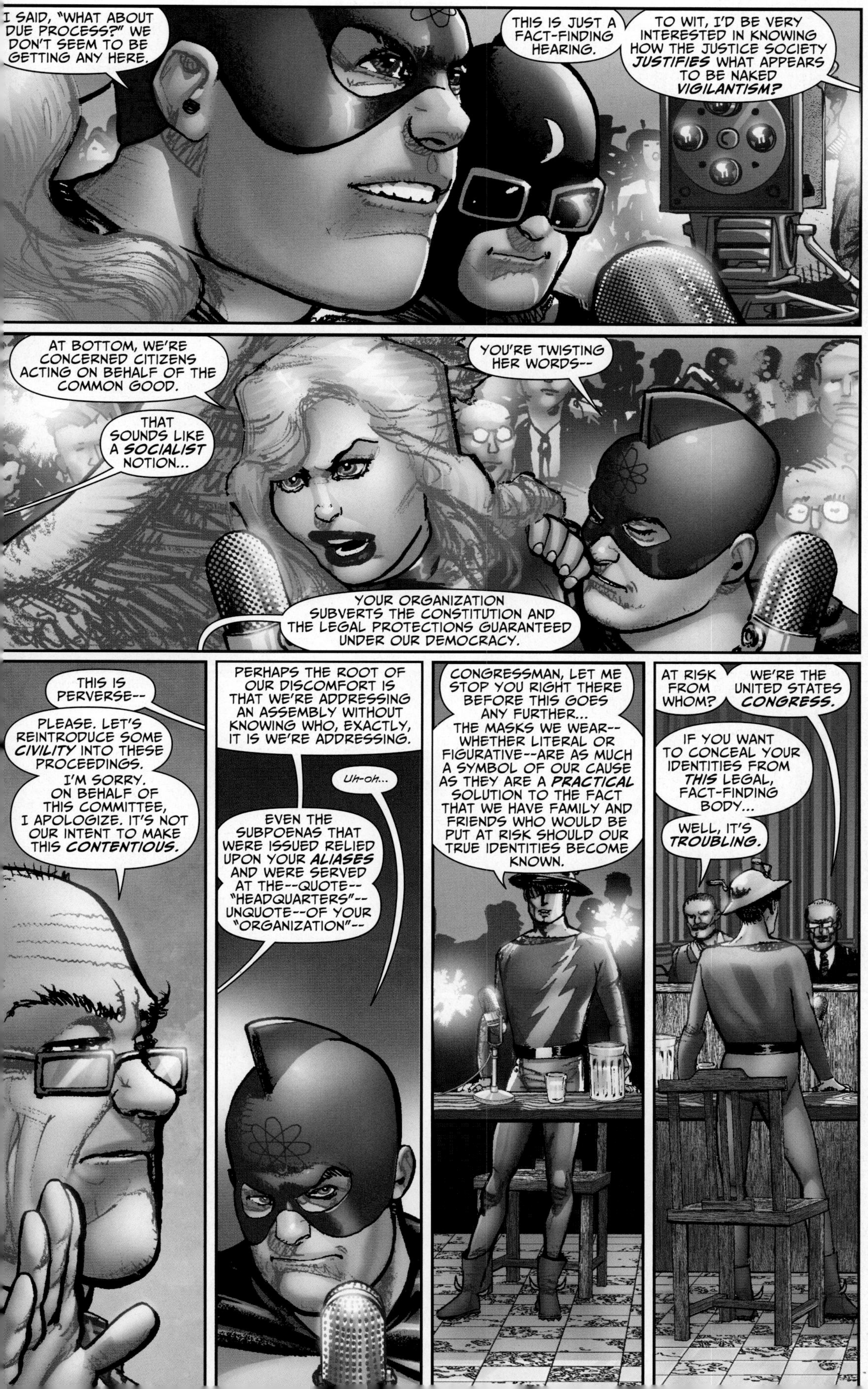

I SAID, "WHAT ABOUT DUE PROCESS?" WE DON'T SEEM TO BE GETTING ANY HERE.
THIS IS JUST A FACT-FINDING HEARING.
TO WIT, I'D BE VERY INTERESTED IN KNOWING HOW THE JUSTICE SOCIETY JUSTIFIES WHAT APPEARS TO BE NAKED VIGILANTISM?
AT BOTTOM, WE'RE CONCERNED CITIZENS ACTING ON BEHALF OF THE COMMON GOOD.
THAT SOUNDS LIKE A SOCIALIST NOTION...
YOU'RE TWISTING HER WORDS--
YOUR ORGANIZATION SUBVERTS THE CONSTITUTION AND THE LEGAL PROTECTIONS GUARANTEED UNDER OUR DEMOCRACY.
THIS IS PERVERSE--
PLEASE. LET'S REINTRODUCE SOME CIVILITY INTO THESE PROCEEDINGS.
I'M SORRY. ON BEHALF OF THIS COMMITTEE, I APOLOGIZE. IT'S NOT OUR INTENT TO MAKE THIS CONTENTIOUS.
PERHAPS THE ROOT OF OUR DISCOMFORT IS THAT WE'RE ADDRESSING AN ASSEMBLY WITHOUT KNOWING WHO, EXACTLY, IT IS WE'RE ADDRESSING.
Uh-oh...
EVEN THE SUBPOENAS THAT WERE ISSUED RELIED UPON YOUR ALIASES AND WERE SERVED AT THE--QUOTE--"HEADQUARTERS"--UNQUOTE--OF YOUR "ORGANIZATION"--
CONGRESSMAN, LET ME STOP YOU RIGHT THERE BEFORE THIS GOES ANY FURTHER...
THE MASKS WE WEAR--WHETHER LITERAL OR FIGURATIVE--ARE AS MUCH A SYMBOL OF OUR CAUSE AS THEY ARE A PRACTICAL SOLUTION TO THE FACT THAT WE HAVE FAMILY AND FRIENDS WHO WOULD BE PUT AT RISK SHOULD OUR TRUE IDENTITIES BECOME KNOWN.
AT RISK FROM WHOM?
WE'RE THE UNITED STATES CONGRESS.
IF YOU WANT TO CONCEAL YOUR IDENTITIES FROM THIS LEGAL, FACT-FINDING BODY...
WELL, IT'S TROUBLING.

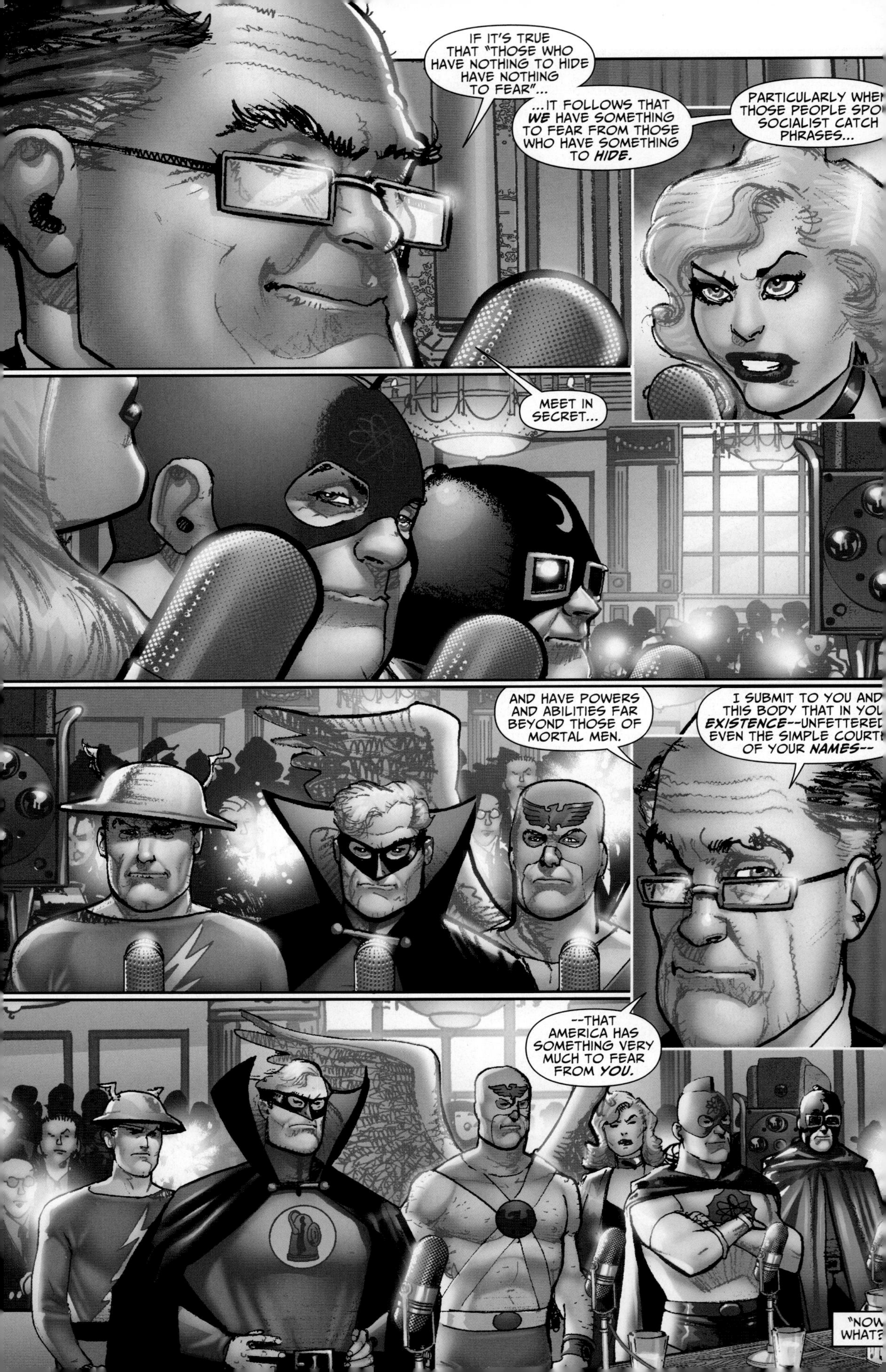

IF IT'S TRUE THAT "THOSE WHO HAVE NOTHING TO HIDE HAVE NOTHING TO FEAR"...
...IT FOLLOWS THAT WE HAVE SOMETHING TO FEAR FROM THOSE WHO HAVE SOMETHING TO HIDE.
PARTICULARLY WHEN THOSE PEOPLE SPO SOCIALIST CATCH PHRASES...
MEET IN SECRET...
AND HAVE POWERS AND ABILITIES FAR BEYOND THOSE OF MORTAL MEN.
I SUBMIT TO YOU AND THIS BODY THAT IN YOU EXISTENCE--UNFETTERED EVEN THE SIMPLE COURT OF YOUR NAMES--
--THAT AMERICA HAS SOMETHING VERY MUCH TO FEAR FROM YOU.
"NOW WHAT?

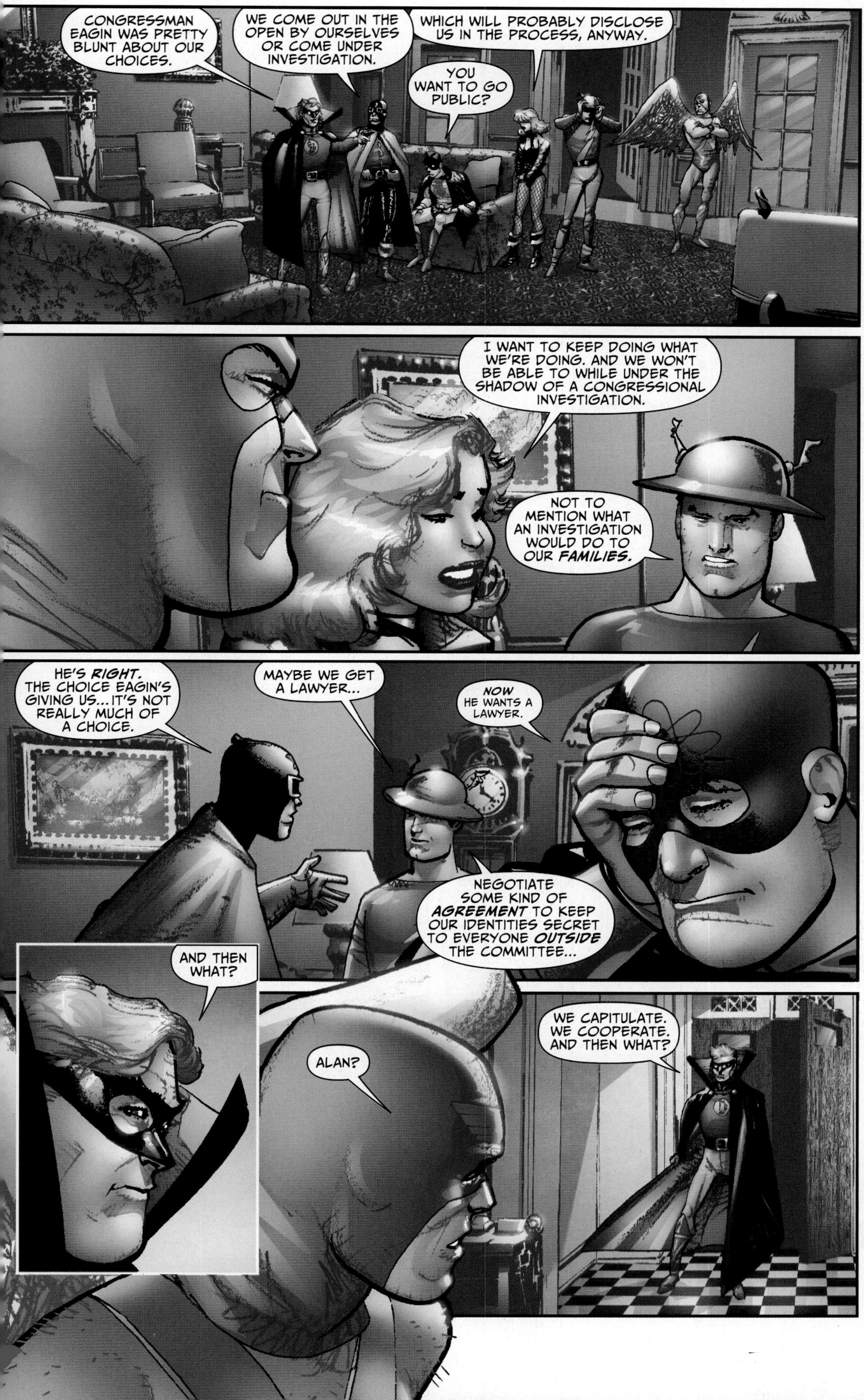
CONGRESSMAN EAGIN WAS PRETTY BLUNT ABOUT OUR CHOICES.
WE COME OUT IN THE OPEN BY OURSELVES OR COME UNDER INVESTIGATION.
YOU WANT TO GO PUBLIC?
WHICH WILL PROBABLY DISCLOSE US IN THE PROCESS, ANYWAY.
I WANT TO KEEP DOING WHAT WE'RE DOING. AND WE WON'T BE ABLE TO WHILE UNDER THE SHADOW OF A CONGRESSIONAL INVESTIGATION.
NOT TO MENTION WHAT AN INVESTIGATION WOULD DO TO OUR *FAMILIES.*
HE'S *RIGHT.* THE CHOICE EAGIN'S GIVING US... IT'S NOT REALLY MUCH OF A CHOICE.
MAYBE WE GET A LAWYER...
*NOW* HE WANTS A LAWYER.
NEGOTIATE SOME KIND OF *AGREEMENT* TO KEEP OUR IDENTITIES SECRET TO EVERYONE *OUTSIDE* THE COMMITTEE...
AND THEN WHAT?
ALAN?
WE CAPITULATE. WE COOPERATE. AND THEN WHAT?

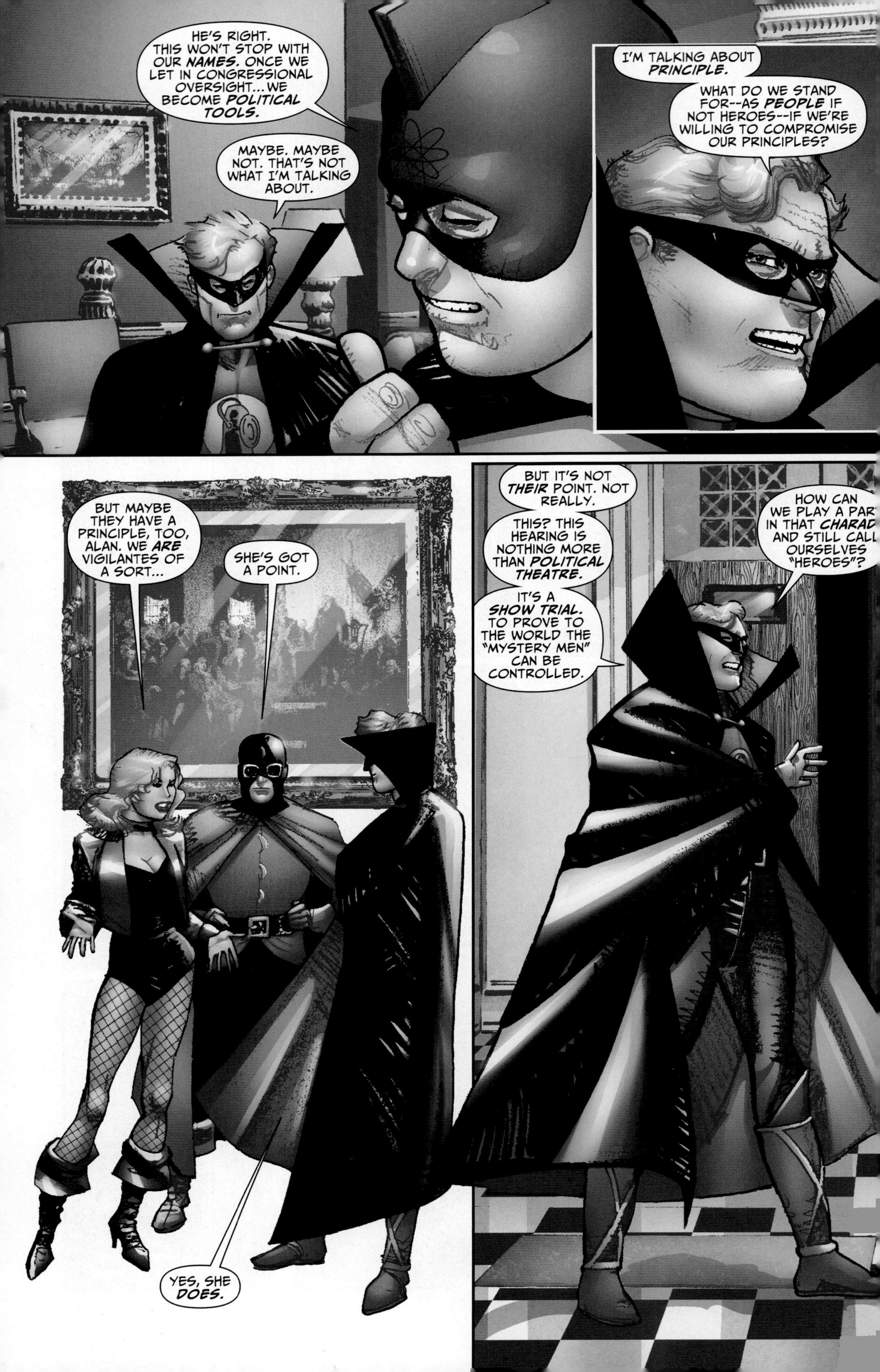
HE'S RIGHT. THIS WON'T STOP WITH OUR *NAMES.* ONCE WE LET IN CONGRESSIONAL OVERSIGHT... WE BECOME *POLITICAL TOOLS.*
MAYBE. MAYBE NOT. THAT'S NOT WHAT I'M TALKING ABOUT.
I'M TALKING ABOUT *PRINCIPLE.*
WHAT DO WE STAND FOR--AS *PEOPLE* IF NOT HEROES--IF WE'RE WILLING TO COMPROMISE OUR PRINCIPLES?
BUT MAYBE THEY HAVE A PRINCIPLE, TOO, ALAN. WE *ARE* VIGILANTES OF A SORT...
SHE'S GOT A POINT.
YES, SHE *DOES.*
BUT IT'S NOT *THEIR* POINT. NOT REALLY.
THIS? THIS HEARING IS NOTHING MORE THAN *POLITICAL THEATRE.*
IT'S A *SHOW TRIAL.* TO PROVE TO THE WORLD THE "MYSTERY MEN" CAN BE CONTROLLED.
HOW CAN WE PLAY A PART IN THAT *CHARADE* AND STILL CALL OURSELVES "HEROES"?

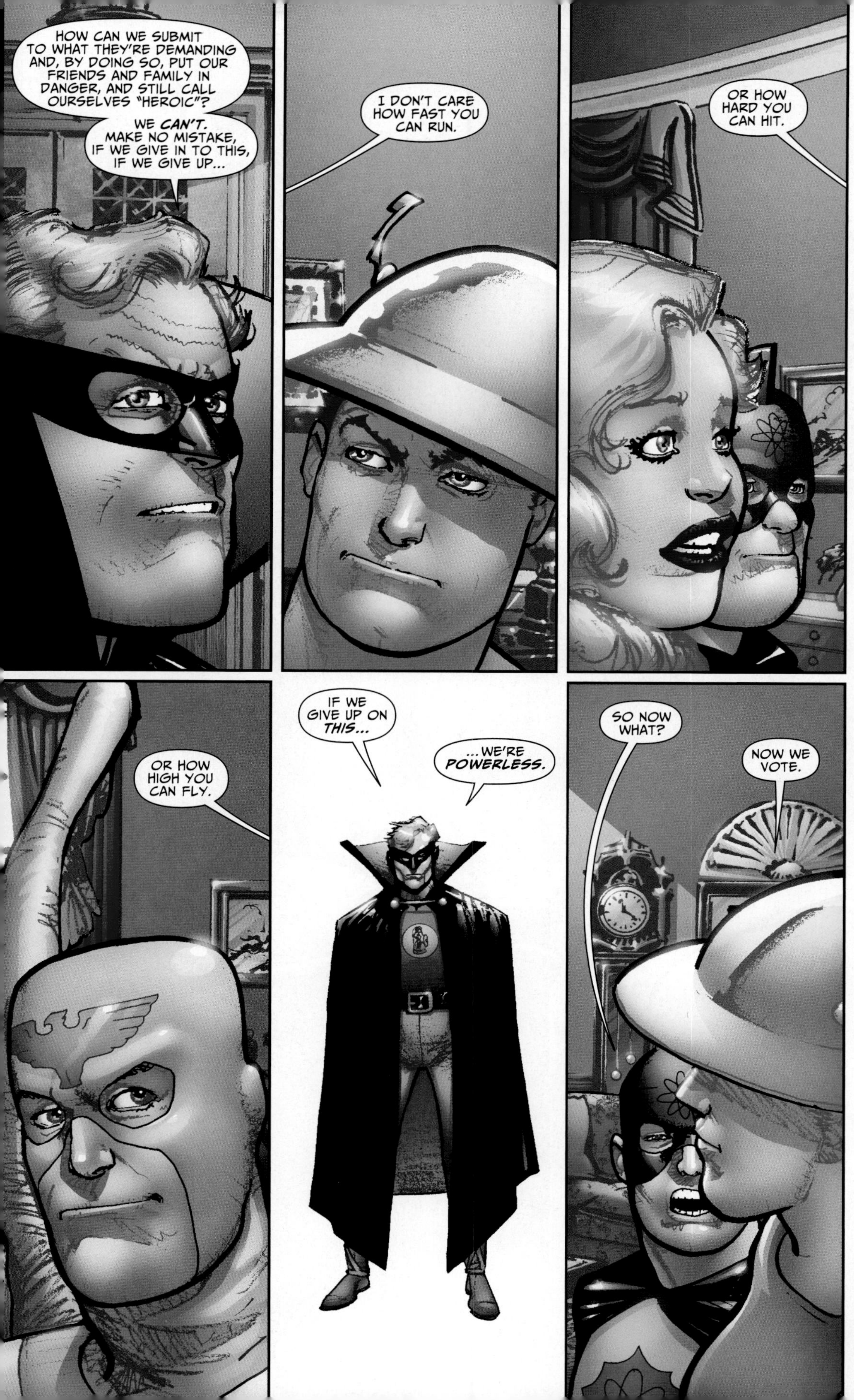
HOW CAN WE SUBMIT TO WHAT THEY'RE DEMANDING AND, BY DOING SO, PUT OUR FRIENDS AND FAMILY IN DANGER, AND STILL CALL OURSELVES "HEROIC"?
WE *CAN'T.* MAKE NO MISTAKE, IF WE GIVE IN TO THIS, IF WE GIVE UP...
I DON'T CARE HOW FAST YOU CAN RUN.
OR HOW HARD YOU CAN HIT.
OR HOW HIGH YOU CAN FLY.
IF WE GIVE UP ON *THIS...*
...WE'RE *POWERLESS.*
SO NOW WHAT?
NOW WE VOTE.

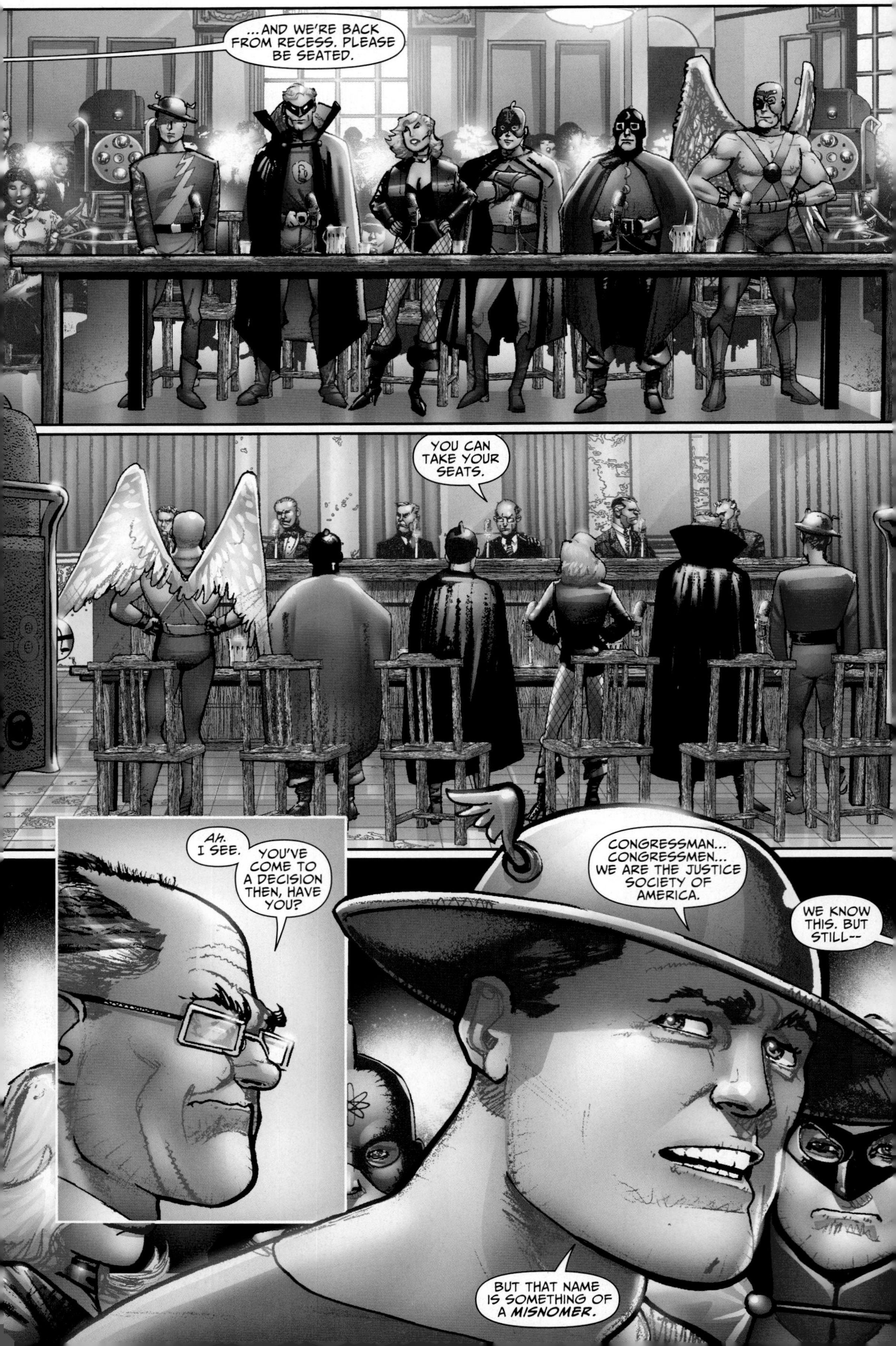
...AND WE'RE BACK FROM RECESS. PLEASE BE SEATED.
YOU CAN TAKE YOUR SEATS.
Ah. I SEE.
YOU'VE COME TO A DECISION THEN, HAVE YOU?
CONGRESSMAN... CONGRESSMEN... WE ARE THE JUSTICE SOCIETY OF AMERICA.
WE KNOW THIS. BUT STILL--
BUT THAT NAME IS SOMETHING OF A MISNOMER.

WHAT WE REALLY ARE IS THE JUSTICE SOCIETY *FOR* AMERICA. AND WE DON'T BELIEVE AMERICA WANTS US TO ENSURE ITS SAFETY WHILE SACRIFICING OUR *OWN*.

WE DON'T BELIEVE AMERICA WANTS US TO PROTECT ITS FREEDOM WHILE FORFEITING OUR *OWN*.

WE DON'T BELIEVE THAT WHAT'S HAPPENING IN THIS ROOM IS WHAT AMERICA WANTS.

WE DON'T BELIEVE IT'S *AMERICAN*.

YOU CALL YOURSELVES THE HOUSE UN-AMERICAN ACTIVITIES COMMITTEE?

MIGHT WE SUGGEST YOU START WITH *YOU*.

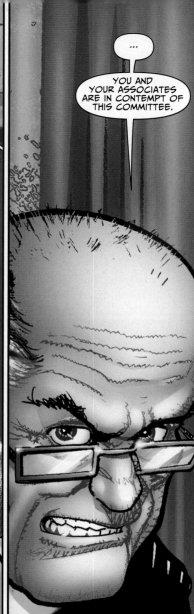

...

YOU AND YOUR ASSOCIATES ARE IN CONTEMPT OF THIS COMMITTEE.

THAT'S THE FIRST THING YOU'VE SAID TODAY I AGREE WITH.

I'M GOING TO CALL FOR A RESOLUTION ASKING THE FEDERAL BUREAU OF INVESTIGATION TO OPEN FILES ON ALL OF YOU.

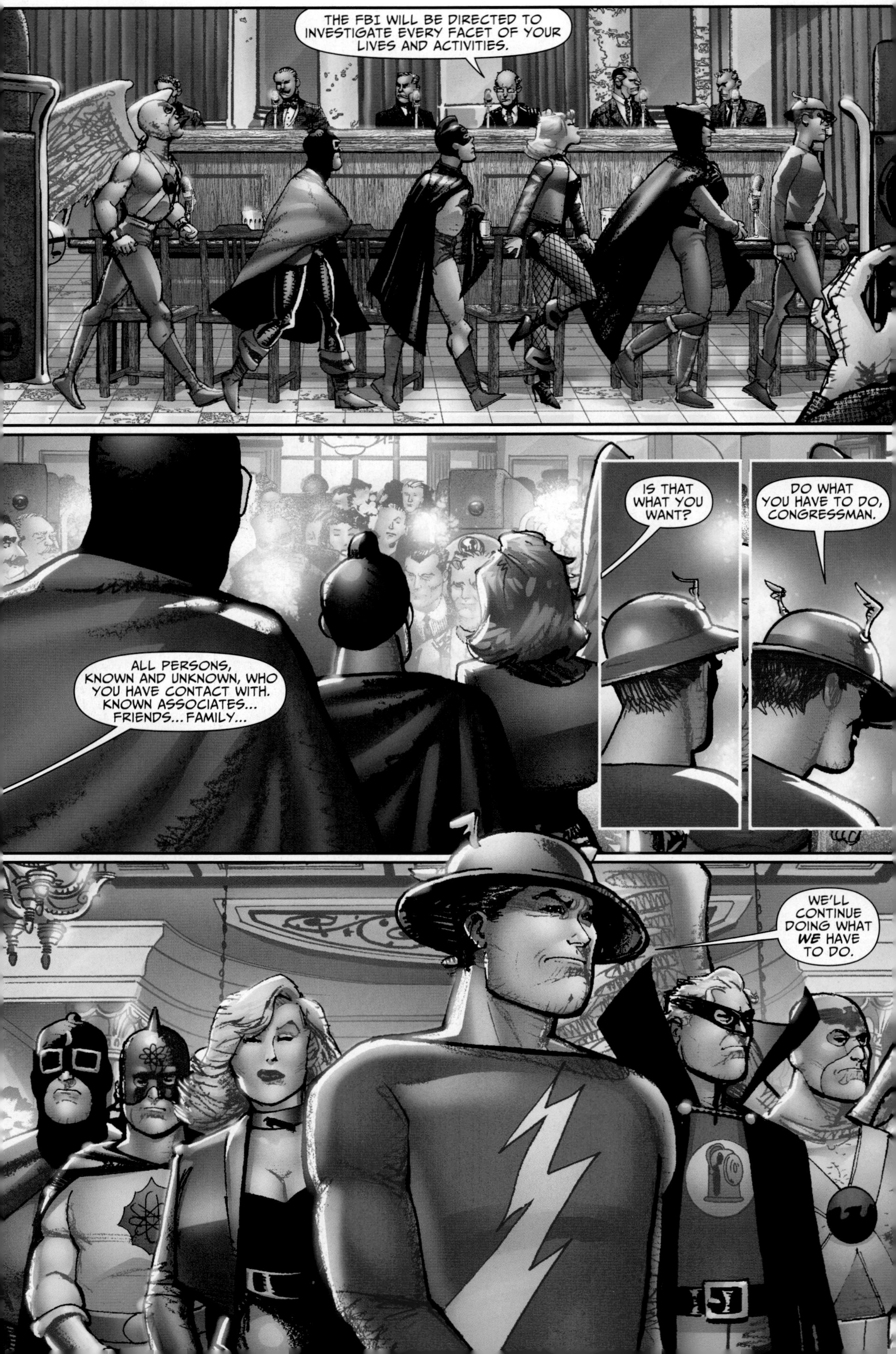
THE FBI WILL BE DIRECTED TO INVESTIGATE EVERY FACET OF YOUR LIVES AND ACTIVITIES.
ALL PERSONS, KNOWN AND UNKNOWN, WHO YOU HAVE CONTACT WITH. KNOWN ASSOCIATES... FRIENDS... FAMILY...
IS THAT WHAT YOU WANT?
DO WHAT YOU HAVE TO DO, CONGRESSMAN.
WE'LL CONTINUE DOING WHAT WE HAVE TO DO.

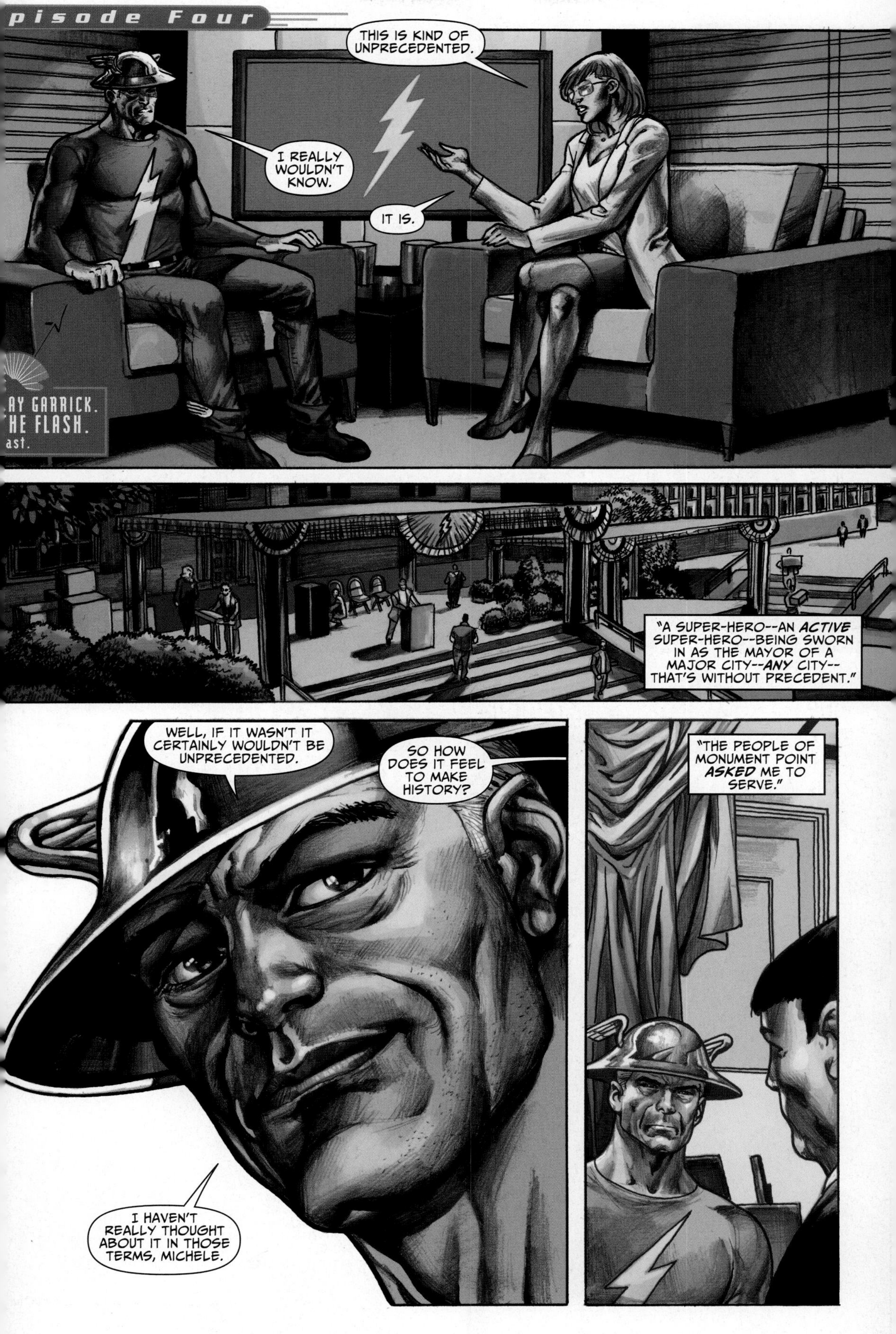
pisode Four
THIS IS KIND OF UNPRECEDENTED.
I REALLY WOULDN'T KNOW.
IT IS.
AY GARRICK.
HE FLASH.
ast.
"A SUPER-HERO--AN ACTIVE SUPER-HERO--BEING SWORN IN AS THE MAYOR OF A MAJOR CITY--ANY CITY--THAT'S WITHOUT PRECEDENT."
WELL, IF IT WASN'T IT CERTAINLY WOULDN'T BE UNPRECEDENTED.
SO HOW DOES IT FEEL TO MAKE HISTORY?
I HAVEN'T REALLY THOUGHT ABOUT IT IN THOSE TERMS, MICHELE.
"THE PEOPLE OF MONUMENT POINT ASKED ME TO SERVE."

YOU MAKE IT SOUND SO SIMPLE.

BECAUSE IT IS.

SPOKEN LIKE A MEMBER OF THE GREATEST GENERATION.

I THINK WE JUST HAD A BETTER *PUBLICIST* THAN OTHER GENERATIONS.

"THE RED BEETLE'S YOUR AGE.

BUT IT'S THAT ETHOS, THAT CALL TO SERVICE... THAT'S WHAT DEFINES YOU AND YOUR PEERS.

NOT JUST ME AND MY PEERS.

"RI...MANHUNTER...

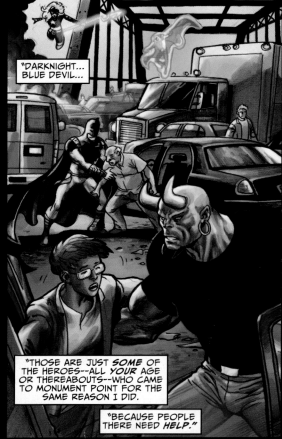

"DARKNIGHT... BLUE DEVIL...

"THOSE ARE JUST *SOME* OF THE HEROES--ALL *YOUR* AGE OR THEREABOUTS--WHO CAME TO MONUMENT POINT FOR THE SAME REASON I DID.

"BECAUSE PEOPLE THERE NEED *HELP*."

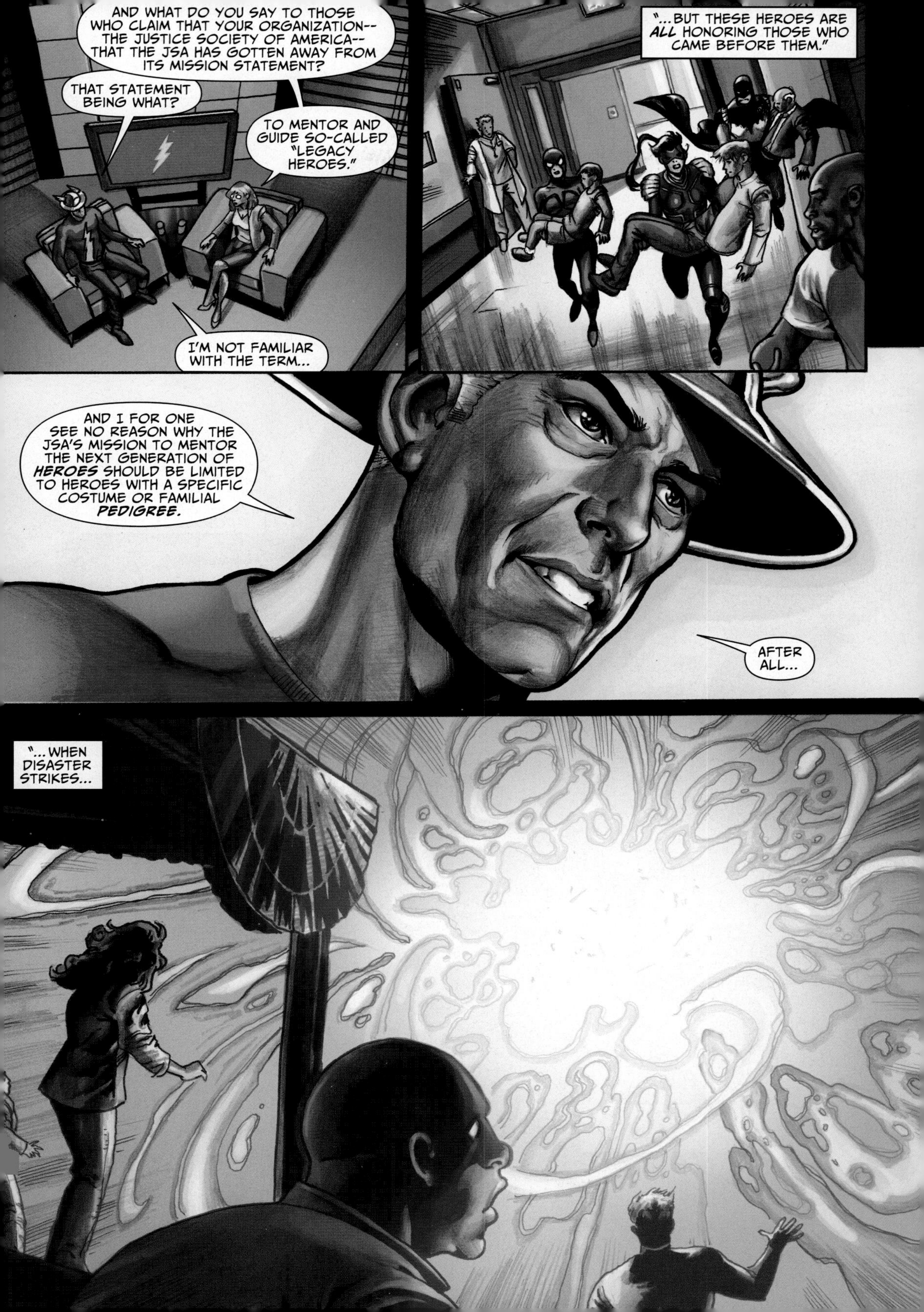
AND WHAT DO YOU SAY TO THOSE WHO CLAIM THAT YOUR ORGANIZATION-- THE JUSTICE SOCIETY OF AMERICA-- THAT THE JSA HAS GOTTEN AWAY FROM ITS MISSION STATEMENT?
THAT STATEMENT BEING WHAT?
TO MENTOR AND GUIDE SO-CALLED "LEGACY HEROES."
I'M NOT FAMILIAR WITH THE TERM...
"...BUT THESE HEROES ARE ALL HONORING THOSE WHO CAME BEFORE THEM."
AND I FOR ONE SEE NO REASON WHY THE JSA'S MISSION TO MENTOR THE NEXT GENERATION OF HEROES SHOULD BE LIMITED TO HEROES WITH A SPECIFIC COSTUME OR FAMILIAL PEDIGREE.
AFTER ALL...
"...WHEN DISASTER STRIKES...

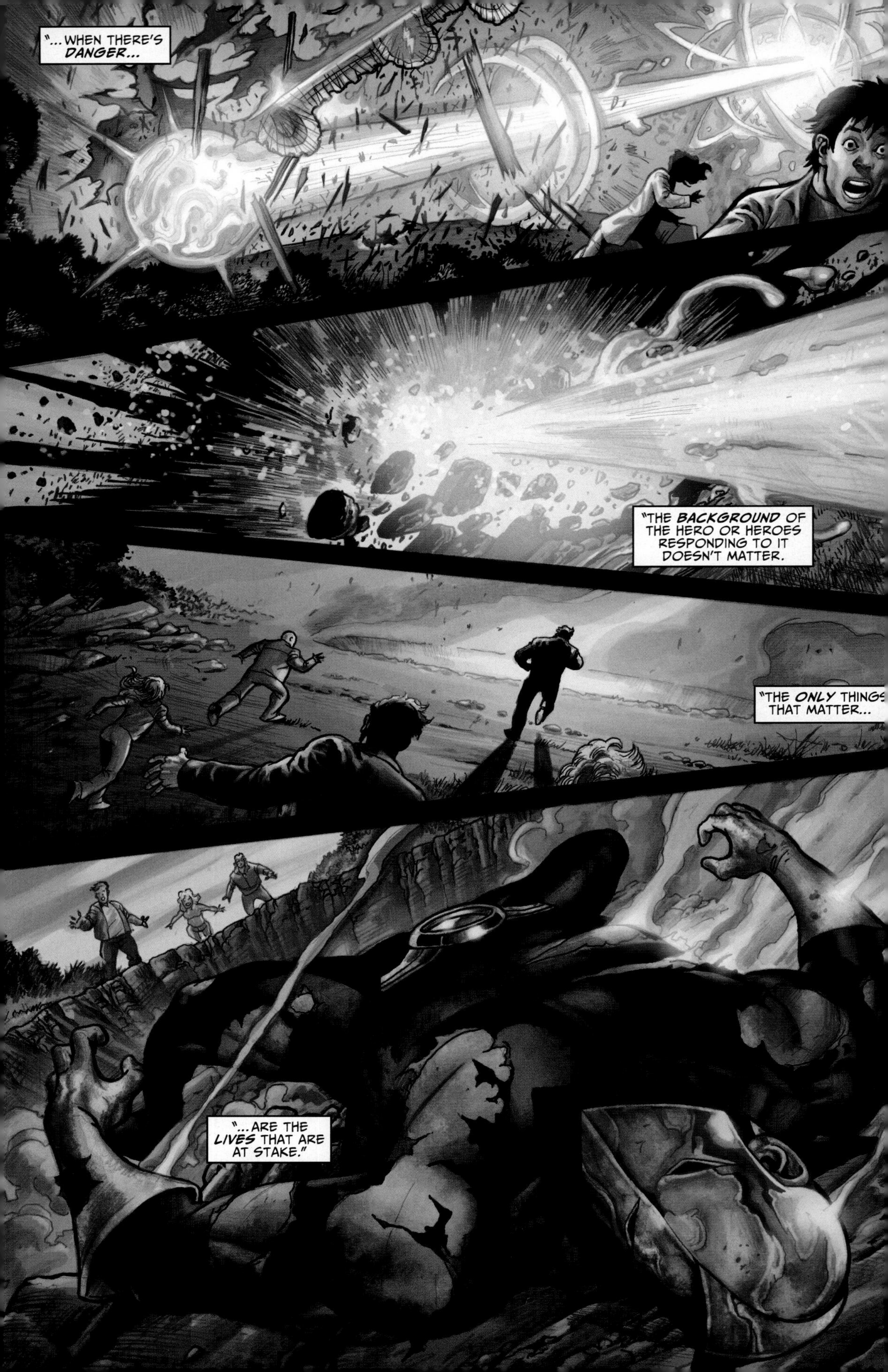
"...WHEN THERE'S *DANGER*...
"THE *BACKGROUND* OF THE HERO OR HEROES RESPONDING TO IT DOESN'T MATTER.
"THE *ONLY* THINGS THAT MATTER...
"...ARE THE *LIVES* THAT ARE AT STAKE."

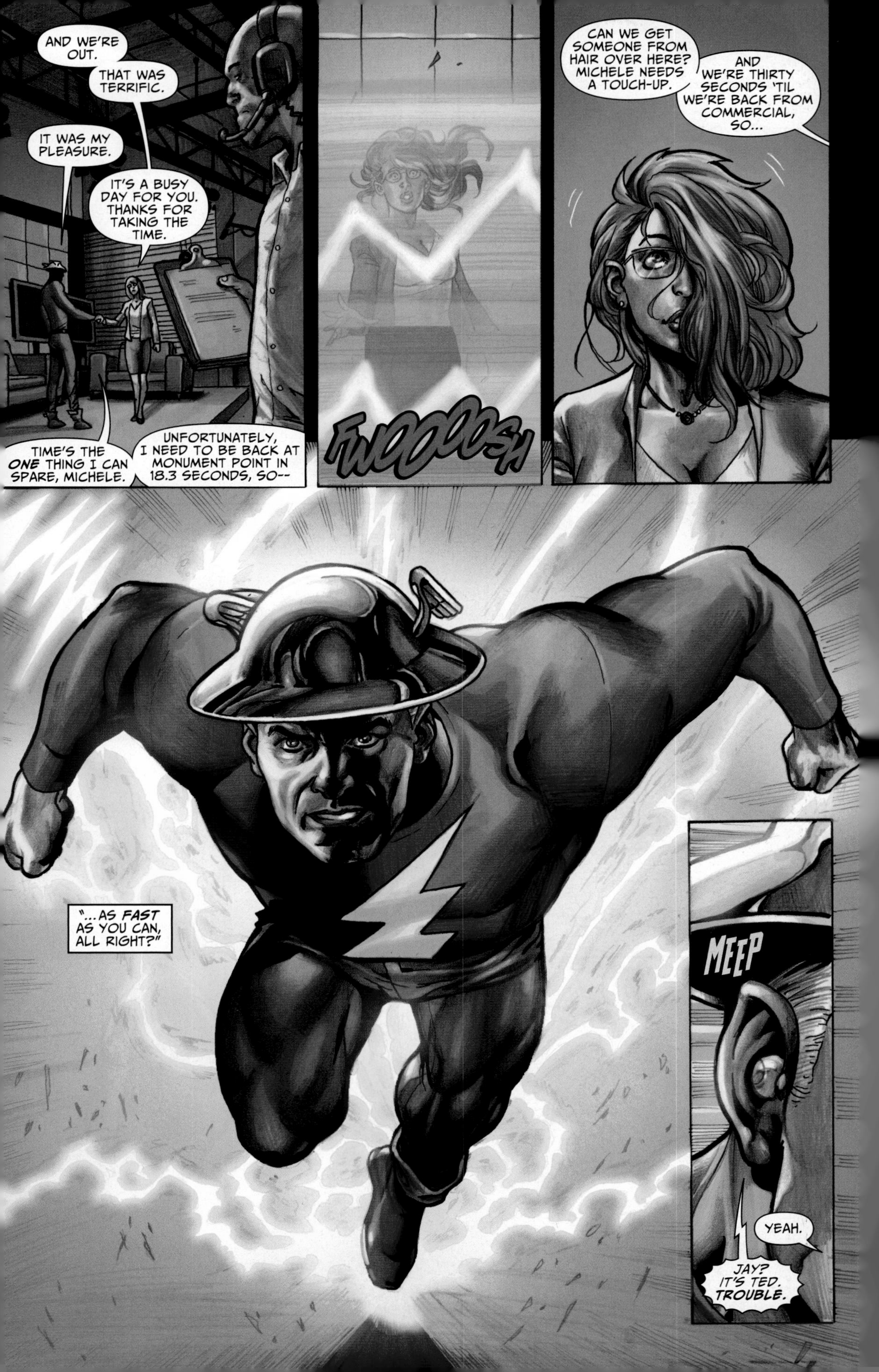
AND WE'RE OUT.
THAT WAS TERRIFIC.
IT WAS MY PLEASURE.
IT'S A BUSY DAY FOR YOU. THANKS FOR TAKING THE TIME.
TIME'S THE ONE THING I CAN SPARE, MICHELE.
UNFORTUNATELY, I NEED TO BE BACK AT MONUMENT POINT IN 18.3 SECONDS, SO--
FWOOOOOSH
CAN WE GET SOMEONE FROM HAIR OVER HERE? MICHELE NEEDS A TOUCH-UP.
AND WE'RE THIRTY SECONDS 'TIL WE'RE BACK FROM COMMERCIAL, SO...
"...AS FAST AS YOU CAN, ALL RIGHT?"
MEEP
YEAH.
JAY? IT'S TED. TROUBLE.

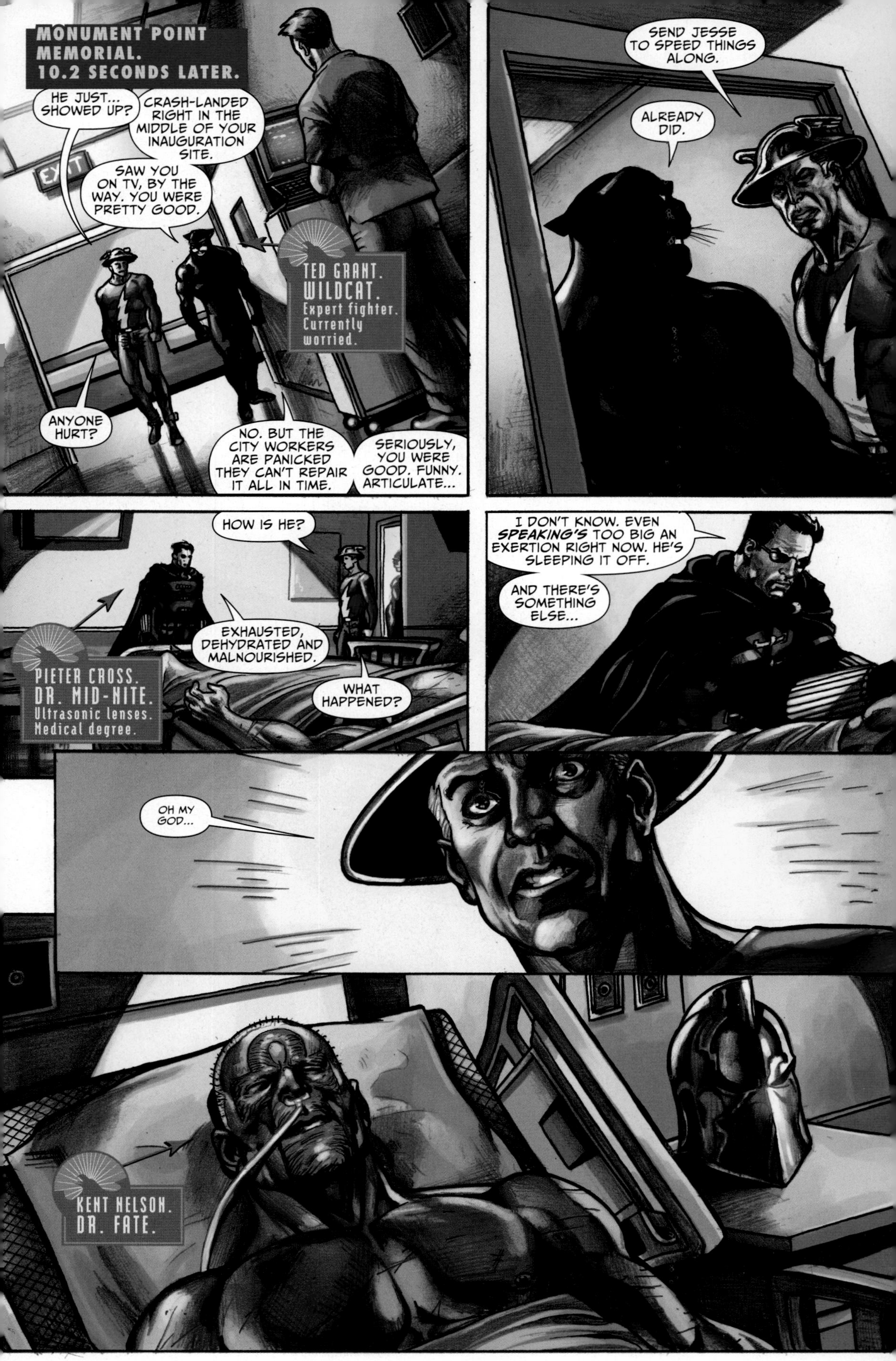

MONUMENT POINT MEMORIAL. 10.2 SECONDS LATER.
HE JUST... SHOWED UP?
CRASH-LANDED RIGHT IN THE MIDDLE OF YOUR INAUGURATION SITE.
SAW YOU ON TV, BY THE WAY. YOU WERE PRETTY GOOD.
EXIT
TED GRANT. WILDCAT. Expert fighter. Currently worried.
ANYONE HURT?
NO. BUT THE CITY WORKERS ARE PANICKED THEY CAN'T REPAIR IT ALL IN TIME.
SERIOUSLY, YOU WERE GOOD. FUNNY. ARTICULATE...
SEND JESSE TO SPEED THINGS ALONG.
ALREADY DID.
HOW IS HE?
EXHAUSTED, DEHYDRATED AND MALNOURISHED.
WHAT HAPPENED?
PIETER CROSS. DR. MID-NITE. Ultrasonic lenses. Medical degree.
I DON'T KNOW. EVEN SPEAKING'S TOO BIG AN EXERTION RIGHT NOW. HE'S SLEEPING IT OFF.
AND THERE'S SOMETHING ELSE...
OH MY GOD...
KENT NELSON. DR. FATE.

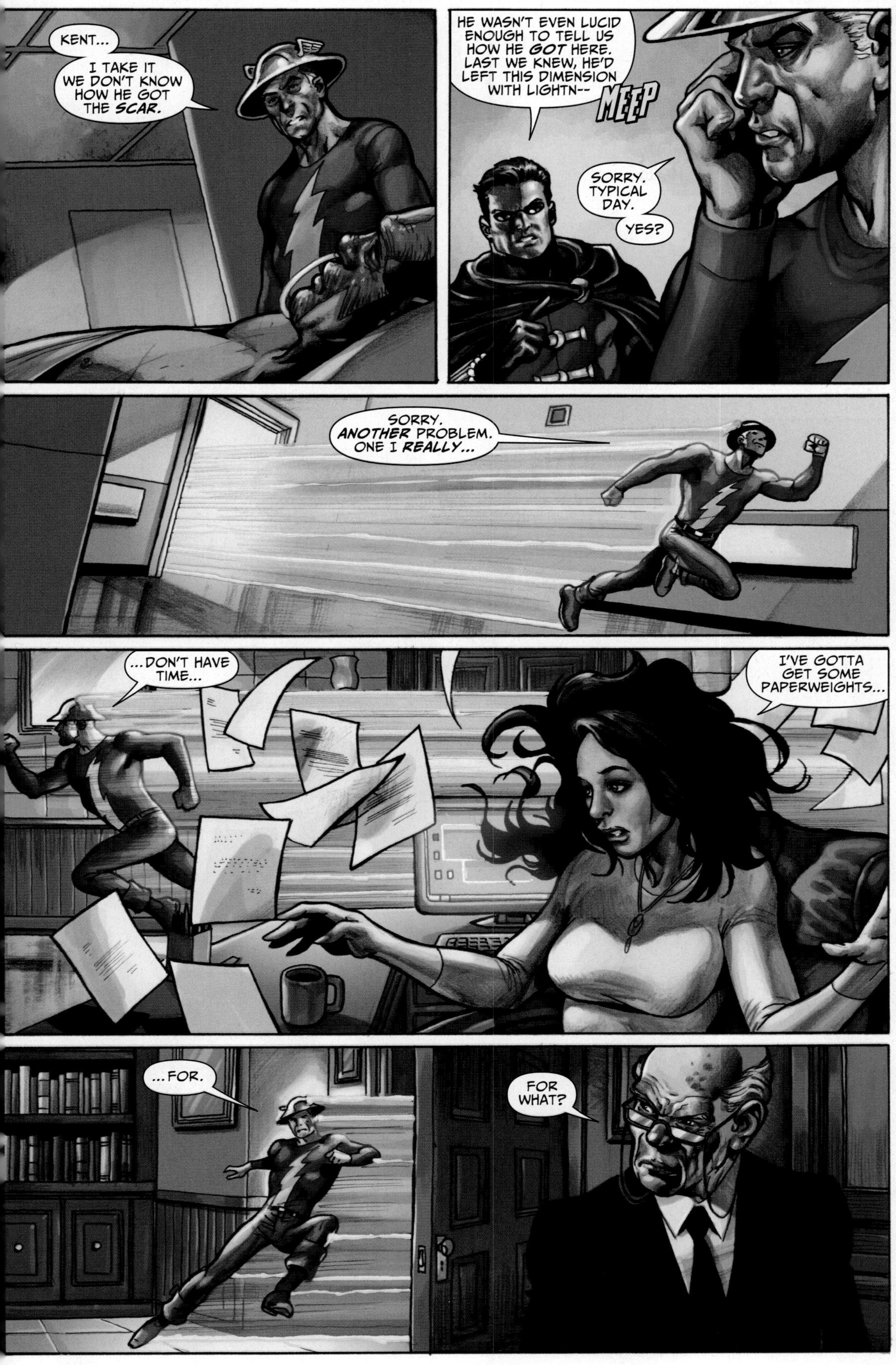
KENT...
I TAKE IT WE DON'T KNOW HOW HE GOT THE SCAR.
HE WASN'T EVEN LUCID ENOUGH TO TELL US HOW HE GOT HERE. LAST WE KNEW, HE'D LEFT THIS DIMENSION WITH LIGHTN--
MEEP
SORRY. TYPICAL DAY.
YES?
SORRY. ANOTHER PROBLEM. ONE I REALLY...
...DON'T HAVE TIME...
I'VE GOTTA GET SOME PAPERWEIGHTS...
...FOR.
FOR WHAT?

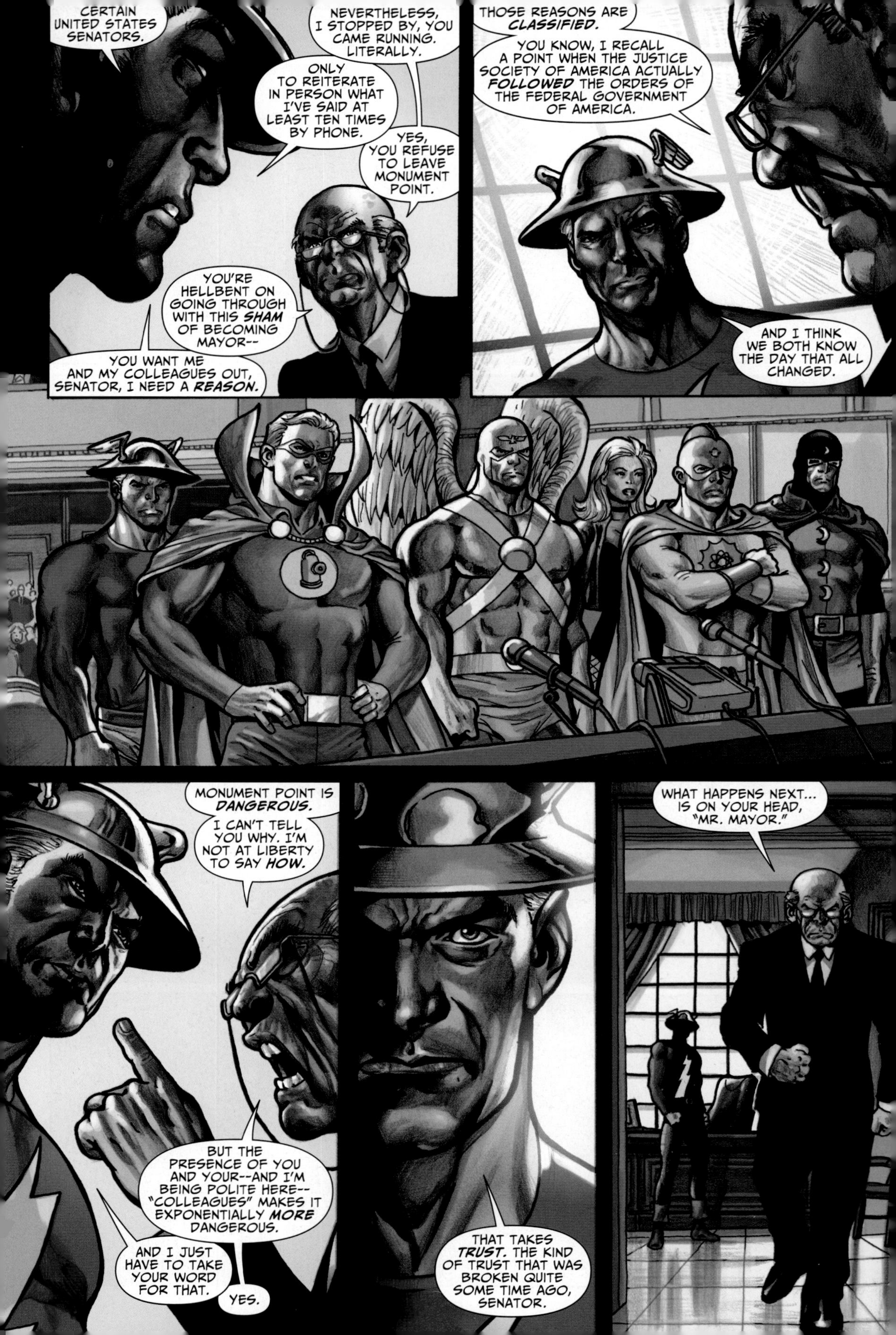
CERTAIN UNITED STATES SENATORS.
NEVERTHELESS, I STOPPED BY, YOU CAME RUNNING. LITERALLY.
ONLY TO REITERATE IN PERSON WHAT I'VE SAID AT LEAST TEN TIMES BY PHONE.
YES, YOU REFUSE TO LEAVE MONUMENT POINT.
YOU'RE HELLBENT ON GOING THROUGH WITH THIS *SHAM* OF BECOMING MAYOR--
YOU WANT ME AND MY COLLEAGUES OUT, SENATOR, I NEED A *REASON.*
THOSE REASONS ARE *CLASSIFIED.*
YOU KNOW, I RECALL A POINT WHEN THE JUSTICE SOCIETY OF AMERICA ACTUALLY *FOLLOWED* THE ORDERS OF THE FEDERAL GOVERNMENT OF AMERICA.
AND I THINK WE BOTH KNOW THE DAY THAT ALL CHANGED.
MONUMENT POINT IS *DANGEROUS.*
I CAN'T TELL YOU WHY. I'M NOT AT LIBERTY TO SAY *HOW.*
BUT THE PRESENCE OF YOU AND YOUR--AND I'M BEING POLITE HERE--"COLLEAGUES" MAKES IT EXPONENTIALLY *MORE* DANGEROUS.
AND I JUST HAVE TO TAKE YOUR WORD FOR THAT.
YES.
THAT TAKES *TRUST.* THE KIND OF TRUST THAT WAS BROKEN QUITE SOME TIME AGO, SENATOR.
WHAT HAPPENS NEXT... IS ON YOUR HEAD, "MR. MAYOR."

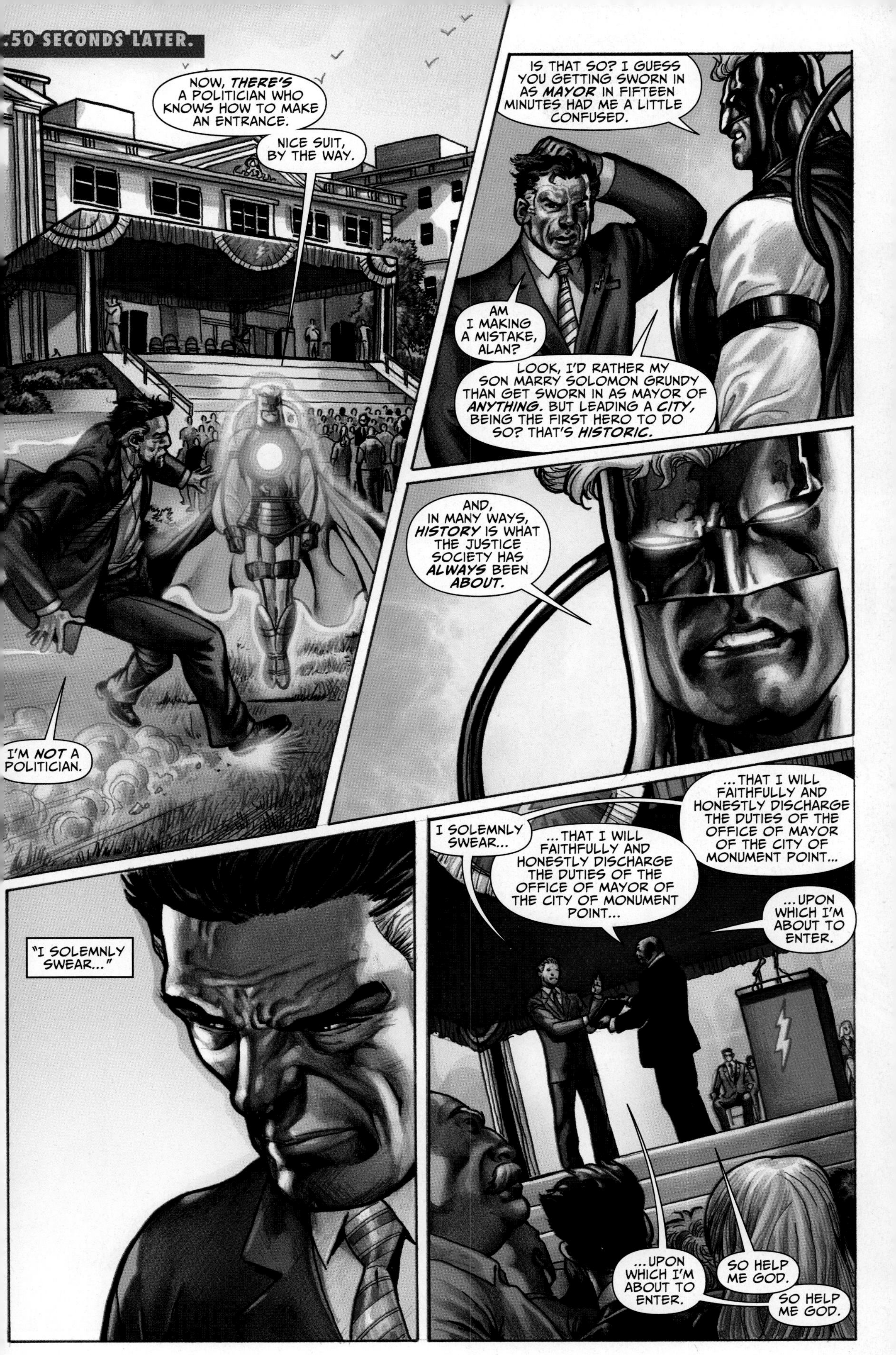
.50 SECONDS LATER.
NOW, THERE'S A POLITICIAN WHO KNOWS HOW TO MAKE AN ENTRANCE.
NICE SUIT, BY THE WAY.
I'M NOT A POLITICIAN.
IS THAT SO? I GUESS YOU GETTING SWORN IN AS MAYOR IN FIFTEEN MINUTES HAD ME A LITTLE CONFUSED.
AM I MAKING A MISTAKE, ALAN?
LOOK, I'D RATHER MY SON MARRY SOLOMON GRUNDY THAN GET SWORN IN AS MAYOR OF ANYTHING. BUT LEADING A CITY, BEING THE FIRST HERO TO DO SO? THAT'S HISTORIC.
AND, IN MANY WAYS, HISTORY IS WHAT THE JUSTICE SOCIETY HAS ALWAYS BEEN ABOUT.
"I SOLEMNLY SWEAR..."
I SOLEMNLY SWEAR...
...THAT I WILL FAITHFULLY AND HONESTLY DISCHARGE THE DUTIES OF THE OFFICE OF MAYOR OF THE CITY OF MONUMENT POINT...
...THAT I WILL FAITHFULLY AND HONESTLY DISCHARGE THE DUTIES OF THE OFFICE OF MAYOR OF THE CITY OF MONUMENT POINT...
...UPON WHICH I'M ABOUT TO ENTER.
...UPON WHICH I'M ABOUT TO ENTER.
SO HELP ME GOD.
SO HELP ME GOD.

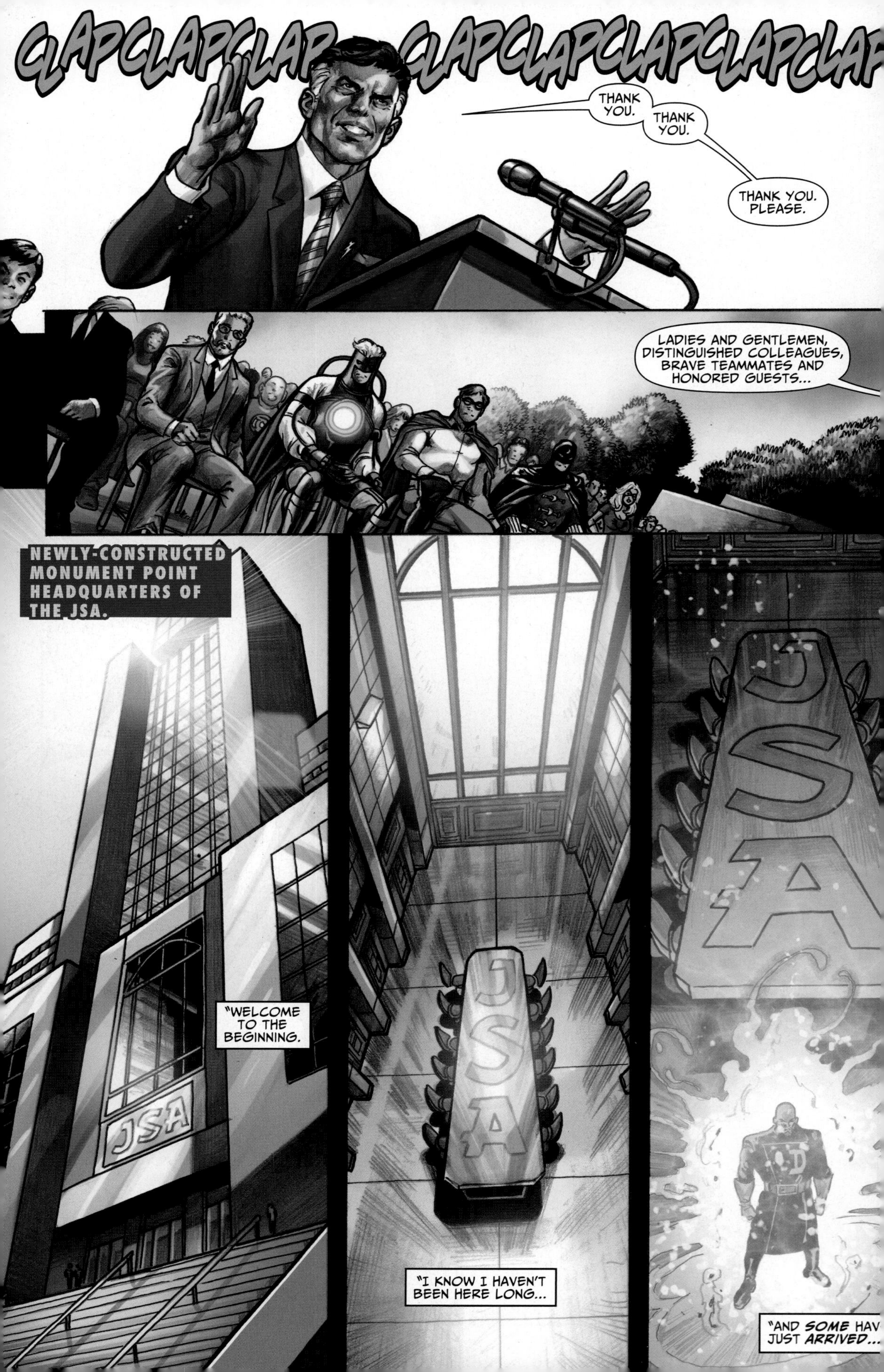
CLAPCLAPCLAP CLAPCLAPCLAPCLAP
THANK YOU.
THANK YOU.
THANK YOU. PLEASE.
LADIES AND GENTLEMEN, DISTINGUISHED COLLEAGUES, BRAVE TEAMMATES AND HONORED GUESTS...
NEWLY-CONSTRUCTED MONUMENT POINT HEADQUARTERS OF THE JSA.
"WELCOME TO THE BEGINNING.
JSA
"I KNOW I HAVEN'T BEEN HERE LONG...
JSA
JSA
"AND SOME HAV JUST ARRIVED...

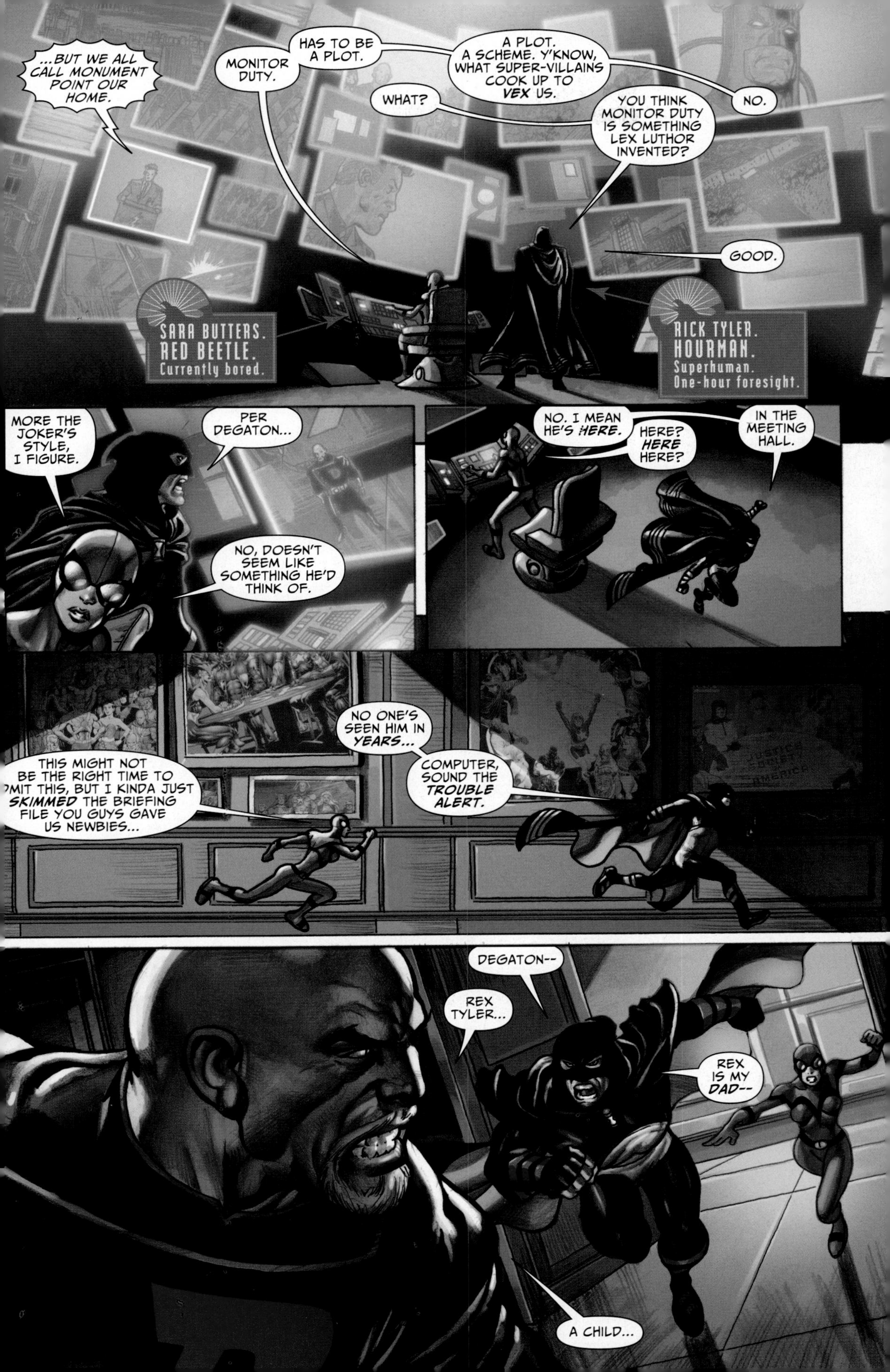
...BUT WE ALL CALL MONUMENT POINT OUR HOME.
MONITOR DUTY.
HAS TO BE A PLOT.
A PLOT. A SCHEME. Y'KNOW, WHAT SUPER-VILLAINS COOK UP TO VEX US.
NO.
WHAT?
YOU THINK MONITOR DUTY IS SOMETHING LEX LUTHOR INVENTED?
GOOD.
SARA BUTTERS. RED BEETLE. Currently bored.
RICK TYLER. HOURMAN. Superhuman. One-hour foresight.
MORE THE JOKER'S STYLE, I FIGURE.
PER DEGATON...
NO, DOESN'T SEEM LIKE SOMETHING HE'D THINK OF.
NO. I MEAN HE'S HERE.
HERE? HERE HERE?
IN THE MEETING HALL.
THIS MIGHT NOT BE THE RIGHT TIME TO
MIT THIS, BUT I KINDA JUST SKIMMED THE BRIEFING FILE YOU GUYS GAVE US NEWBIES...
NO ONE'S SEEN HIM IN YEARS...
COMPUTER, SOUND THE TROUBLE ALERT.
DEGATON--
REX TYLER...
REX IS MY DAD--
A CHILD...

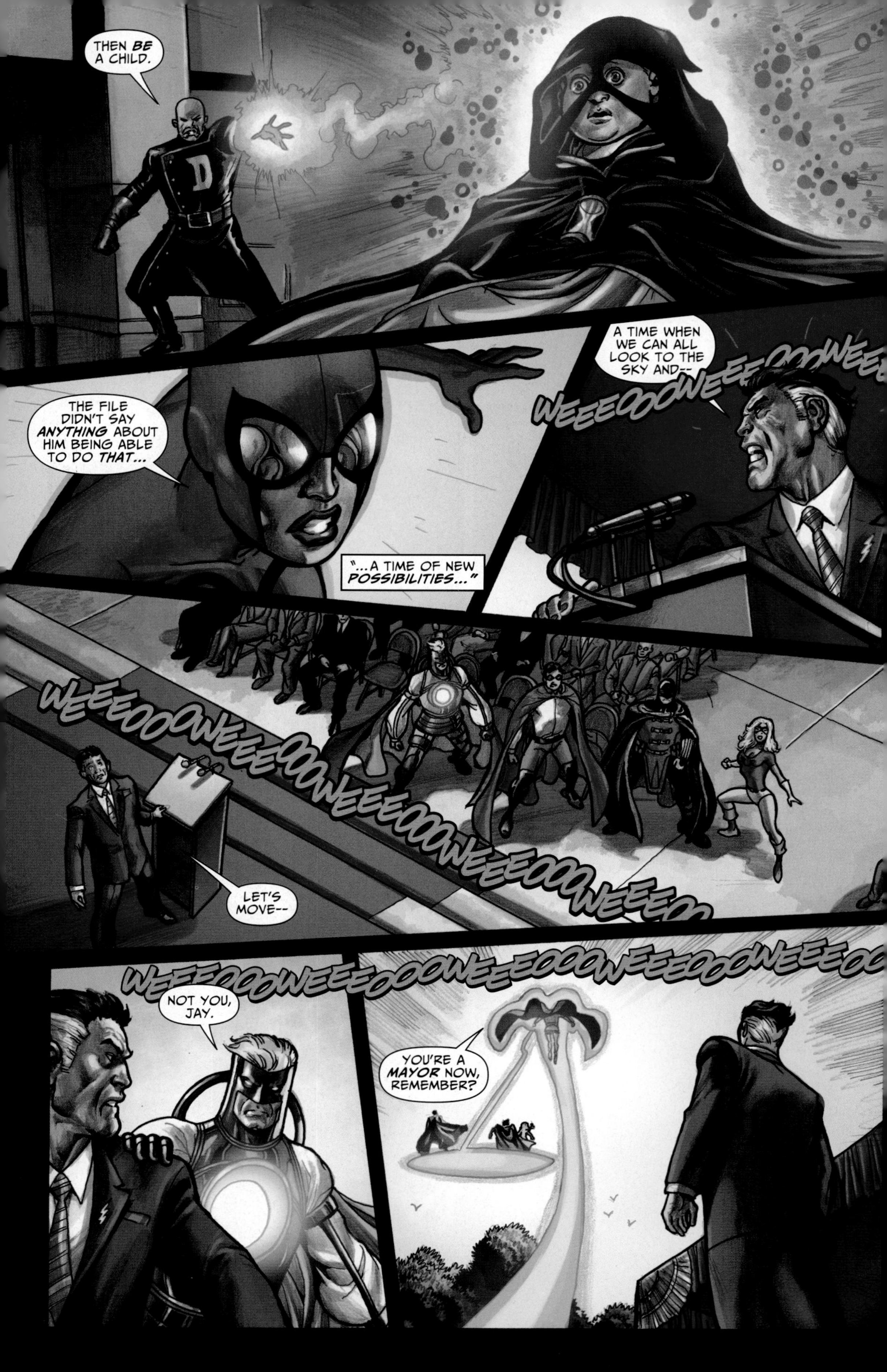
THEN BE A CHILD.
THE FILE DIDN'T SAY ANYTHING ABOUT HIM BEING ABLE TO DO THAT...
A TIME WHEN WE CAN ALL LOOK TO THE SKY AND--
WEEEOOOWEEEOOOWEE
"...A TIME OF NEW POSSIBILITIES..."
WEEEOOOWEEEOOOWEEEOOOWEEEOOOWEEEOO
LET'S MOVE--
WEEEOOOWEEEOOOWEEEOOOWEEEOOOWEEEOO
NOT YOU, JAY.
YOU'RE A MAYOR NOW, REMEMBER?

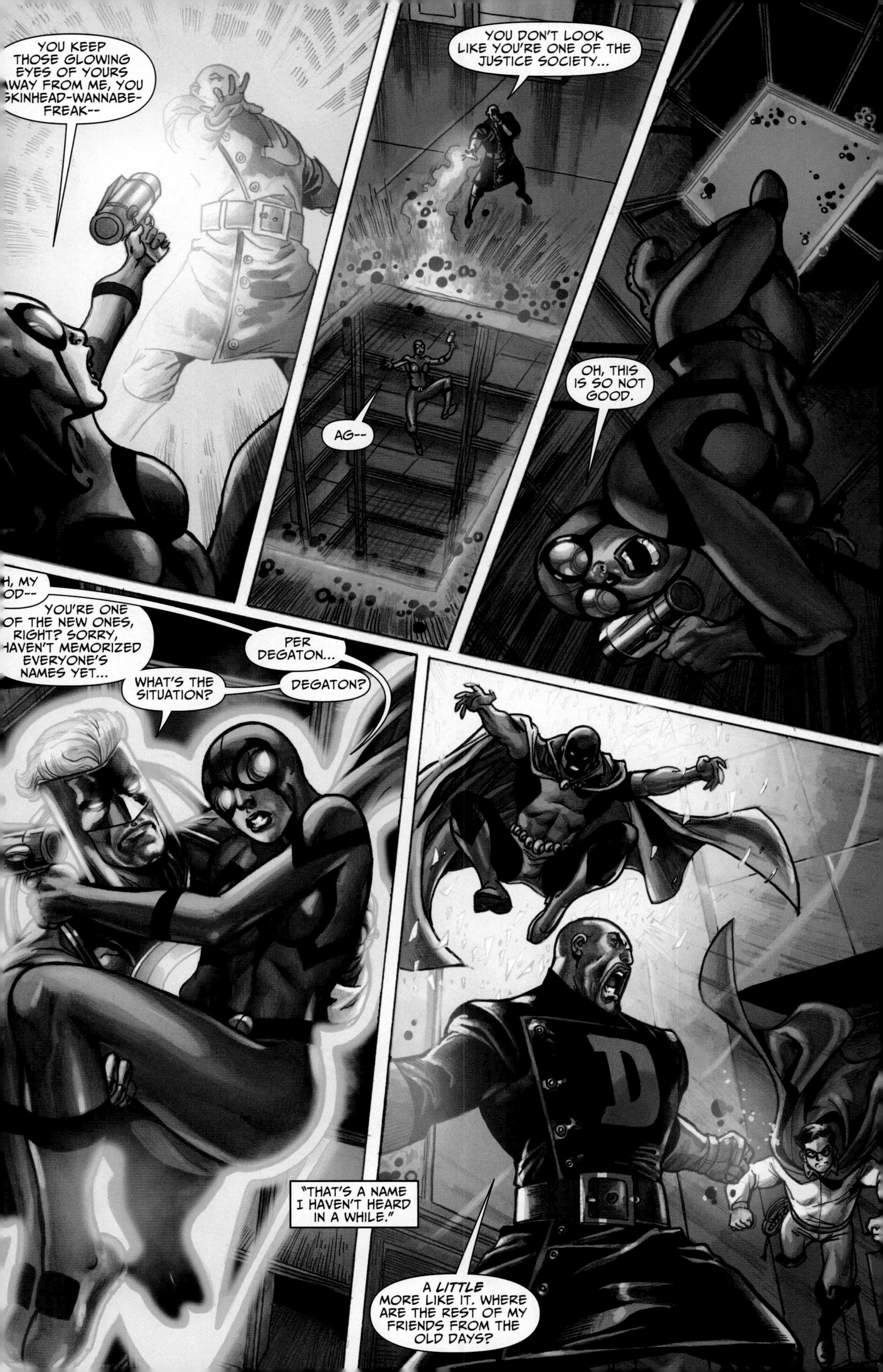
YOU KEEP THOSE GLOWING EYES OF YOURS AWAY FROM ME, YOU SKINHEAD-WANNABE-FREAK--
YOU DON'T LOOK LIKE YOU'RE ONE OF THE JUSTICE SOCIETY...
AG--
OH, THIS IS SO NOT GOOD.
H, MY OD--
YOU'RE ONE OF THE NEW ONES, RIGHT? SORRY, HAVEN'T MEMORIZED EVERYONE'S NAMES YET...
PER DEGATON...
WHAT'S THE SITUATION?
DEGATON?
"THAT'S A NAME I HAVEN'T HEARD IN A WHILE."
A *LITTLE* MORE LIKE IT. WHERE ARE THE REST OF MY FRIENDS FROM THE OLD DAYS?

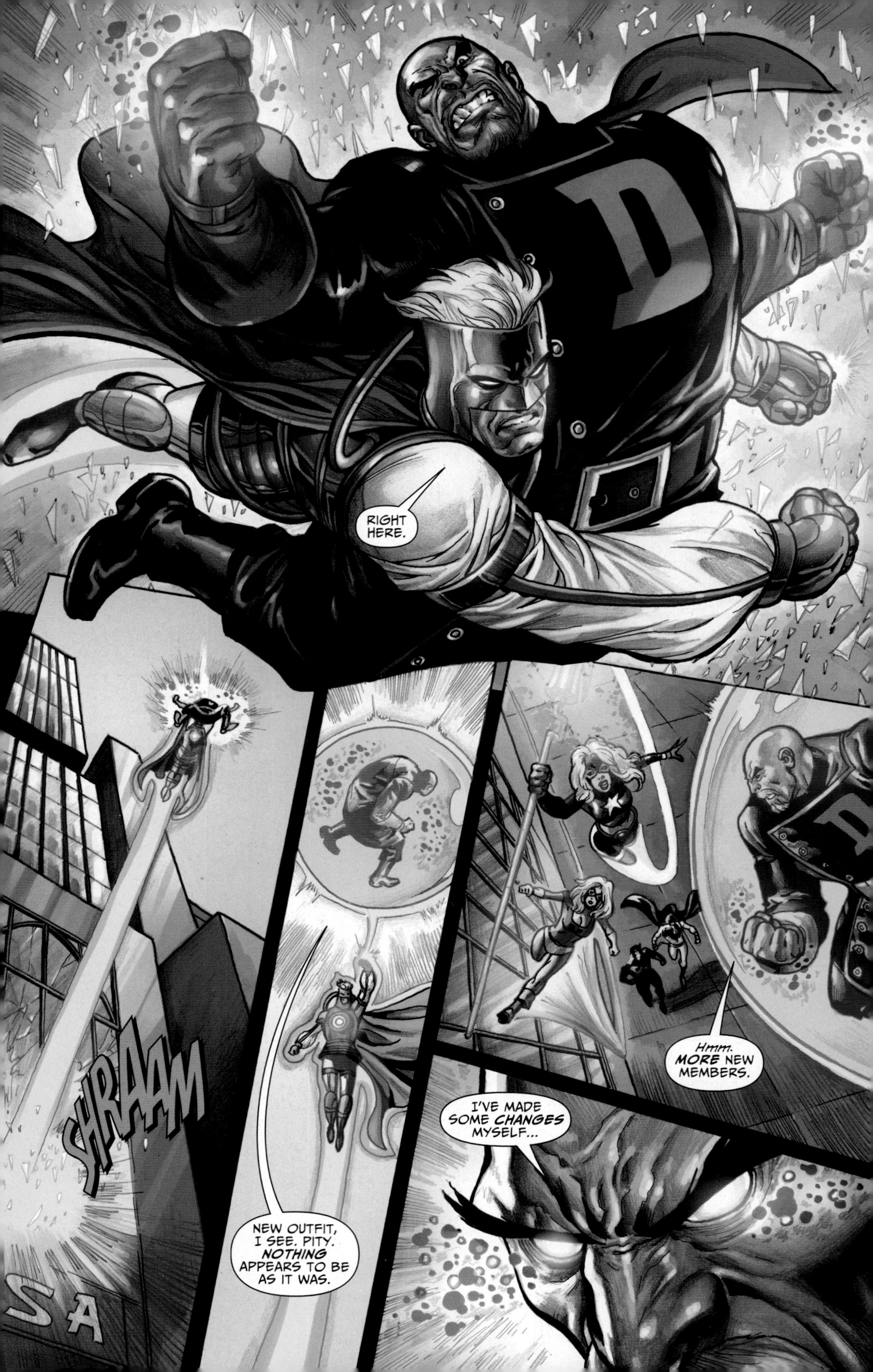
RIGHT HERE.
SHRAAM
NEW OUTFIT, I SEE. PITY. *NOTHING* APPEARS TO BE AS IT WAS.
*Hmm.* ***MORE*** NEW MEMBERS.
I'VE MADE SOME ***CHANGES*** MYSELF...

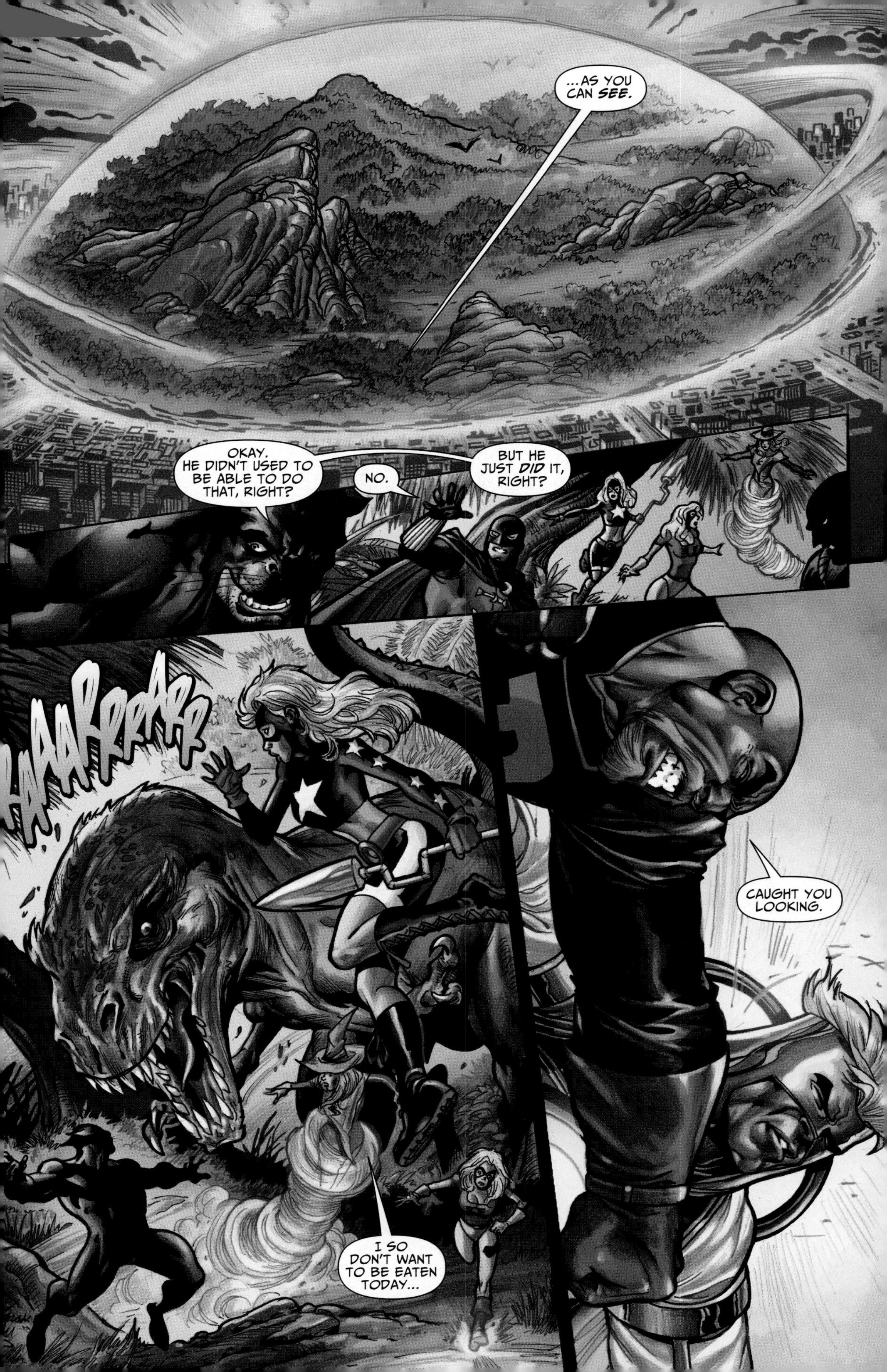
...AS YOU CAN *SEE*.
OKAY. HE DIDN'T USED TO BE ABLE TO DO THAT, RIGHT?
NO.
BUT HE JUST *DID* IT, RIGHT?
RAARRRARR
I SO DON'T WANT TO BE EATEN TODAY...
CAUGHT YOU LOOKING.

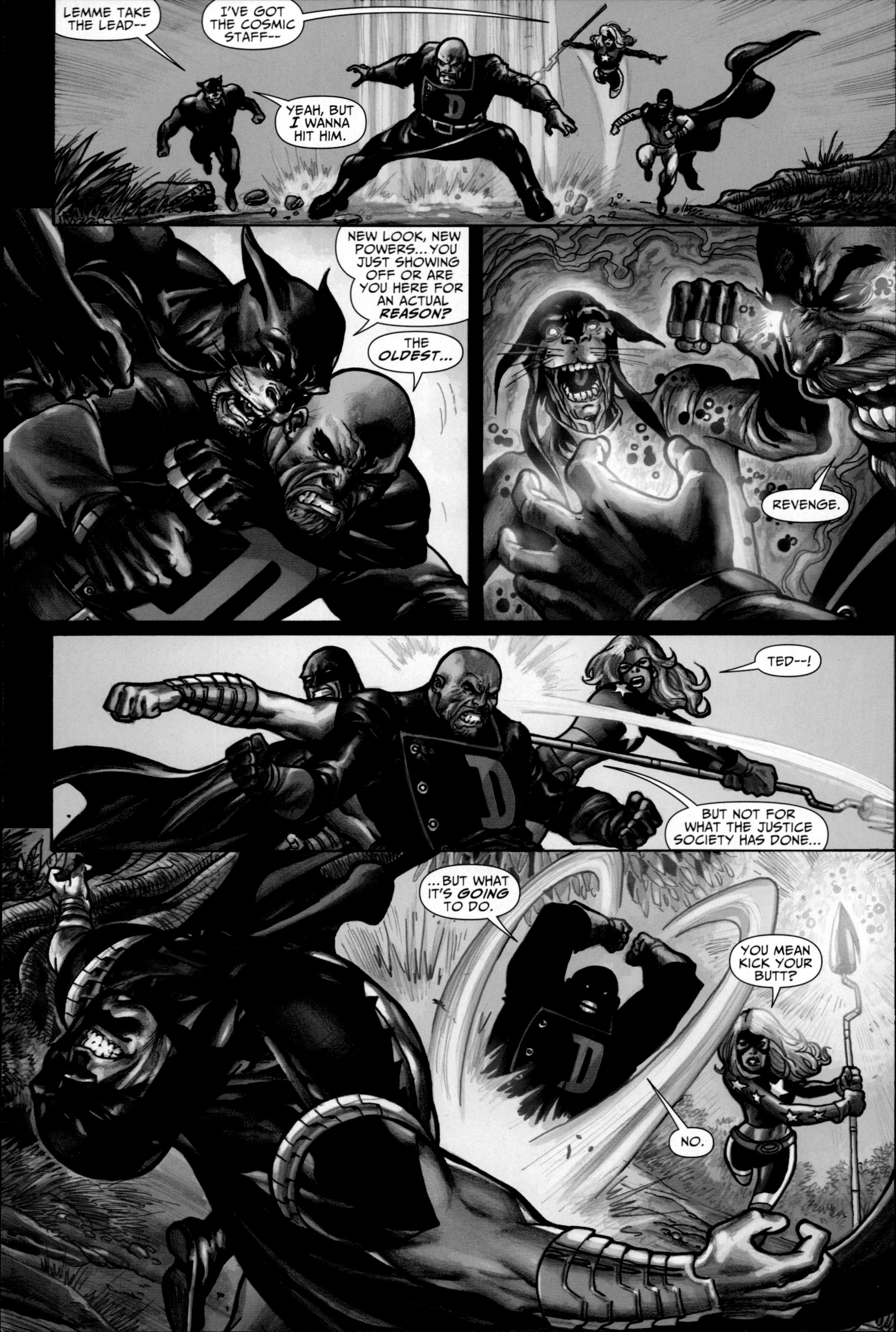

LEMME TAKE THE LEAD--
I'VE GOT THE COSMIC STAFF--
YEAH, BUT I WANNA HIT HIM.
NEW LOOK, NEW POWERS... YOU JUST SHOWING OFF OR ARE YOU HERE FOR AN ACTUAL REASON?
THE OLDEST...
REVENGE.
TED--!
BUT NOT FOR WHAT THE JUSTICE SOCIETY HAS DONE...
...BUT WHAT IT'S GOING TO DO.
YOU MEAN KICK YOUR BUTT?
NO.

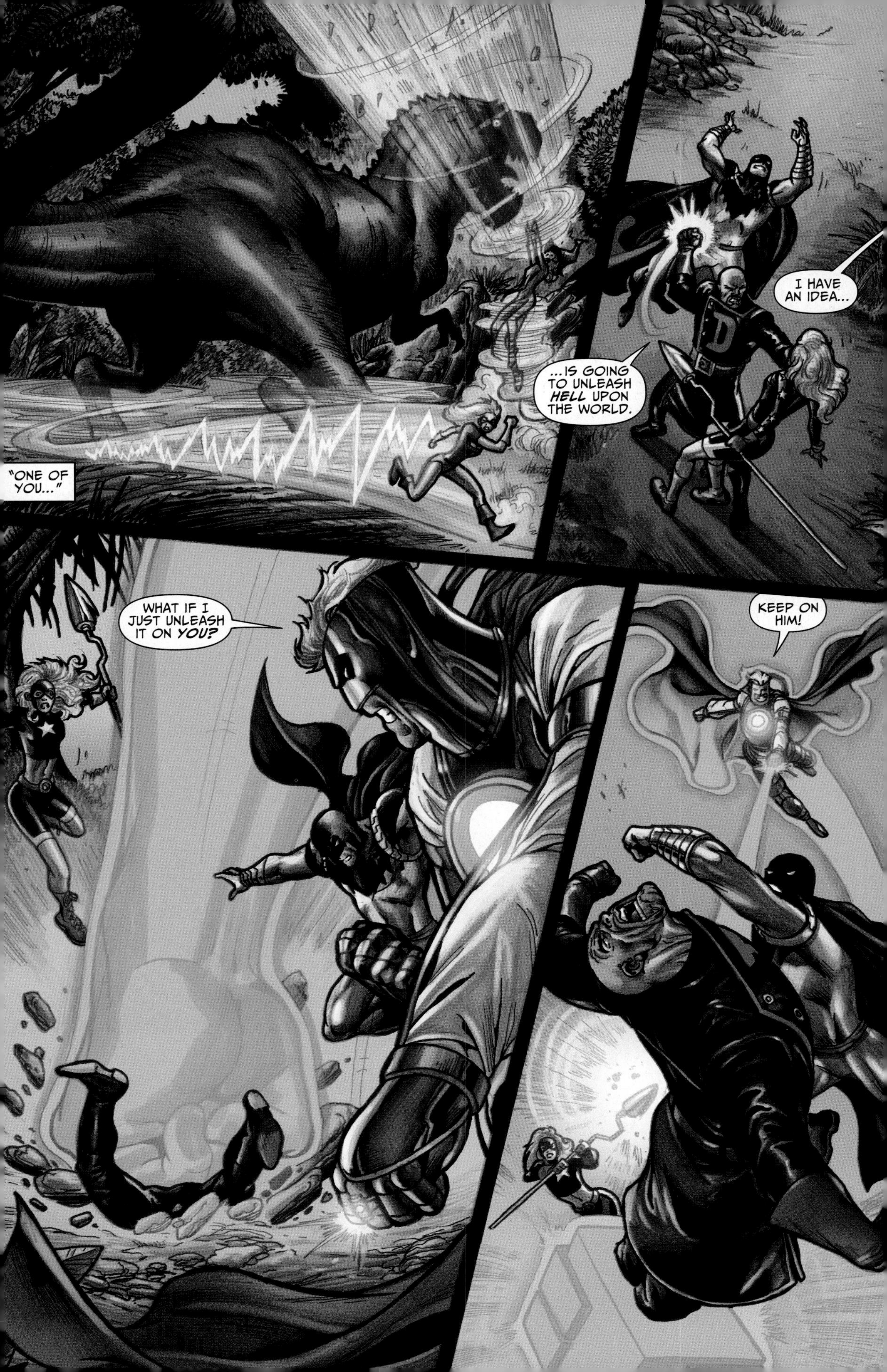
"ONE OF YOU..."
...IS GOING TO UNLEASH *HELL* UPON THE WORLD.
I HAVE AN IDEA...
WHAT IF I JUST UNLEASH IT ON *YOU?*
KEEP ON HIM!

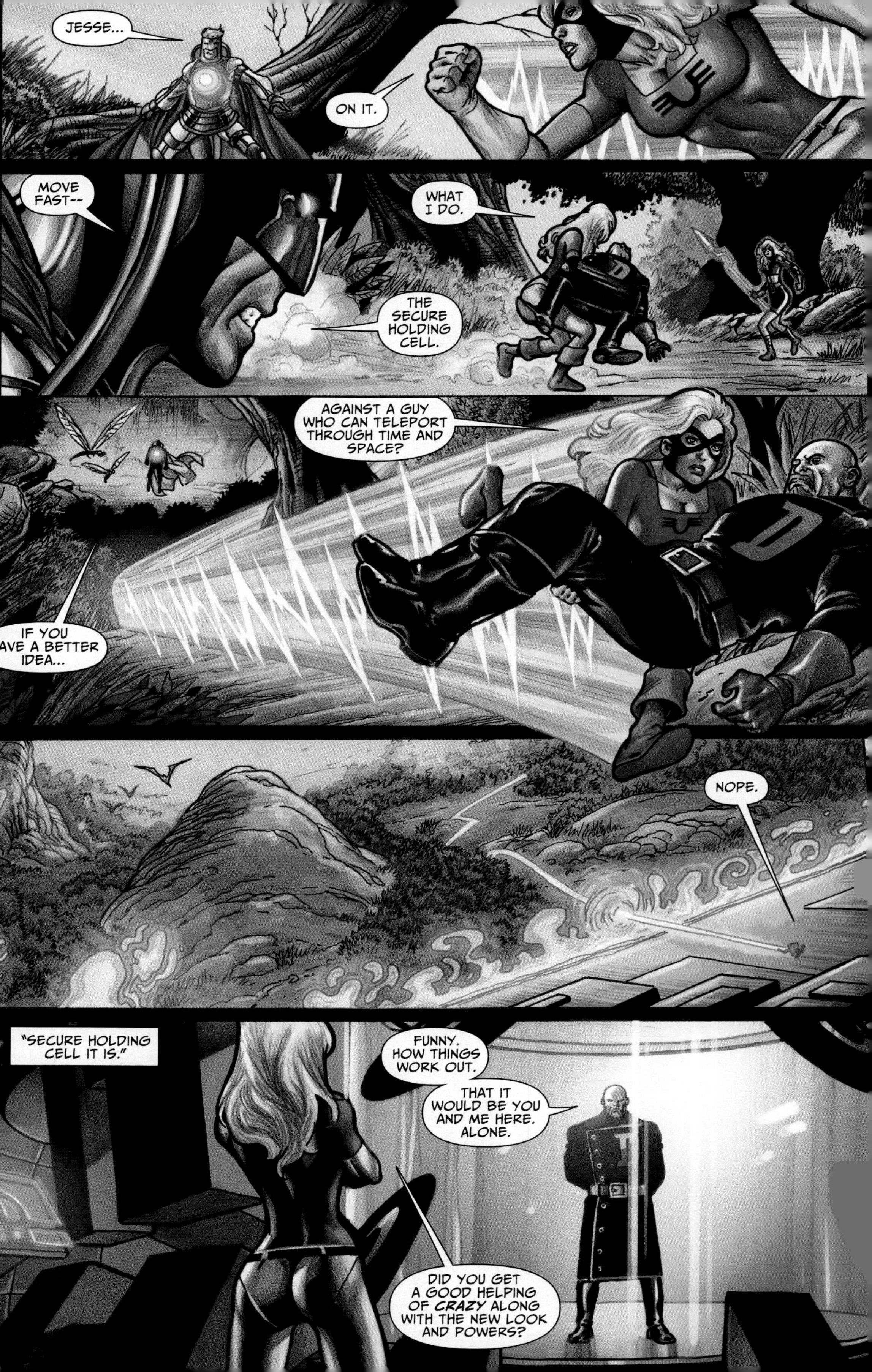
JESSE...
ON IT.
MOVE FAST--
WHAT I DO.
THE SECURE HOLDING CELL.
AGAINST A GUY WHO CAN TELEPORT THROUGH TIME AND SPACE?
IF YOU HAVE A BETTER IDEA...
NOPE.
"SECURE HOLDING CELL IT IS."
FUNNY. HOW THINGS WORK OUT.
THAT IT WOULD BE YOU AND ME HERE. ALONE.
DID YOU GET A GOOD HELPING OF CRAZY ALONG WITH THE NEW LOOK AND POWERS?

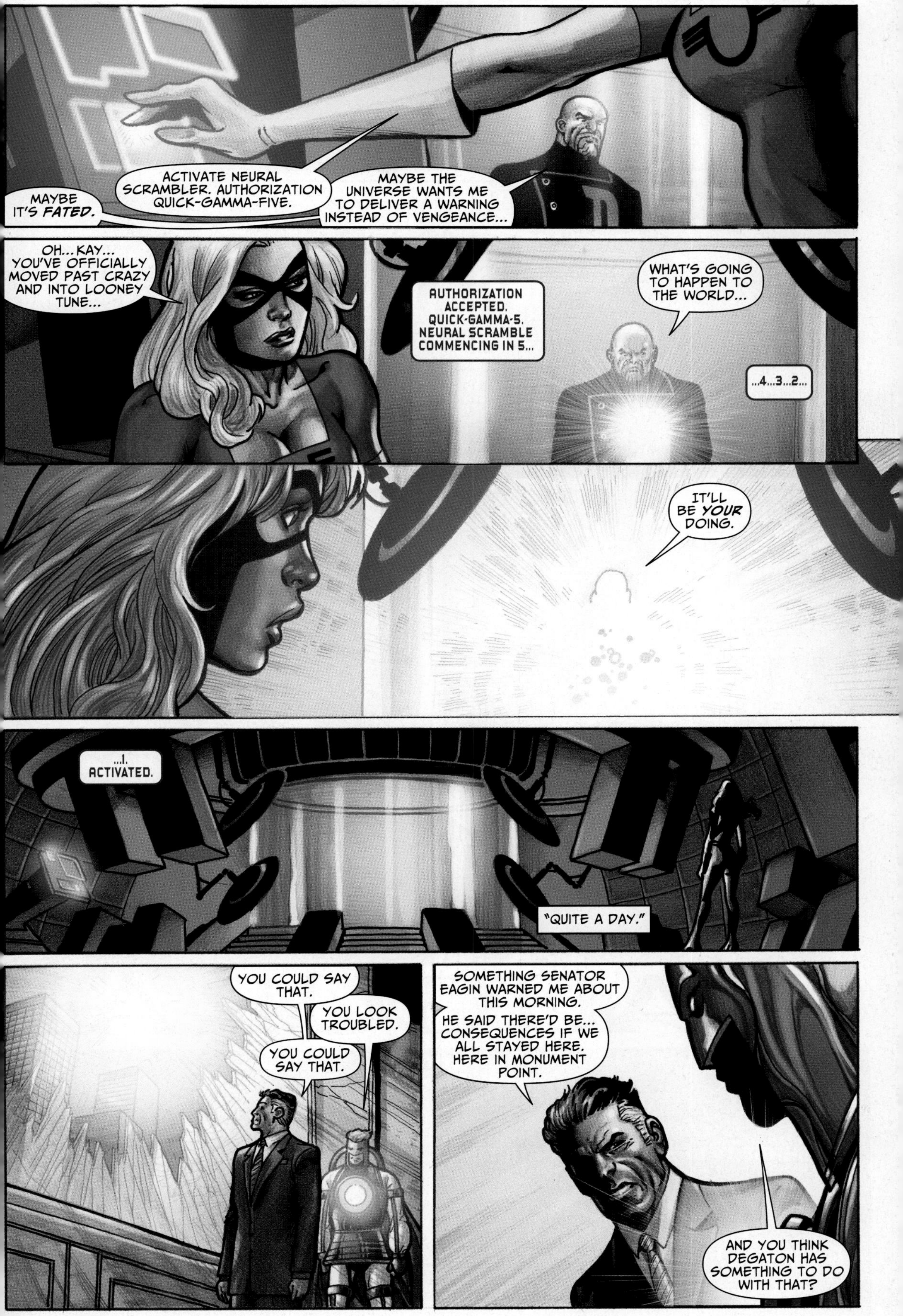
MAYBE IT'S *FATED.*
ACTIVATE NEURAL SCRAMBLER. AUTHORIZATION QUICK-GAMMA-FIVE.
MAYBE THE UNIVERSE WANTS ME TO DELIVER A WARNING INSTEAD OF VENGEANCE...
OH... KAY... YOU'VE OFFICIALLY MOVED PAST CRAZY AND INTO LOONEY TUNE...
AUTHORIZATION ACCEPTED. QUICK-GAMMA-5. NEURAL SCRAMBLE COMMENCING IN 5...
WHAT'S GOING TO HAPPEN TO THE WORLD...
...4...3...2...
IT'LL BE *YOUR* DOING.
...1. ACTIVATED.
"QUITE A DAY."
YOU COULD SAY THAT.
YOU LOOK TROUBLED.
YOU COULD SAY THAT.
SOMETHING SENATOR EAGIN WARNED ME ABOUT THIS MORNING.
HE SAID THERE'D BE... CONSEQUENCES IF WE ALL STAYED HERE. HERE IN MONUMENT POINT.
AND YOU THINK DEGATON HAS SOMETHING TO DO WITH THAT?

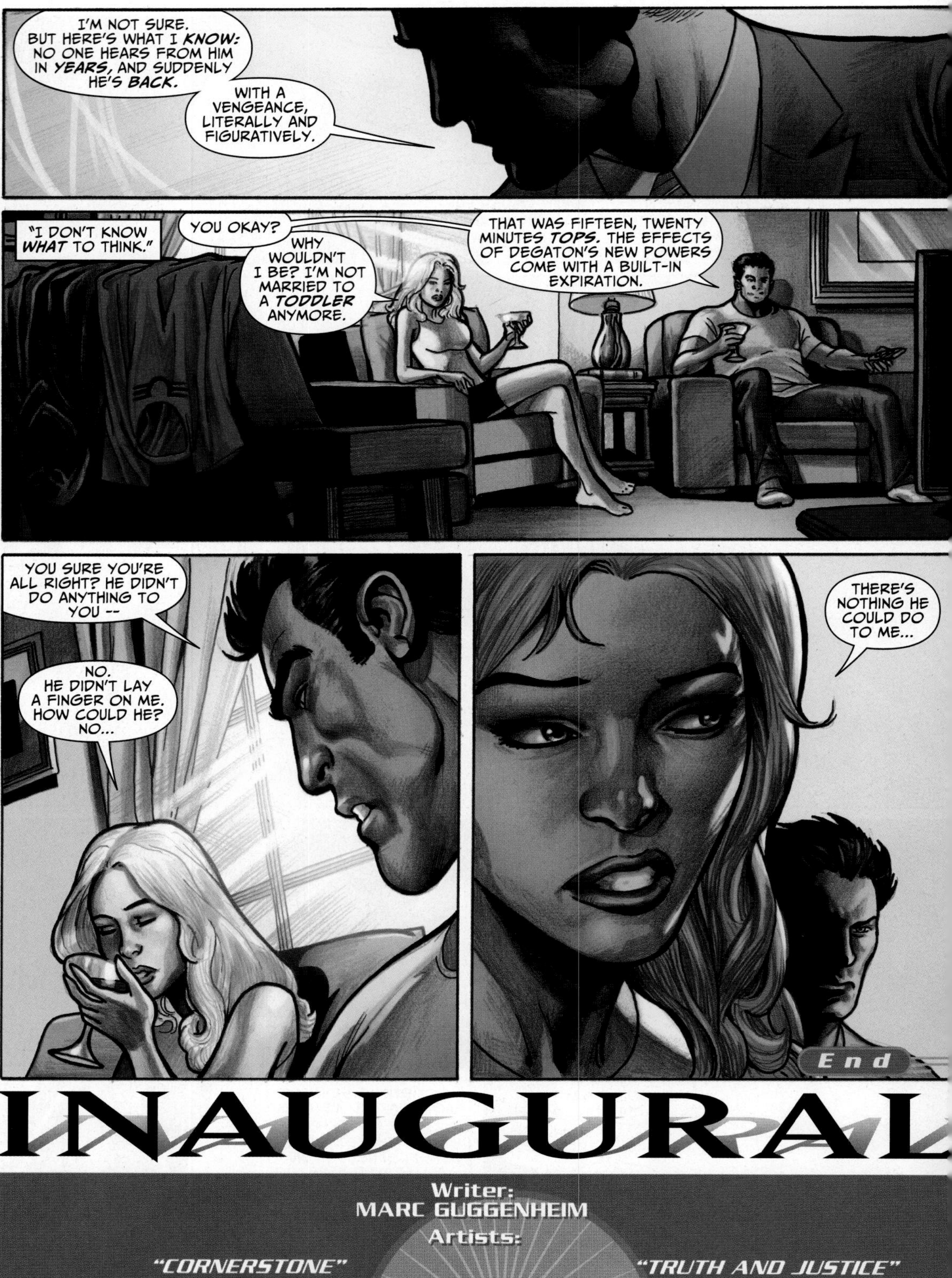
I'M NOT SURE. BUT HERE'S WHAT I KNOW: NO ONE HEARS FROM HIM IN YEARS, AND SUDDENLY HE'S BACK.
WITH A VENGEANCE, LITERALLY AND FIGURATIVELY.
"I DON'T KNOW WHAT TO THINK."
YOU OKAY?
WHY WOULDN'T I BE? I'M NOT MARRIED TO A TODDLER ANYMORE.
THAT WAS FIFTEEN, TWENTY MINUTES TOPS. THE EFFECTS OF DEGATON'S NEW POWERS COME WITH A BUILT-IN EXPIRATION.
YOU SURE YOU'RE ALL RIGHT? HE DIDN'T DO ANYTHING TO YOU --
NO. HE DIDN'T LAY A FINGER ON ME. HOW COULD HE? NO...
THERE'S NOTHING HE COULD DO TO ME...
End

# INAUGURAL

Writer:
MARC GUGGENHEIM

Artists:

"CORNERSTONE"
GEORGE PÉREZ and SCOTT KOBLISH
Colored by HI-FI

"TRUTH AND JUSTICE"
HOWARD CHAYKIN
Colored by JESUS ABURTOV

"INFINITUM"
FREDDIE WILLIAMS II
Colored by RICHARD and TANYA HORIE

"INAUGURAL"
TOM DERENICK
Colored by MIKE ATIYEH

ROB LEIGH, Letterer · Cover by FELIPE MASSAFERA · Variant cover by DARWYN COOKE
CHRIS CONROY, Associate Editor · KATE STEWART, Assistant Editor · JOEY CAVALIERI, Editor

Cover by VICTOR IBÁÑEZ

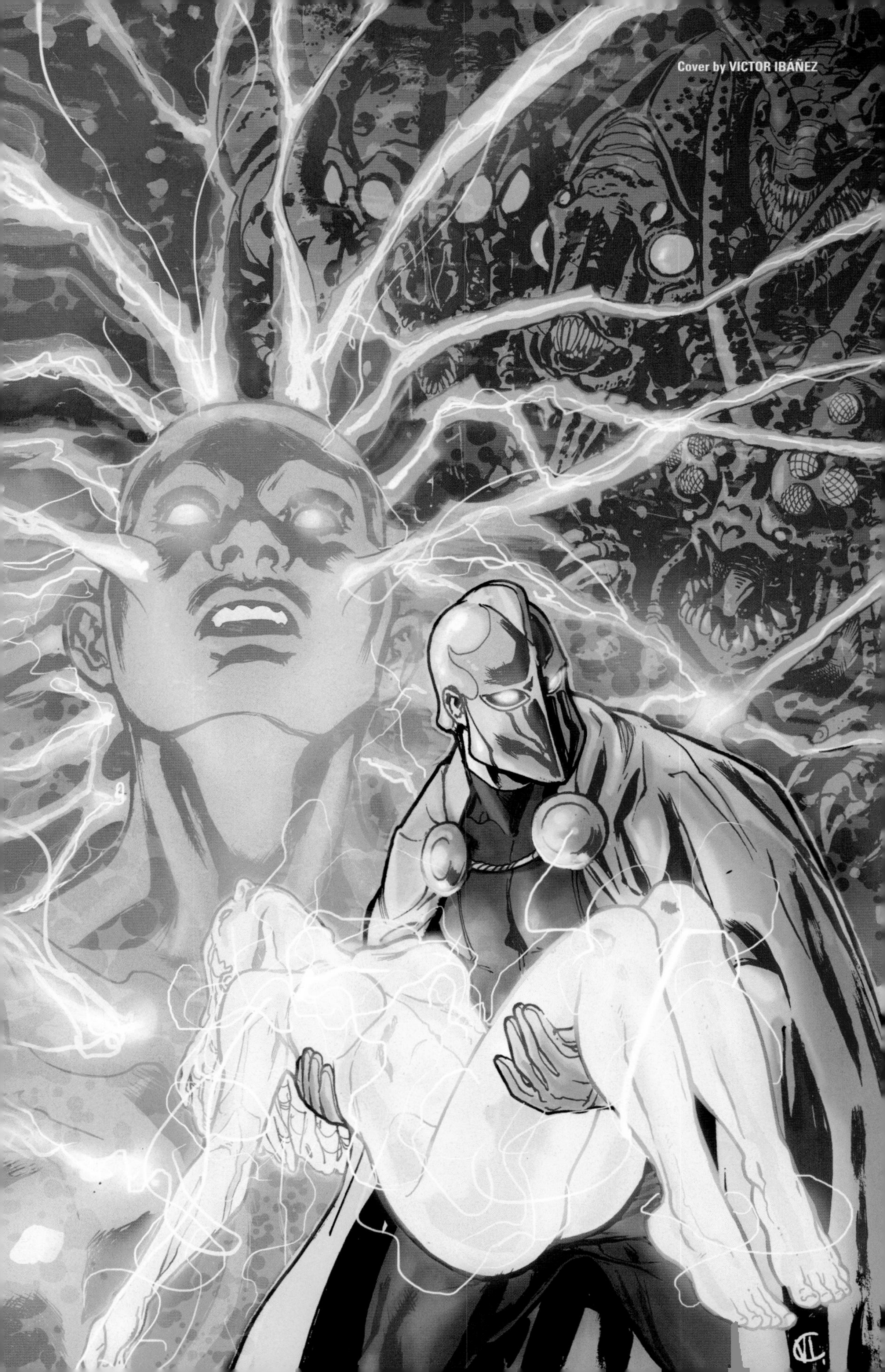

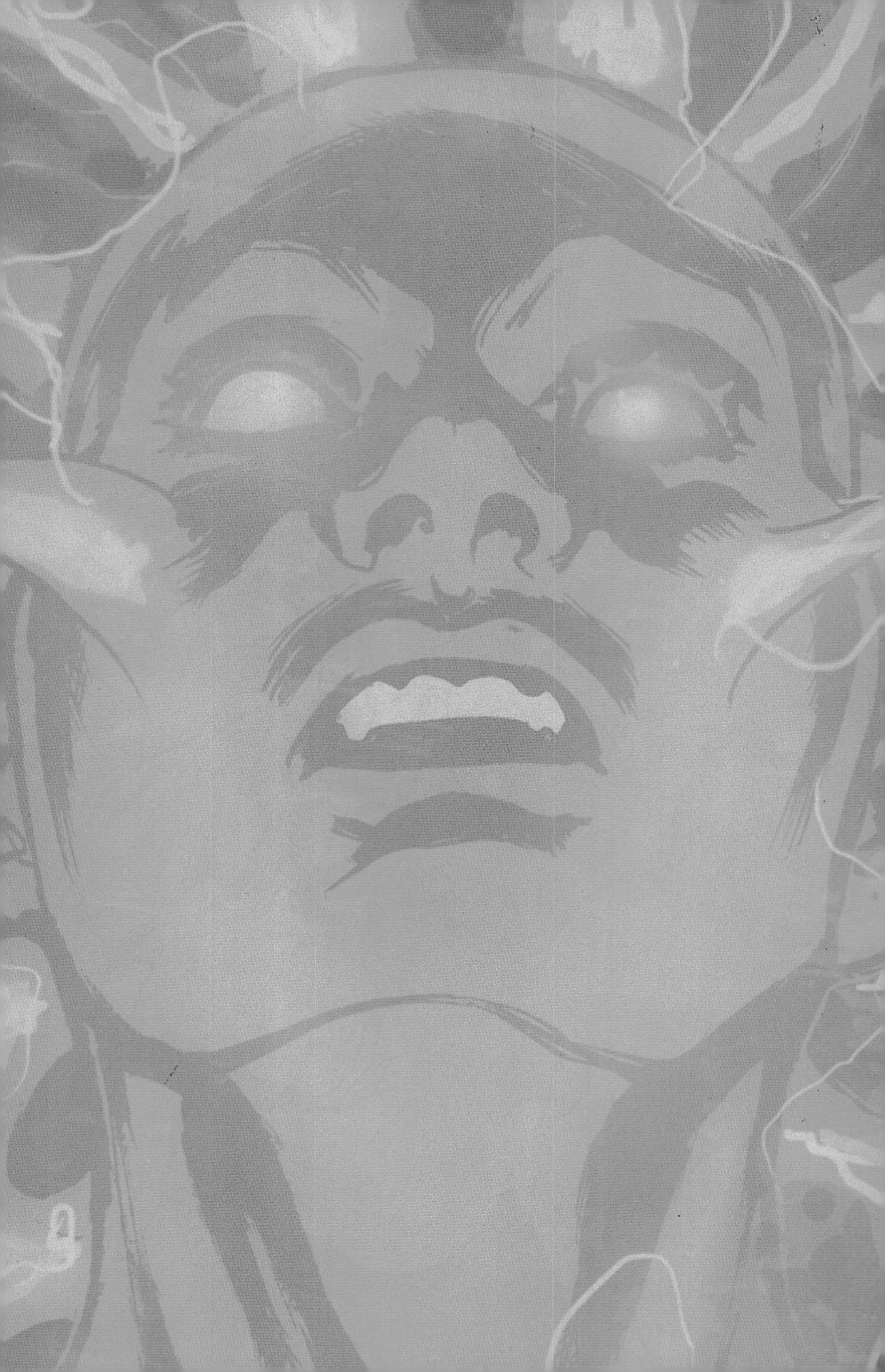

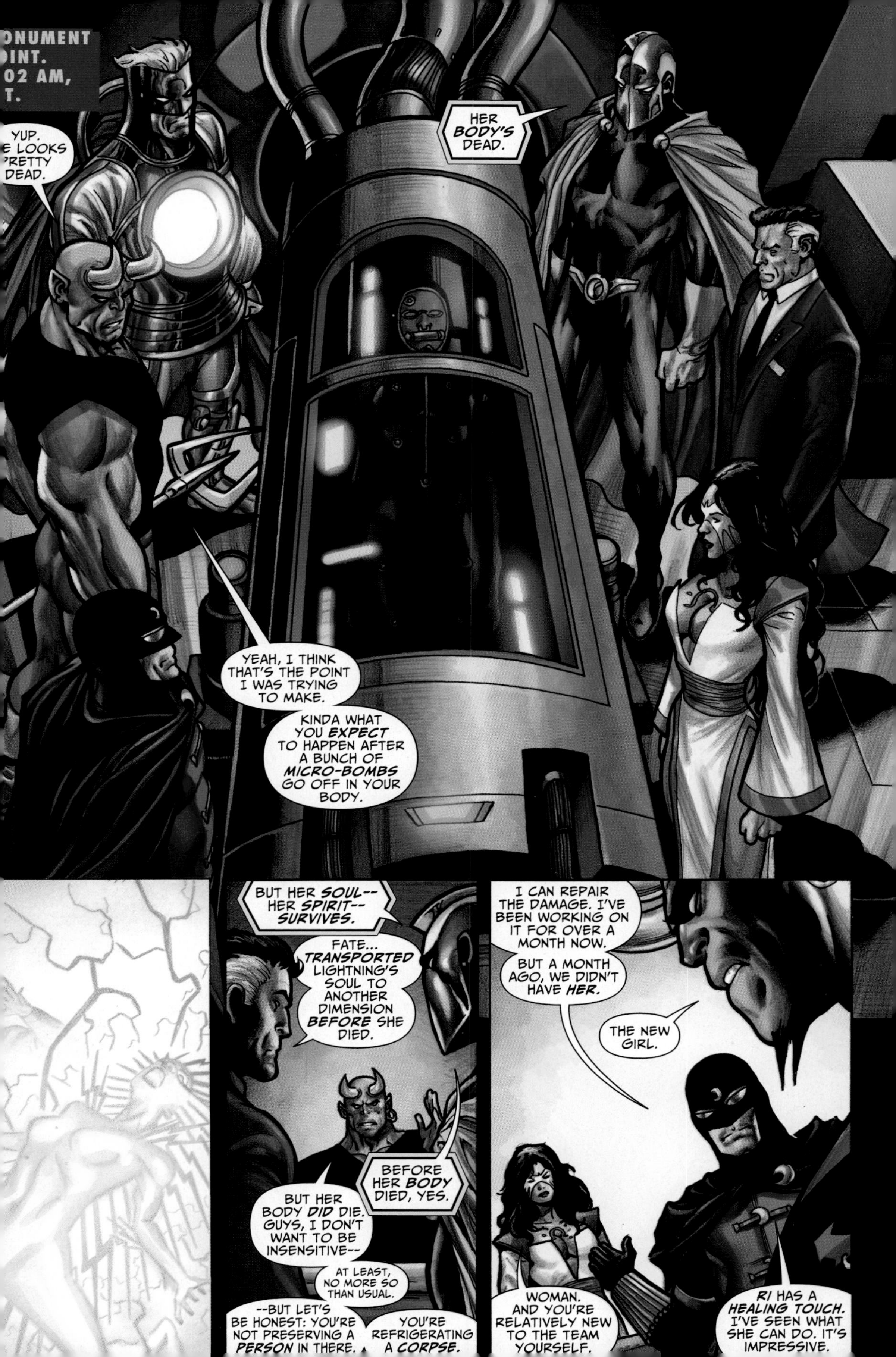
ONUMENT
OINT.
02 AM,
T.
YUP.
E LOOKS
PRETTY
DEAD.
HER BODY'S DEAD.
YEAH, I THINK THAT'S THE POINT I WAS TRYING TO MAKE.
KINDA WHAT YOU EXPECT TO HAPPEN AFTER A BUNCH OF MICRO-BOMBS GO OFF IN YOUR BODY.
BUT HER SOUL-- HER SPIRIT-- SURVIVES.
FATE... TRANSPORTED LIGHTNING'S SOUL TO ANOTHER DIMENSION BEFORE SHE DIED.
BEFORE HER BODY DIED, YES.
BUT HER BODY DID DIE. GUYS, I DON'T WANT TO BE INSENSITIVE--
AT LEAST, NO MORE SO THAN USUAL.
--BUT LET'S BE HONEST: YOU'RE NOT PRESERVING A PERSON IN THERE.
YOU'RE REFRIGERATING A CORPSE.
I CAN REPAIR THE DAMAGE. I'VE BEEN WORKING ON IT FOR OVER A MONTH NOW.
BUT A MONTH AGO, WE DIDN'T HAVE HER.
THE NEW GIRL.
WOMAN. AND YOU'RE RELATIVELY NEW TO THE TEAM YOURSELF.
RI HAS A HEALING TOUCH. I'VE SEEN WHAT SHE CAN DO. IT'S IMPRESSIVE.

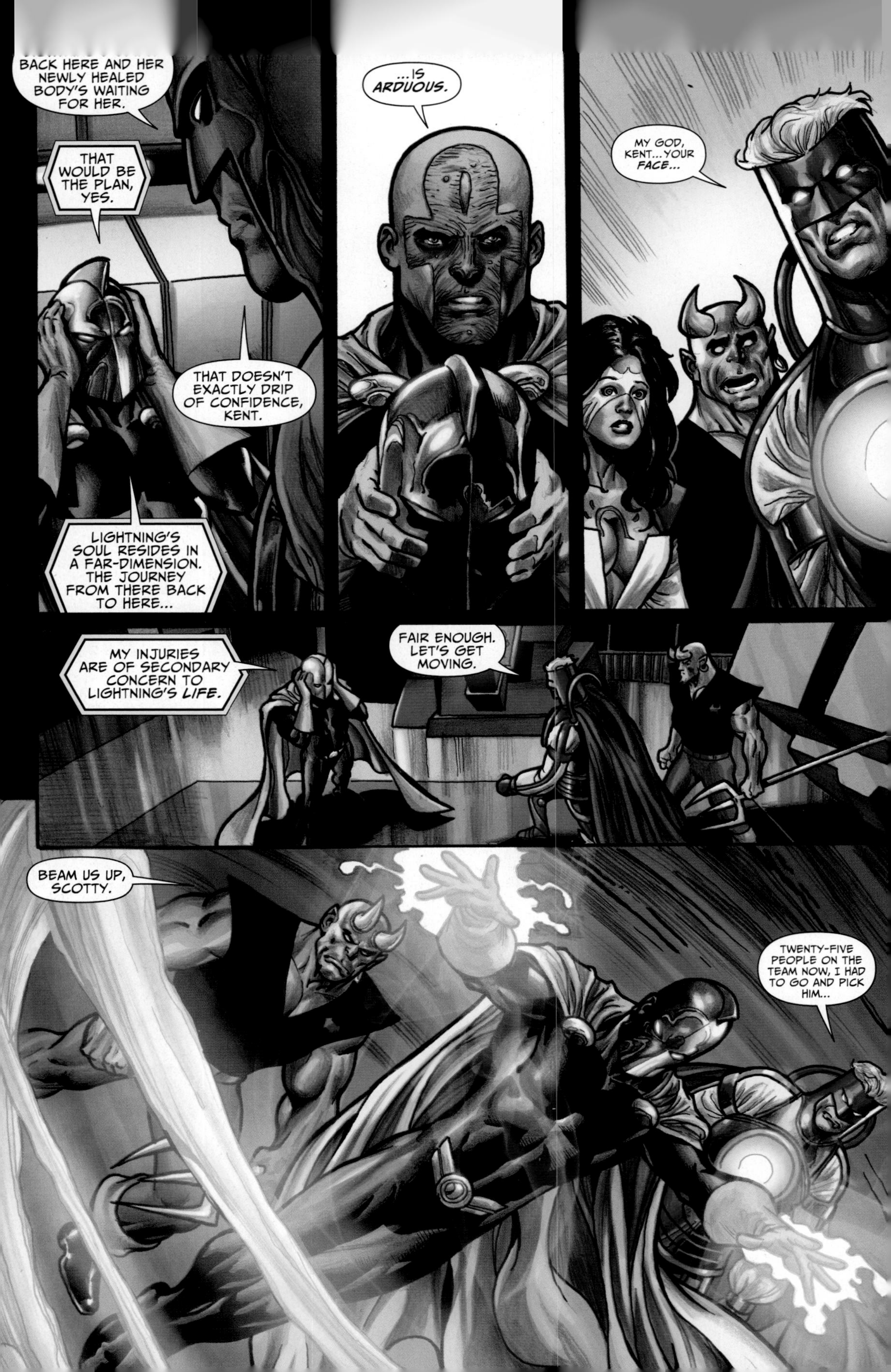
BACK HERE AND HER NEWLY HEALED BODY'S WAITING FOR HER.
THAT WOULD BE THE PLAN, YES.
THAT DOESN'T EXACTLY DRIP OF CONFIDENCE, KENT.
LIGHTNING'S SOUL RESIDES IN A FAR-DIMENSION. THE JOURNEY FROM THERE BACK TO HERE...
...IS *ARDUOUS.*
MY GOD, KENT... YOUR *FACE...*
MY INJURIES ARE OF SECONDARY CONCERN TO LIGHTNING'S *LIFE.*
FAIR ENOUGH. LET'S GET MOVING.
BEAM US UP, SCOTTY.
TWENTY-FIVE PEOPLE ON THE TEAM NOW, I HAD TO GO AND PICK HIM...

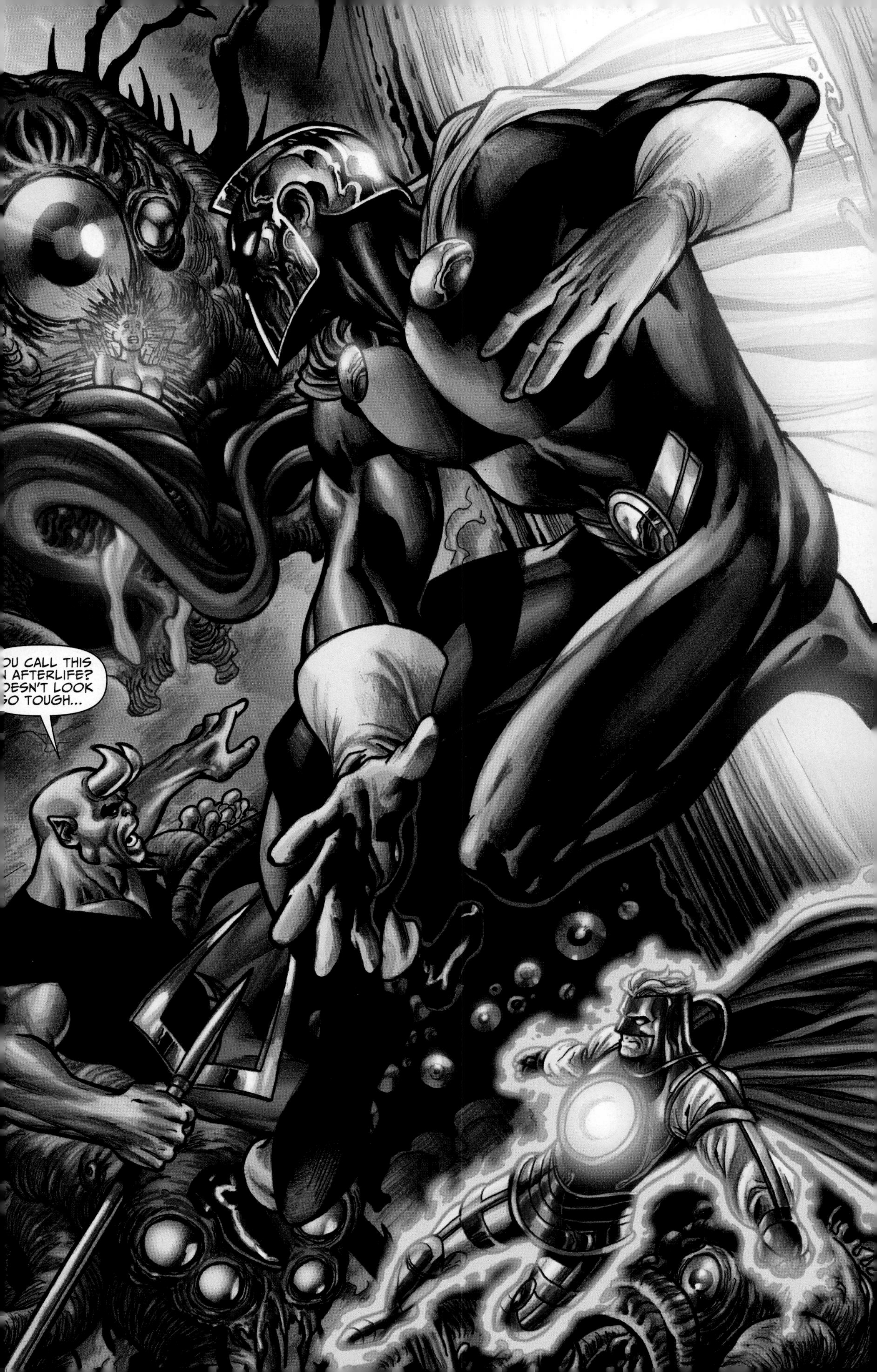
OU CALL THIS N AFTERLIFE? DESN'T LOOK SO TOUGH...

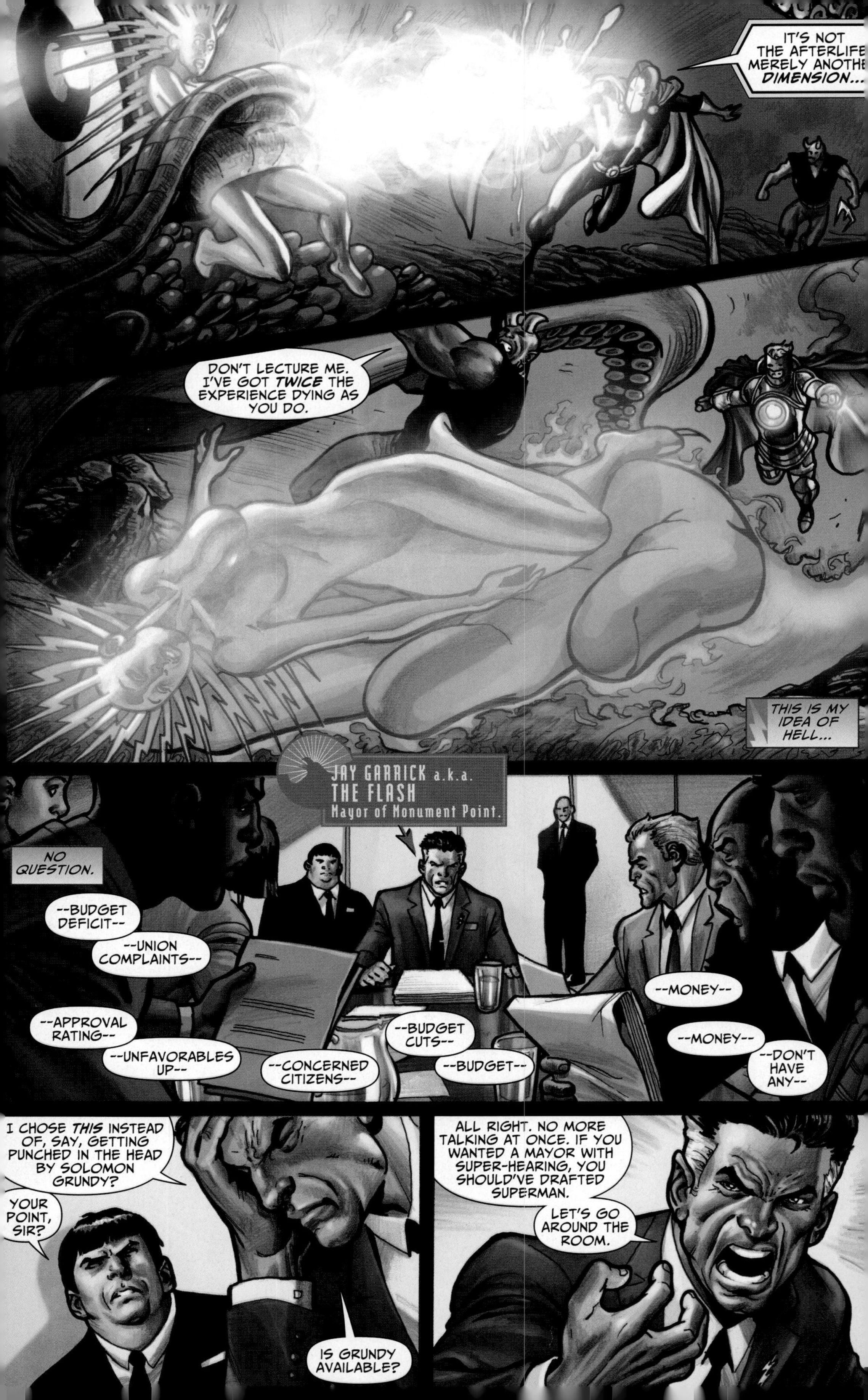
IT'S NOT THE AFTERLIFE MERELY ANOTHE DIMENSION...
DON'T LECTURE ME. I'VE GOT TWICE THE EXPERIENCE DYING AS YOU DO.
THIS IS MY IDEA OF HELL...
JAY GARRICK a.k.a. THE FLASH Mayor of Monument Point.
NO QUESTION.
--BUDGET DEFICIT--
--UNION COMPLAINTS--
--APPROVAL RATING--
--UNFAVORABLES UP--
--CONCERNED CITIZENS--
--BUDGET CUTS--
--BUDGET--
--MONEY--
--MONEY--
--DON'T HAVE ANY--
I CHOSE THIS INSTEAD OF, SAY, GETTING PUNCHED IN THE HEAD BY SOLOMON GRUNDY?
YOUR POINT, SIR?
IS GRUNDY AVAILABLE?
ALL RIGHT. NO MORE TALKING AT ONCE. IF YOU WANTED A MAYOR WITH SUPER-HEARING, YOU SHOULD'VE DRAFTED SUPERMAN.
LET'S GO AROUND THE ROOM.

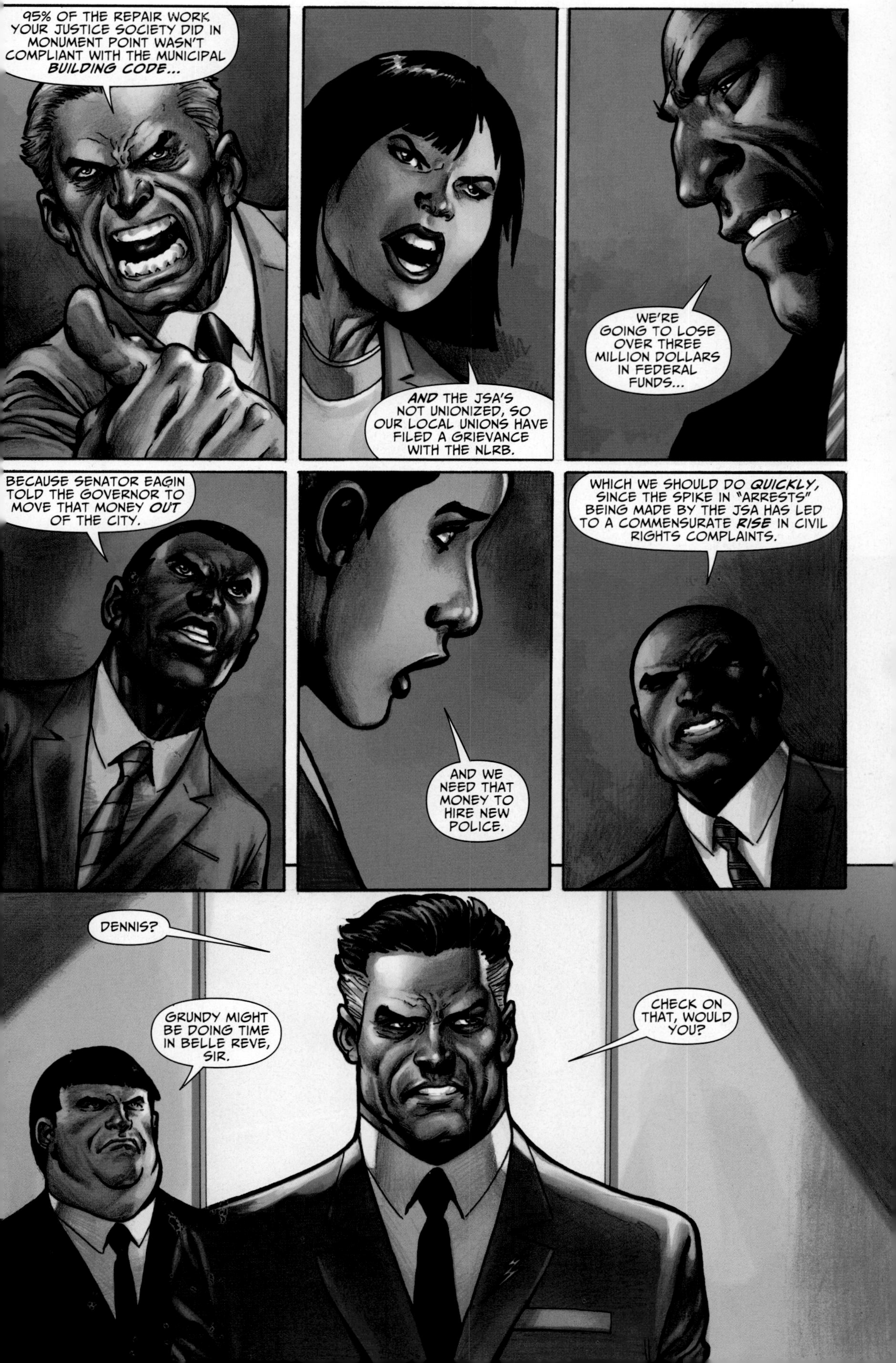
95% OF THE REPAIR WORK YOUR JUSTICE SOCIETY DID IN MONUMENT POINT WASN'T COMPLIANT WITH THE MUNICIPAL *BUILDING CODE...*
*AND* THE JSA'S NOT UNIONIZED, SO OUR LOCAL UNIONS HAVE FILED A GRIEVANCE WITH THE NLRB.
WE'RE GOING TO LOSE OVER THREE MILLION DOLLARS IN FEDERAL FUNDS...
BECAUSE SENATOR EAGIN TOLD THE GOVERNOR TO MOVE THAT MONEY *OUT* OF THE CITY.
AND WE NEED THAT MONEY TO HIRE NEW POLICE.
WHICH WE SHOULD DO *QUICKLY*, SINCE THE SPIKE IN "ARRESTS" BEING MADE BY THE JSA HAS LED TO A COMMENSURATE *RISE* IN CIVIL RIGHTS COMPLAINTS.
DENNIS?
GRUNDY MIGHT BE DOING TIME IN BELLE REVE, SIR.
CHECK ON THAT, WOULD YOU?

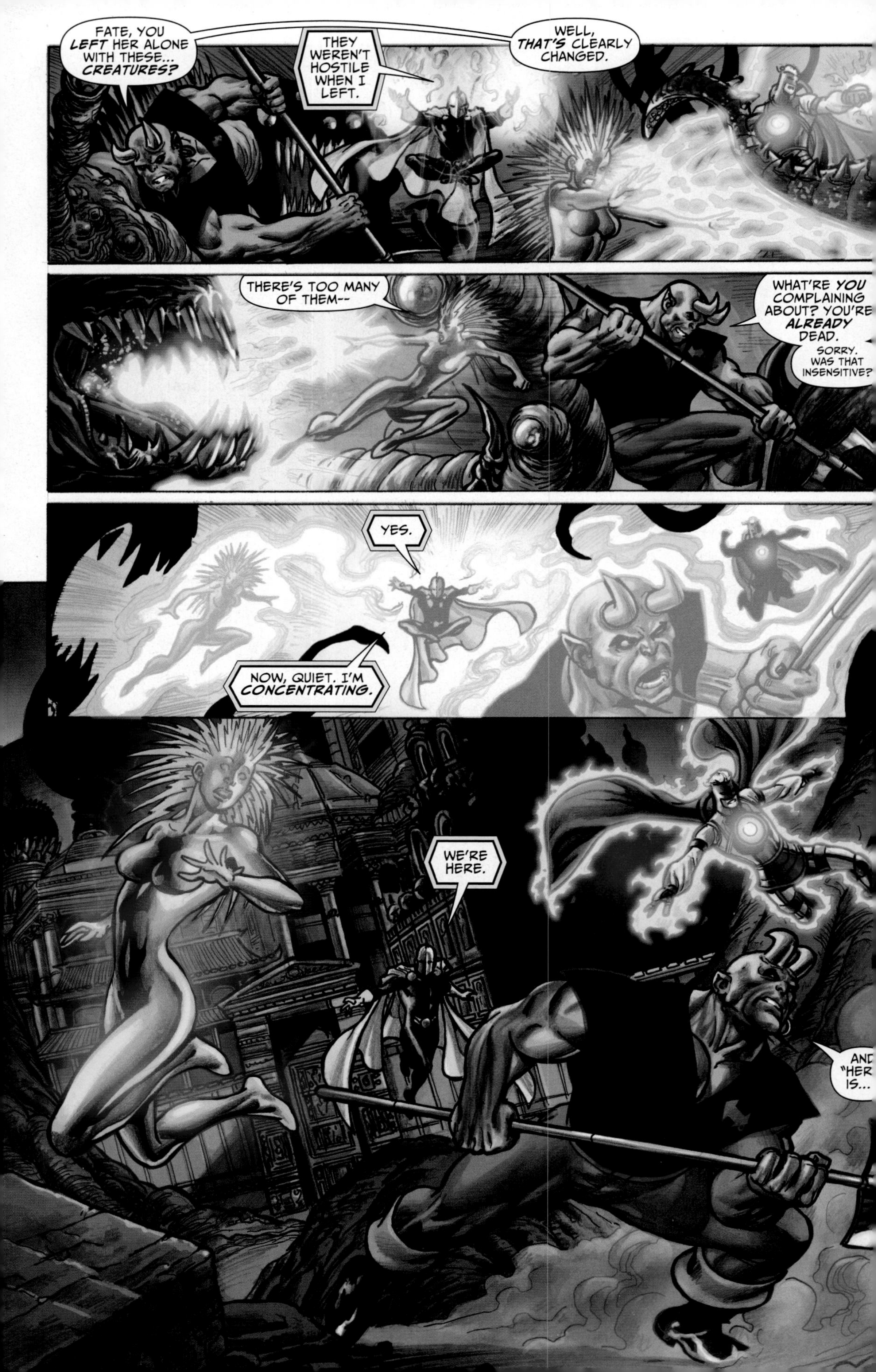
FATE, YOU LEFT HER ALONE WITH THESE... CREATURES?
THEY WEREN'T HOSTILE WHEN I LEFT.
WELL, THAT'S CLEARLY CHANGED.
THERE'S TOO MANY OF THEM--
WHAT'RE YOU COMPLAINING ABOUT? YOU'RE ALREADY DEAD.
SORRY. WAS THAT INSENSITIVE?
YES.
NOW, QUIET. I'M CONCENTRATING.
WE'RE HERE.
AND "HER" IS...

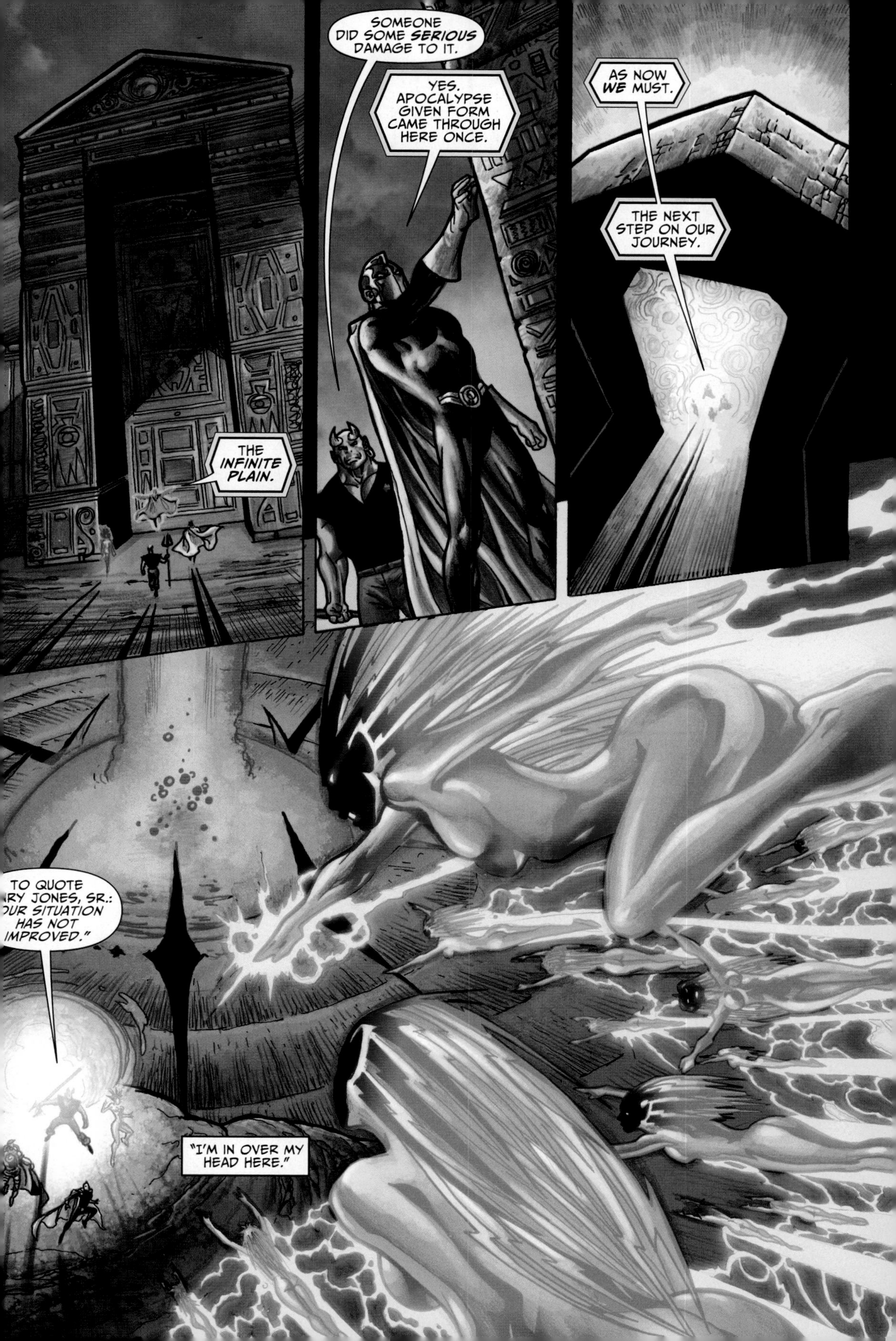
THE INFINITE PLAIN.
SOMEONE DID SOME SERIOUS DAMAGE TO IT.
YES. APOCALYPSE GIVEN FORM CAME THROUGH HERE ONCE.
AS NOW WE MUST.
THE NEXT STEP ON OUR JOURNEY.
TO QUOTE ARY JONES, SR.: OUR SITUATION HAS NOT IMPROVED."
"I'M IN OVER MY HEAD HERE."

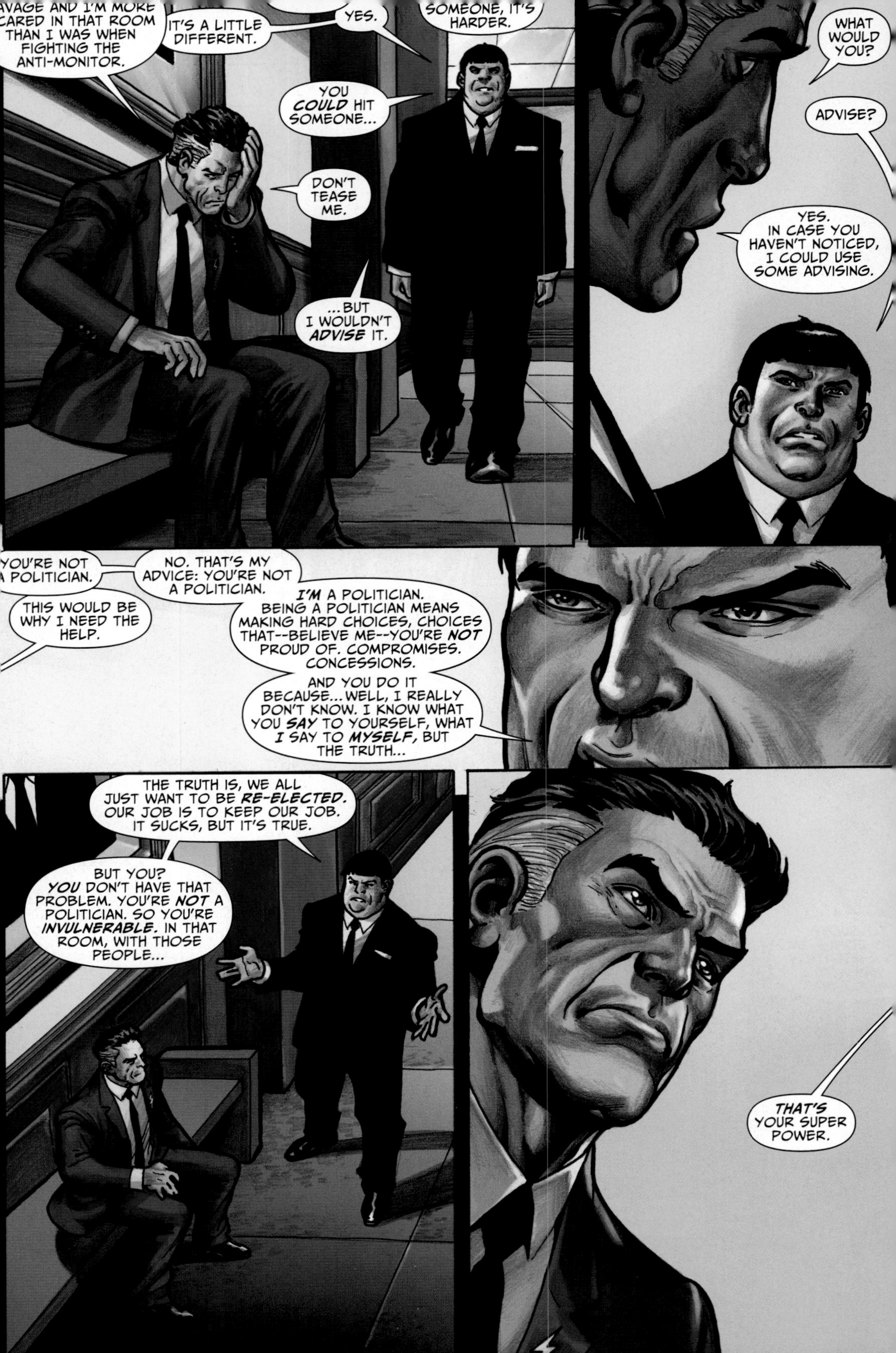
AVAGE AND I'M MORE CARED IN THAT ROOM THAN I WAS WHEN FIGHTING THE ANTI-MONITOR.
IT'S A LITTLE DIFFERENT.
YES.
SOMEONE, IT'S HARDER.
YOU COULD HIT SOMEONE...
DON'T TEASE ME.
...BUT I WOULDN'T ADVISE IT.
WHAT WOULD YOU?
ADVISE?
YES. IN CASE YOU HAVEN'T NOTICED, I COULD USE SOME ADVISING.
YOU'RE NOT A POLITICIAN.
NO. THAT'S MY ADVICE: YOU'RE NOT A POLITICIAN.
THIS WOULD BE WHY I NEED THE HELP.
I'M A POLITICIAN. BEING A POLITICIAN MEANS MAKING HARD CHOICES, CHOICES THAT--BELIEVE ME--YOU'RE NOT PROUD OF. COMPROMISES. CONCESSIONS.
AND YOU DO IT BECAUSE...WELL, I REALLY DON'T KNOW. I KNOW WHAT YOU SAY TO YOURSELF, WHAT I SAY TO MYSELF, BUT THE TRUTH...
THE TRUTH IS, WE ALL JUST WANT TO BE RE-ELECTED. OUR JOB IS TO KEEP OUR JOB. IT SUCKS, BUT IT'S TRUE.
BUT YOU? YOU DON'T HAVE THAT PROBLEM. YOU'RE NOT A POLITICIAN. SO YOU'RE INVULNERABLE. IN THAT ROOM, WITH THOSE PEOPLE...
THAT'S YOUR SUPER POWER.

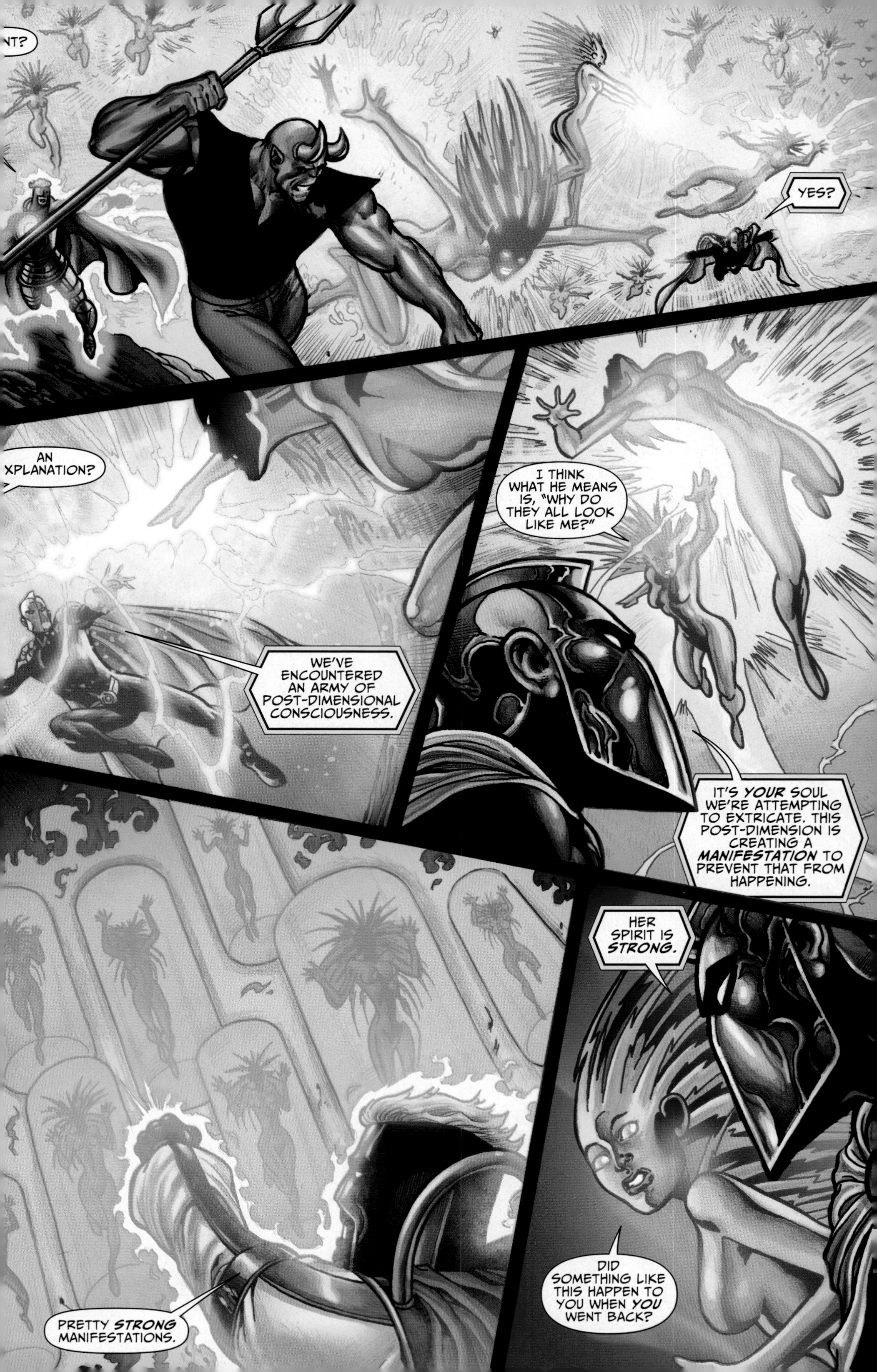
NT?
YES?
AN XPLANATION?
I THINK WHAT HE MEANS IS, "WHY DO THEY ALL LOOK LIKE ME?"
WE'VE ENCOUNTERED AN ARMY OF POST-DIMENSIONAL CONSCIOUSNESS.
IT'S YOUR SOUL WE'RE ATTEMPTING TO EXTRICATE. THIS POST-DIMENSION IS CREATING A MANIFESTATION TO PREVENT THAT FROM HAPPENING.
HER SPIRIT IS STRONG.
PRETTY STRONG MANIFESTATIONS.
DID SOMETHING LIKE THIS HAPPEN TO YOU WHEN YOU WENT BACK?

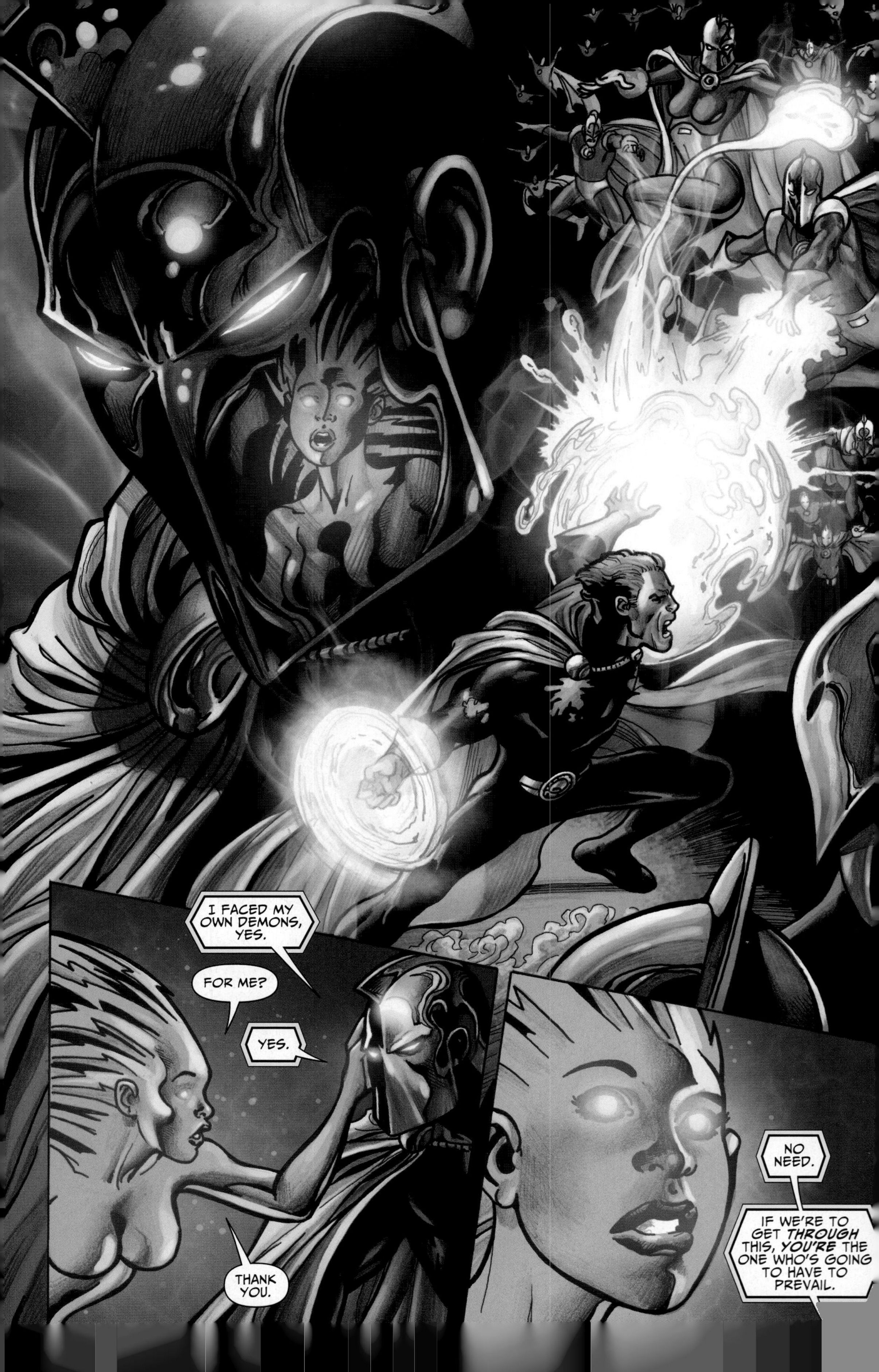
I FACED MY OWN DEMONS, YES.
FOR ME?
YES.
THANK YOU.
NO NEED.
IF WE'RE TO GET *THROUGH* THIS, *YOU'RE* THE ONE WHO'S GOING TO HAVE TO PREVAIL.

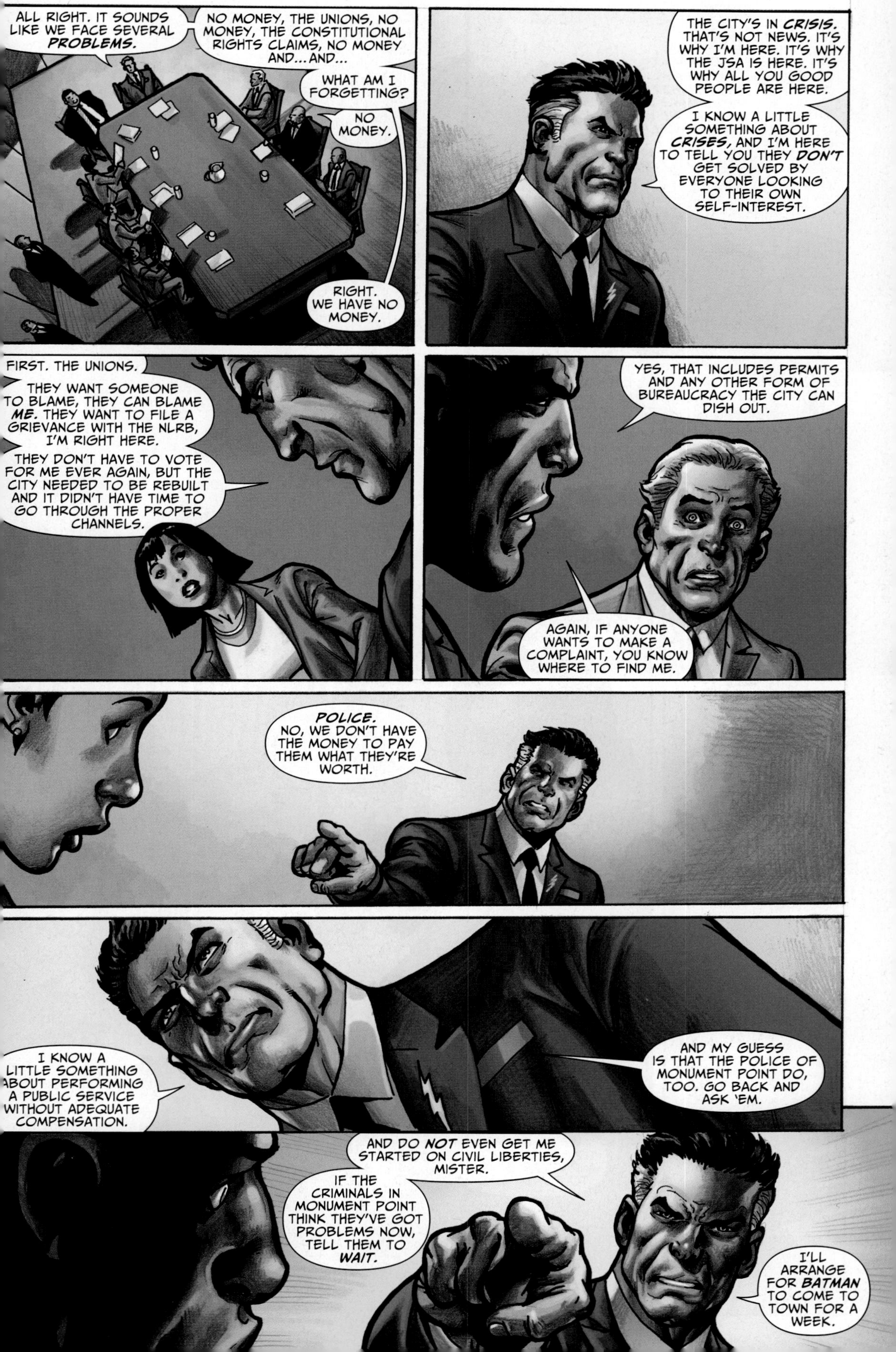
ALL RIGHT. IT SOUNDS LIKE WE FACE SEVERAL PROBLEMS.
NO MONEY, THE UNIONS, NO MONEY, THE CONSTITUTIONAL RIGHTS CLAIMS, NO MONEY AND... AND...
WHAT AM I FORGETTING?
NO MONEY.
RIGHT. WE HAVE NO MONEY.
THE CITY'S IN CRISIS. THAT'S NOT NEWS. IT'S WHY I'M HERE. IT'S WHY THE JSA IS HERE. IT'S WHY ALL YOU GOOD PEOPLE ARE HERE.
I KNOW A LITTLE SOMETHING ABOUT CRISES, AND I'M HERE TO TELL YOU THEY DON'T GET SOLVED BY EVERYONE LOOKING TO THEIR OWN SELF-INTEREST.
FIRST. THE UNIONS.
THEY WANT SOMEONE TO BLAME, THEY CAN BLAME ME. THEY WANT TO FILE A GRIEVANCE WITH THE NLRB, I'M RIGHT HERE.
THEY DON'T HAVE TO VOTE FOR ME EVER AGAIN, BUT THE CITY NEEDED TO BE REBUILT AND IT DIDN'T HAVE TIME TO GO THROUGH THE PROPER CHANNELS.
YES, THAT INCLUDES PERMITS AND ANY OTHER FORM OF BUREAUCRACY THE CITY CAN DISH OUT.
AGAIN, IF ANYONE WANTS TO MAKE A COMPLAINT, YOU KNOW WHERE TO FIND ME.
POLICE. NO, WE DON'T HAVE THE MONEY TO PAY THEM WHAT THEY'RE WORTH.
I KNOW A LITTLE SOMETHING ABOUT PERFORMING A PUBLIC SERVICE WITHOUT ADEQUATE COMPENSATION.
AND MY GUESS IS THAT THE POLICE OF MONUMENT POINT DO, TOO. GO BACK AND ASK 'EM.
AND DO NOT EVEN GET ME STARTED ON CIVIL LIBERTIES, MISTER.
IF THE CRIMINALS IN MONUMENT POINT THINK THEY'VE GOT PROBLEMS NOW, TELL THEM TO WAIT.
I'LL ARRANGE FOR BATMAN TO COME TO TOWN FOR A WEEK.

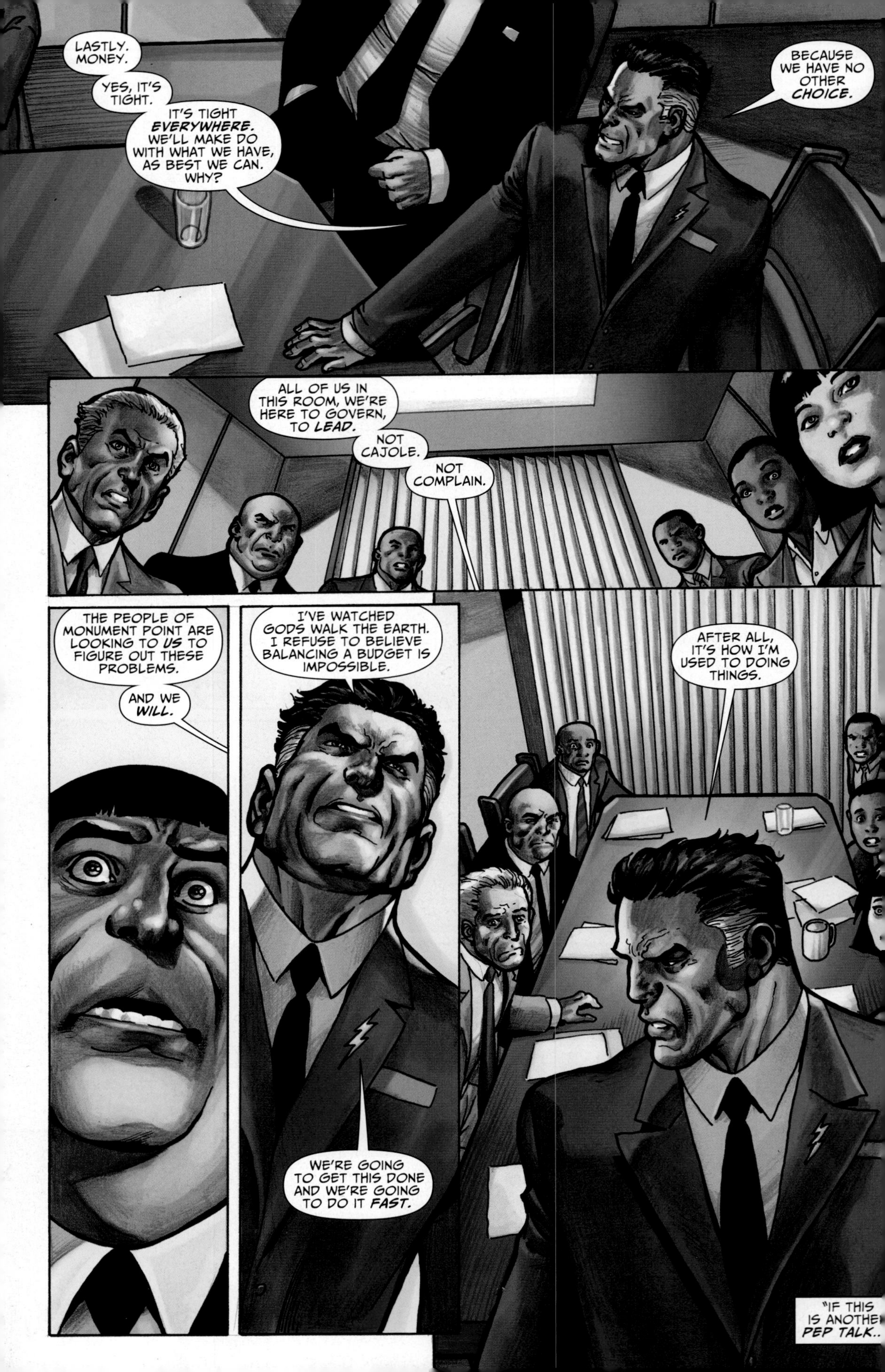
LASTLY. MONEY.
YES, IT'S TIGHT.
IT'S TIGHT EVERYWHERE. WE'LL MAKE DO WITH WHAT WE HAVE, AS BEST WE CAN. WHY?
BECAUSE WE HAVE NO OTHER CHOICE.
ALL OF US IN THIS ROOM, WE'RE HERE TO GOVERN, TO LEAD.
NOT CAJOLE.
NOT COMPLAIN.
THE PEOPLE OF MONUMENT POINT ARE LOOKING TO US TO FIGURE OUT THESE PROBLEMS.
AND WE WILL.
I'VE WATCHED GODS WALK THE EARTH. I REFUSE TO BELIEVE BALANCING A BUDGET IS IMPOSSIBLE.
WE'RE GOING TO GET THIS DONE AND WE'RE GOING TO DO IT FAST.
AFTER ALL, IT'S HOW I'M USED TO DOING THINGS.
"IF THIS IS ANOTHE PEP TALK..

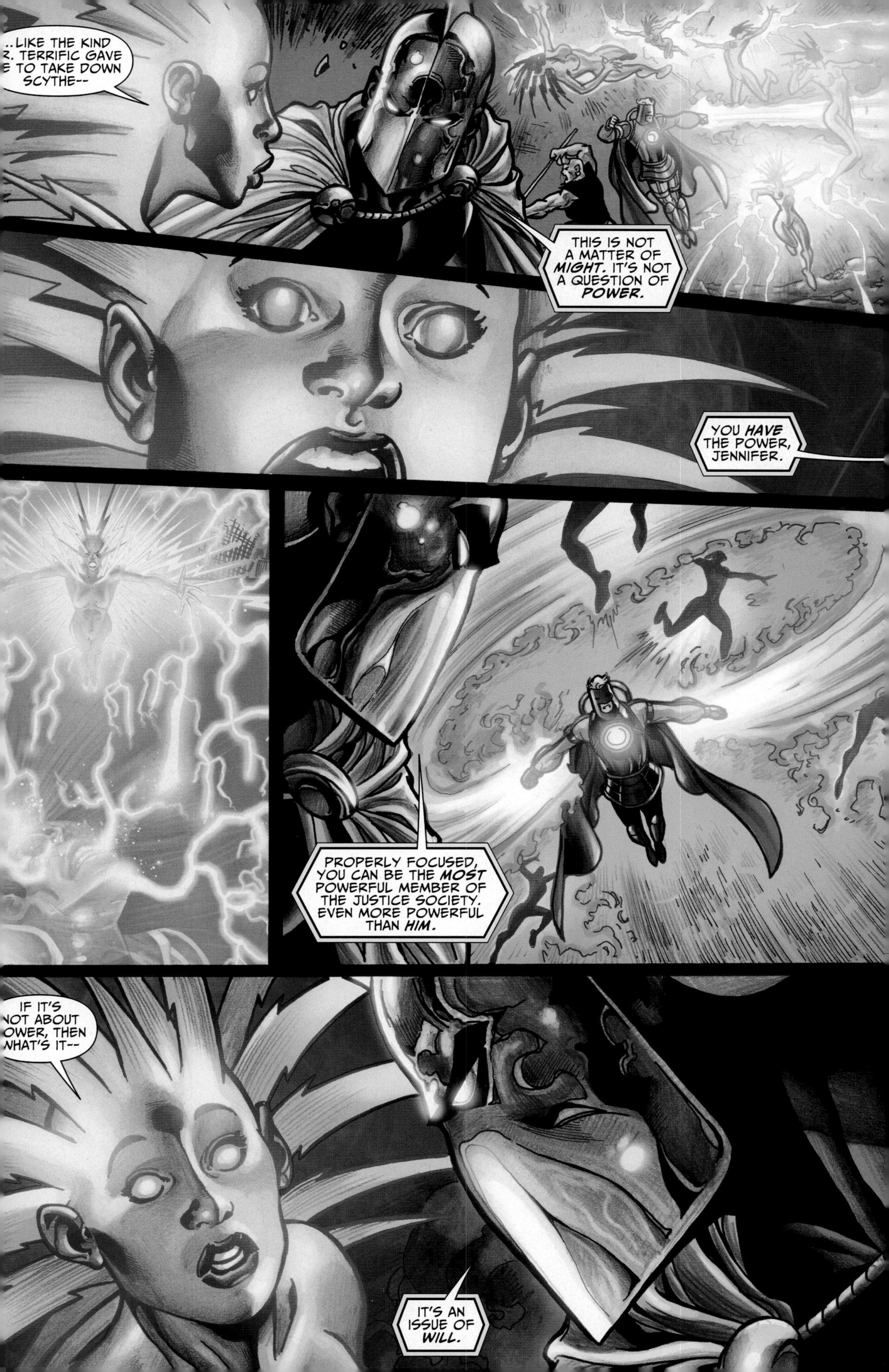
..LIKE THE KIND R. TERRIFIC GAVE E TO TAKE DOWN SCYTHE--
THIS IS NOT A MATTER OF MIGHT. IT'S NOT A QUESTION OF POWER.
YOU HAVE THE POWER, JENNIFER.
PROPERLY FOCUSED, YOU CAN BE THE MOST POWERFUL MEMBER OF THE JUSTICE SOCIETY. EVEN MORE POWERFUL THAN HIM.
IF IT'S NOT ABOUT OWER, THEN WHAT'S IT--
IT'S AN ISSUE OF WILL.

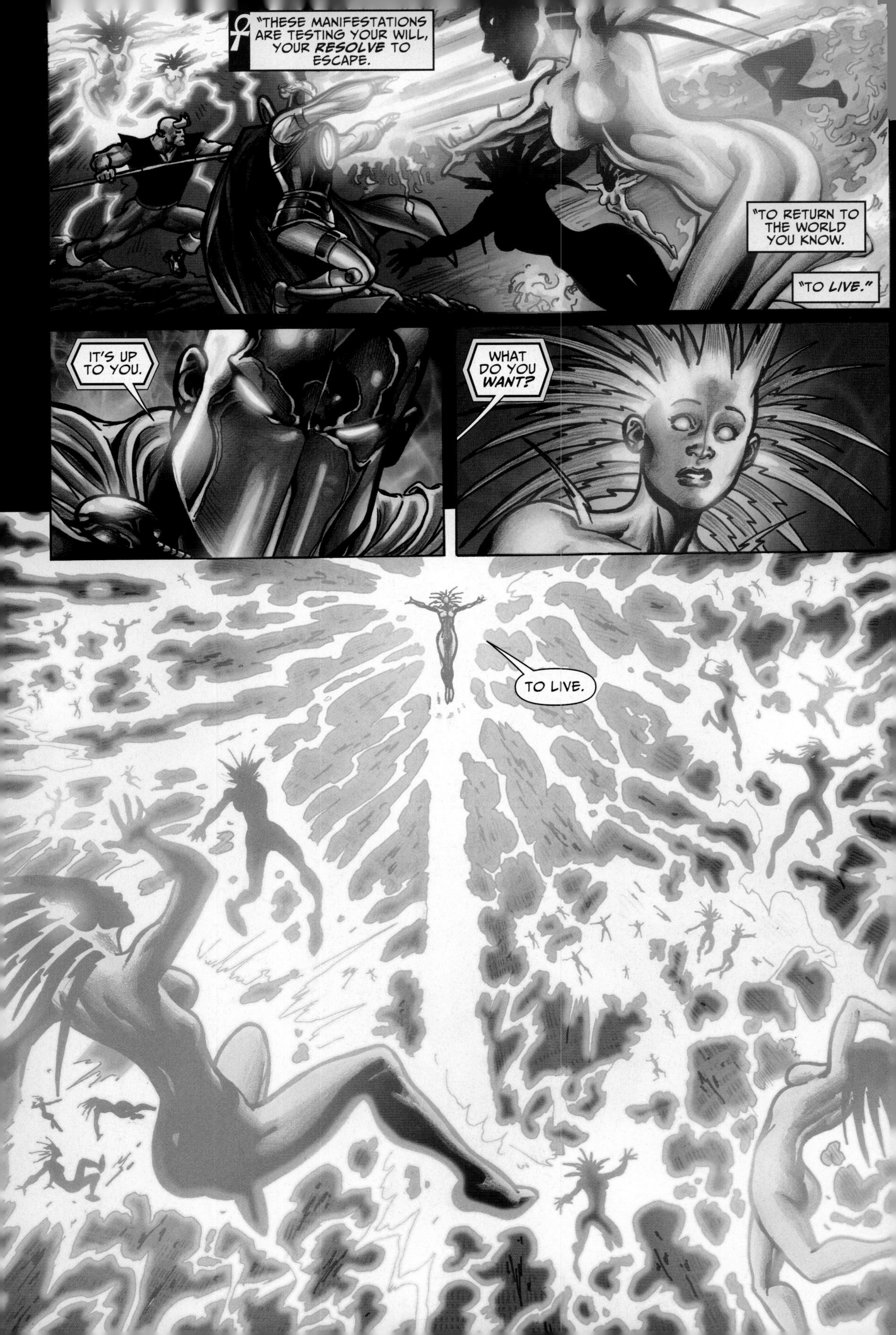
"THESE MANIFESTATIONS ARE TESTING YOUR WILL, YOUR RESOLVE TO ESCAPE.
"TO RETURN TO THE WORLD YOU KNOW.
"TO LIVE."
IT'S UP TO YOU.
WHAT DO YOU WANT?
TO LIVE.

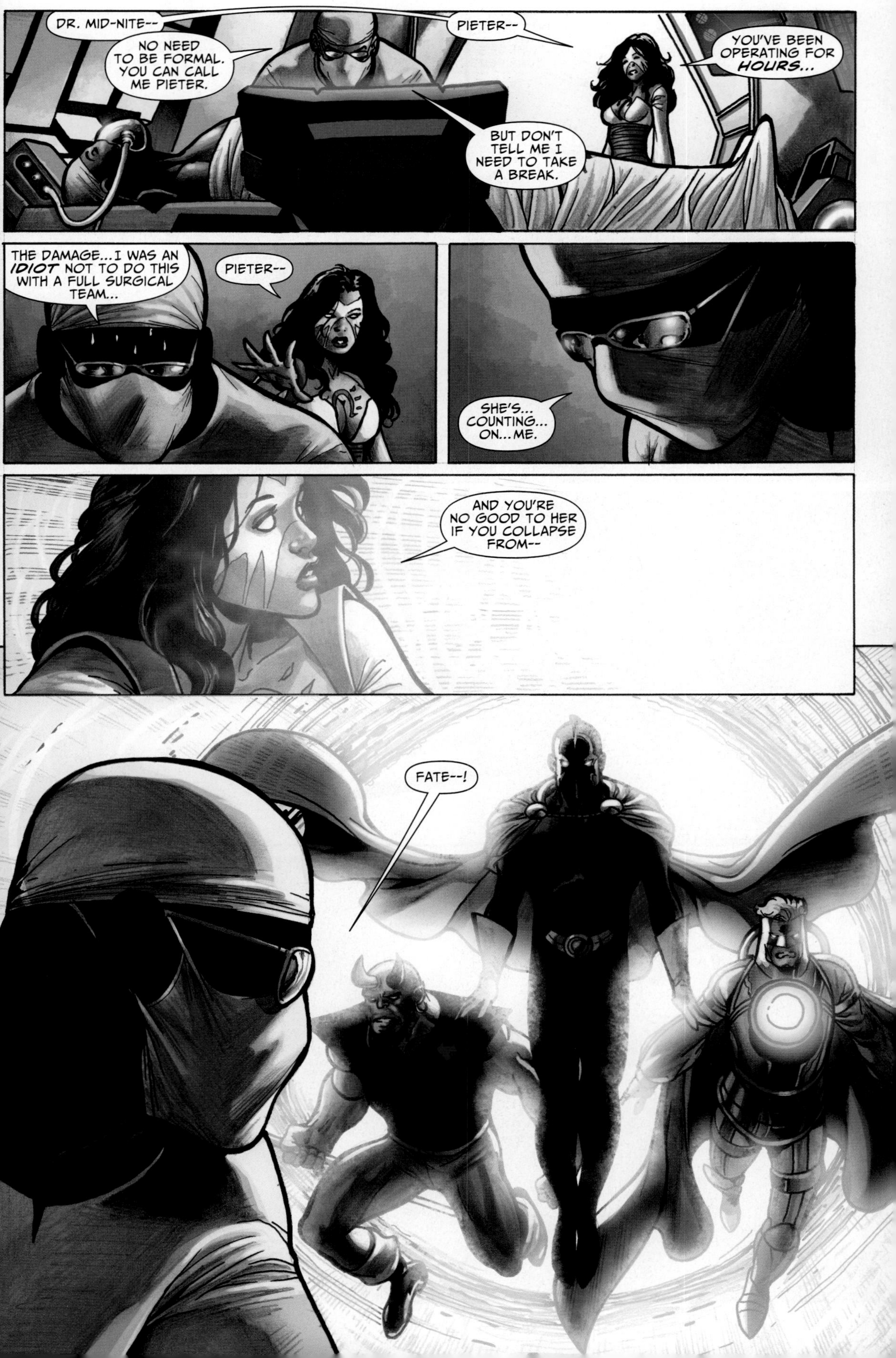
DR. MID-NITE--
NO NEED TO BE FORMAL. YOU CAN CALL ME PIETER.
PIETER--
YOU'VE BEEN OPERATING FOR HOURS...
BUT DON'T TELL ME I NEED TO TAKE A BREAK.
THE DAMAGE...I WAS AN IDIOT NOT TO DO THIS WITH A FULL SURGICAL TEAM...
PIETER--
SHE'S... COUNTING... ON...ME.
AND YOU'RE NO GOOD TO HER IF YOU COLLAPSE FROM--
FATE--!

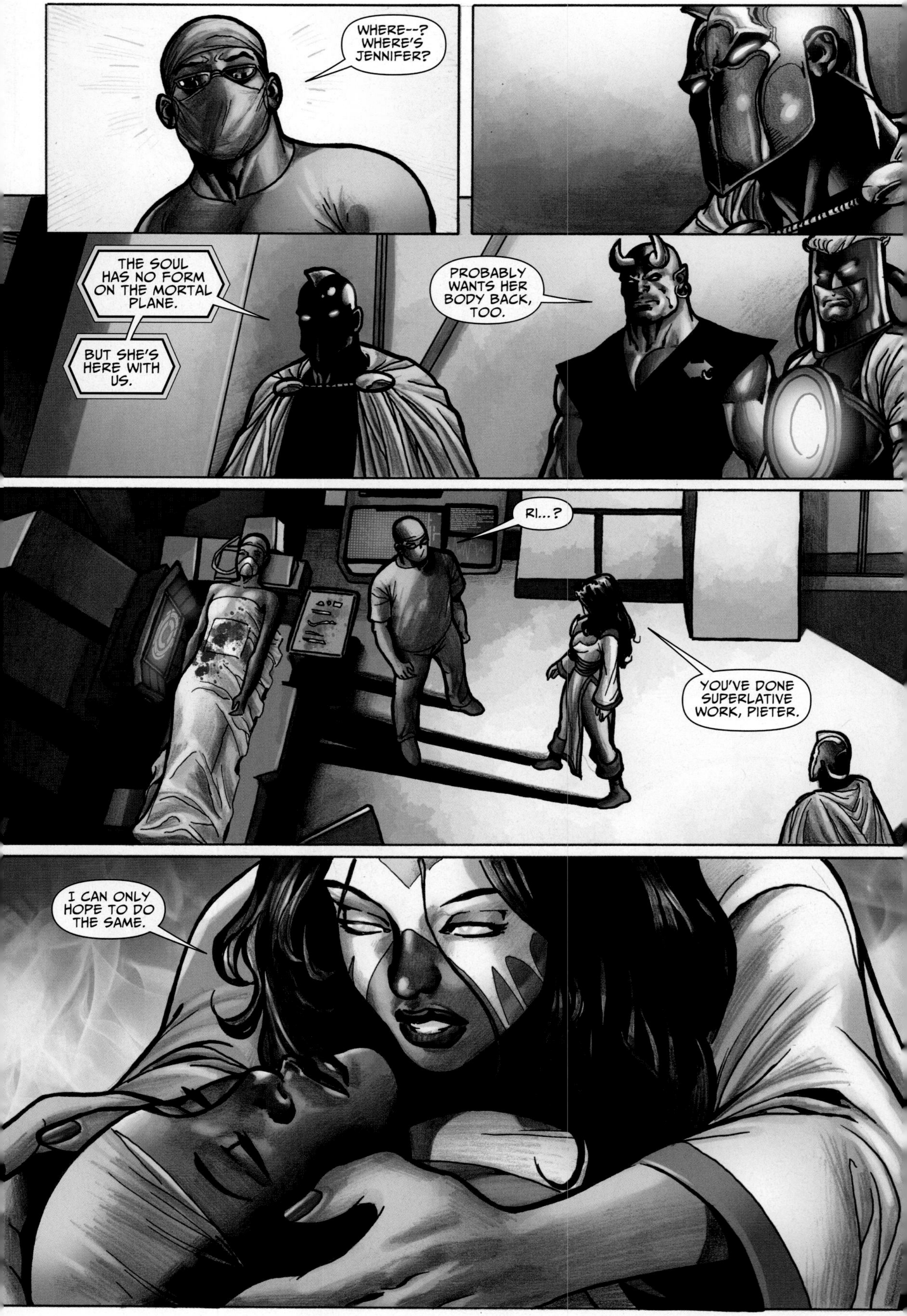
WHERE--? WHERE'S JENNIFER?
THE SOUL HAS NO FORM ON THE MORTAL PLANE.
BUT SHE'S HERE WITH US.
PROBABLY WANTS HER BODY BACK, TOO.
RI...?
YOU'VE DONE SUPERLATIVE WORK, PIETER.
I CAN ONLY HOPE TO DO THE SAME.

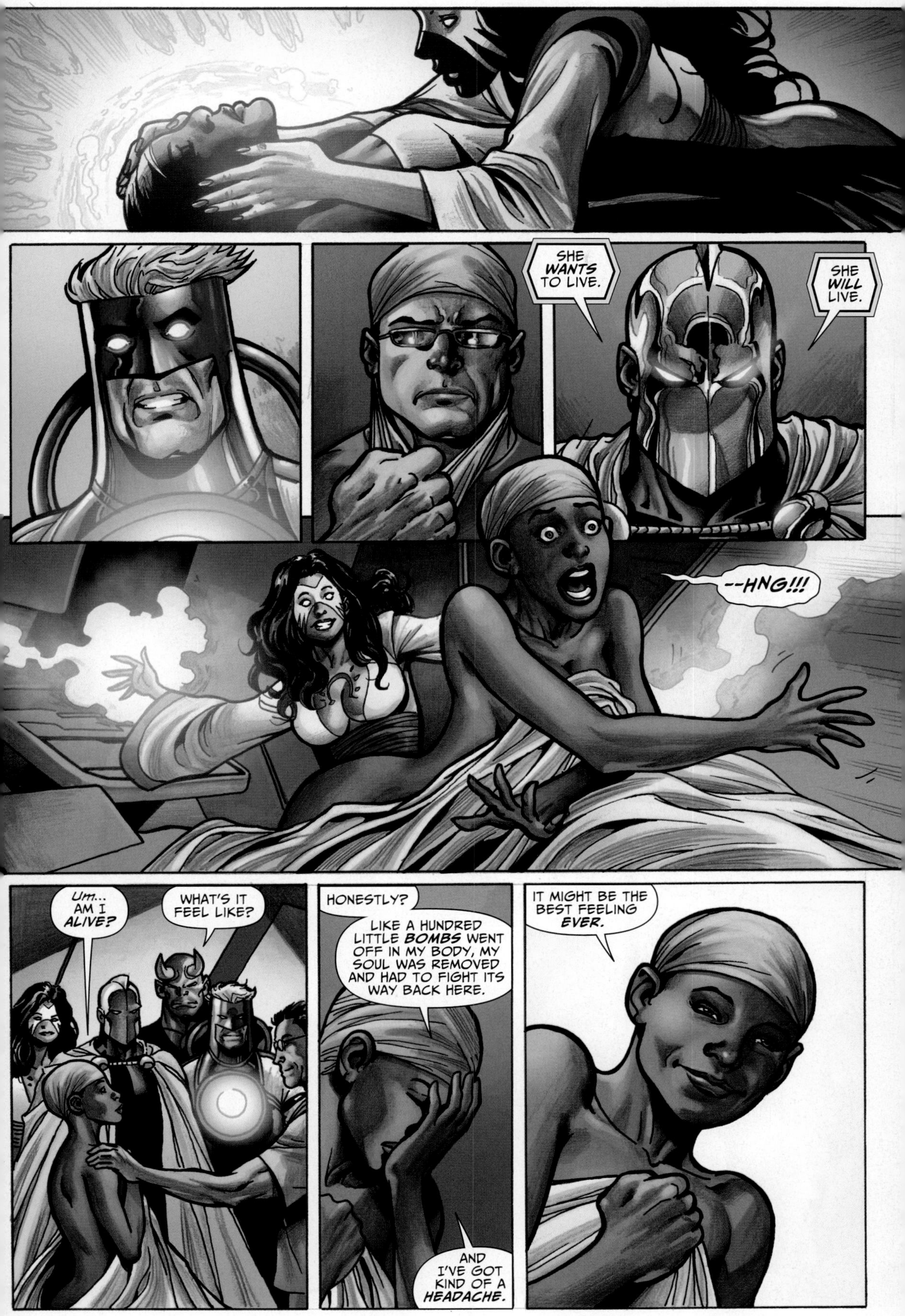

SHE WANTS TO LIVE.
SHE WILL LIVE.
--HNG!!!
Um... AM I ALIVE?
WHAT'S IT FEEL LIKE?
HONESTLY?
LIKE A HUNDRED LITTLE BOMBS WENT OFF IN MY BODY, MY SOUL WAS REMOVED AND HAD TO FIGHT ITS WAY BACK HERE.
AND I'VE GOT KIND OF A HEADACHE.
IT MIGHT BE THE BEST FEELING EVER.

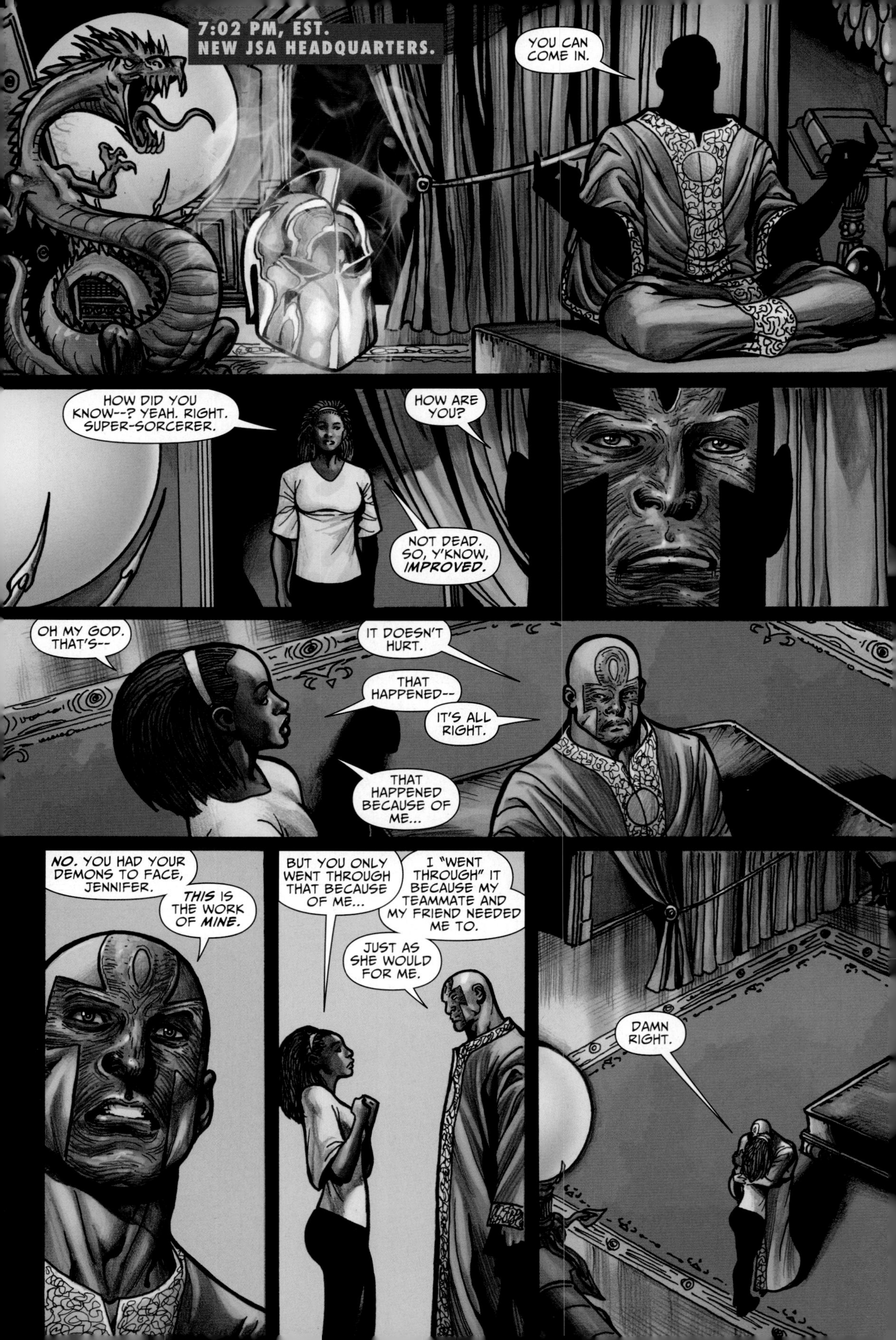
7:02 PM, EST.
NEW JSA HEADQUARTERS.
YOU CAN COME IN.
HOW DID YOU KNOW--? YEAH. RIGHT. SUPER-SORCERER.
HOW ARE YOU?
NOT DEAD. SO, Y'KNOW, *IMPROVED.*
OH MY GOD. THAT'S--
IT DOESN'T HURT.
THAT HAPPENED--
IT'S ALL RIGHT.
THAT HAPPENED BECAUSE OF ME...
**NO.** YOU HAD YOUR DEMONS TO FACE, JENNIFER.
*THIS* IS THE WORK OF *MINE.*
BUT YOU ONLY WENT THROUGH THAT BECAUSE OF ME...
I "WENT THROUGH" IT BECAUSE MY TEAMMATE AND MY FRIEND NEEDED ME TO.
JUST AS SHE WOULD FOR ME.
DAMN RIGHT.

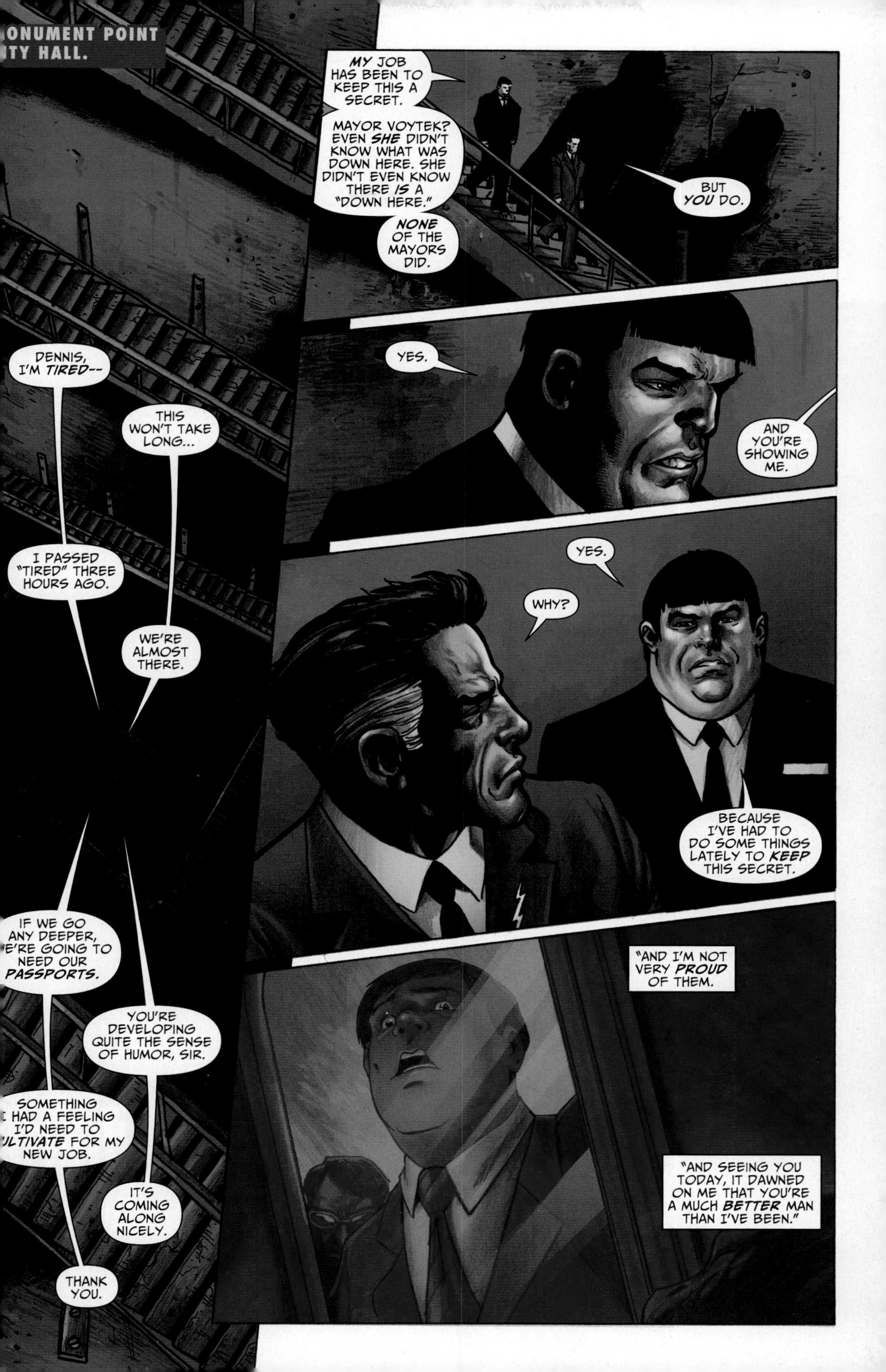

ONUMENT POINT
TY HALL.
MY JOB HAS BEEN TO KEEP THIS A SECRET.
MAYOR VOYTEK? EVEN SHE DIDN'T KNOW WHAT WAS DOWN HERE. SHE DIDN'T EVEN KNOW THERE IS A "DOWN HERE."
NONE OF THE MAYORS DID.
BUT YOU DO.
YES.
AND YOU'RE SHOWING ME.
YES.
WHY?
BECAUSE I'VE HAD TO DO SOME THINGS LATELY TO KEEP THIS SECRET.
"AND I'M NOT VERY PROUD OF THEM.
"AND SEEING YOU TODAY, IT DAWNED ON ME THAT YOU'RE A MUCH BETTER MAN THAN I'VE BEEN."
DENNIS, I'M TIRED--
THIS WON'T TAKE LONG...
I PASSED "TIRED" THREE HOURS AGO.
WE'RE ALMOST THERE.
IF WE GO ANY DEEPER, 'E'RE GOING TO NEED OUR PASSPORTS.
YOU'RE DEVELOPING QUITE THE SENSE OF HUMOR, SIR.
SOMETHING I HAD A FEELING I'D NEED TO ULTIVATE FOR MY NEW JOB.
IT'S COMING ALONG NICELY.
THANK YOU.

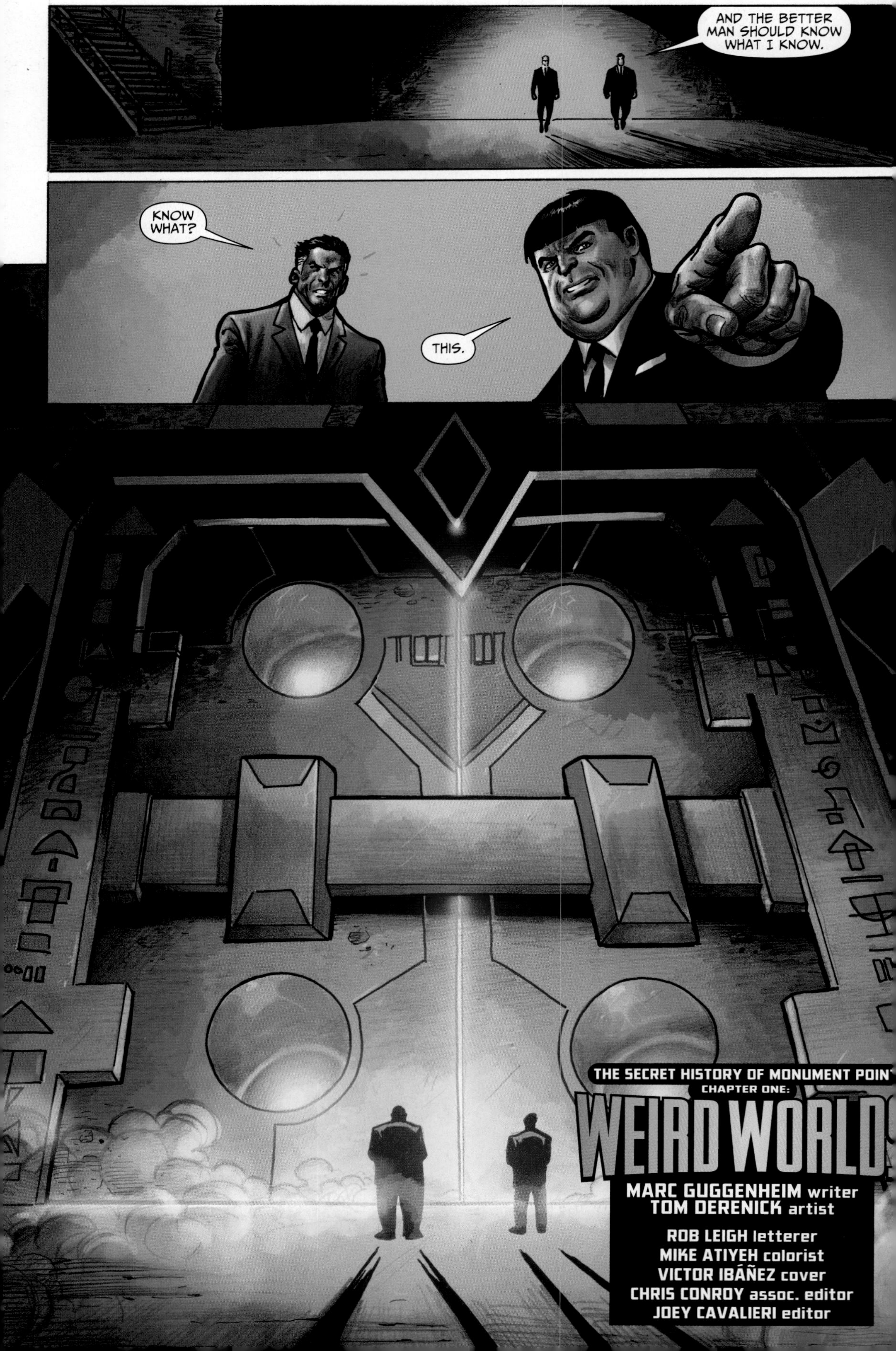
AND THE BETTER MAN SHOULD KNOW WHAT I KNOW.
KNOW WHAT?
THIS.
THE SECRET HISTORY OF MONUMENT POINT
CHAPTER ONE:
WEIRD WORLDS
MARC GUGGENHEIM writer
TOM DERENICK artist
ROB LEIGH letterer
MIKE ATIYEH colorist
VICTOR IBÁÑEZ cover
CHRIS CONROY assoc. editor
JOEY CAVALIERI editor

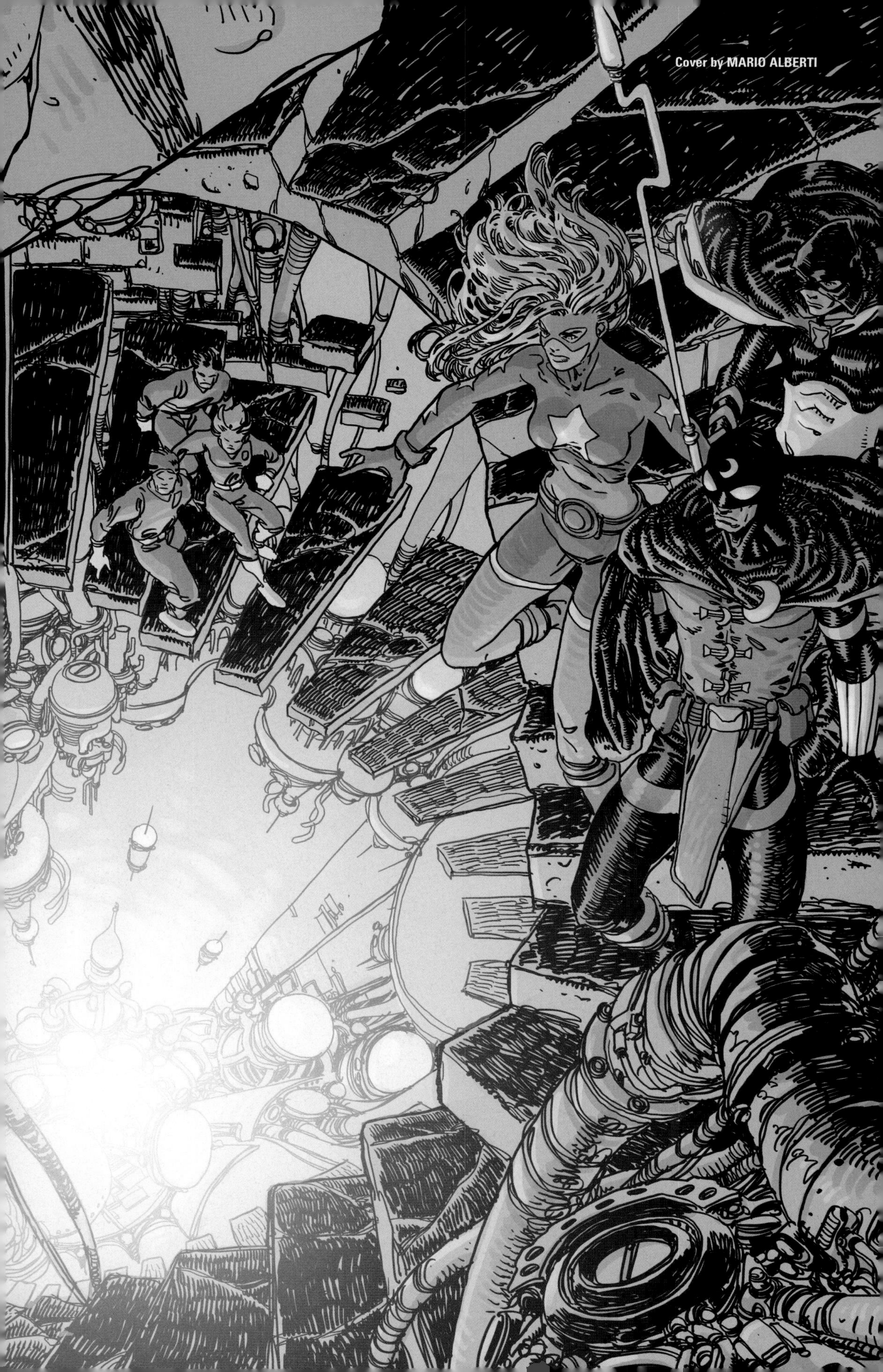

Cover by MARIO ALBERTI

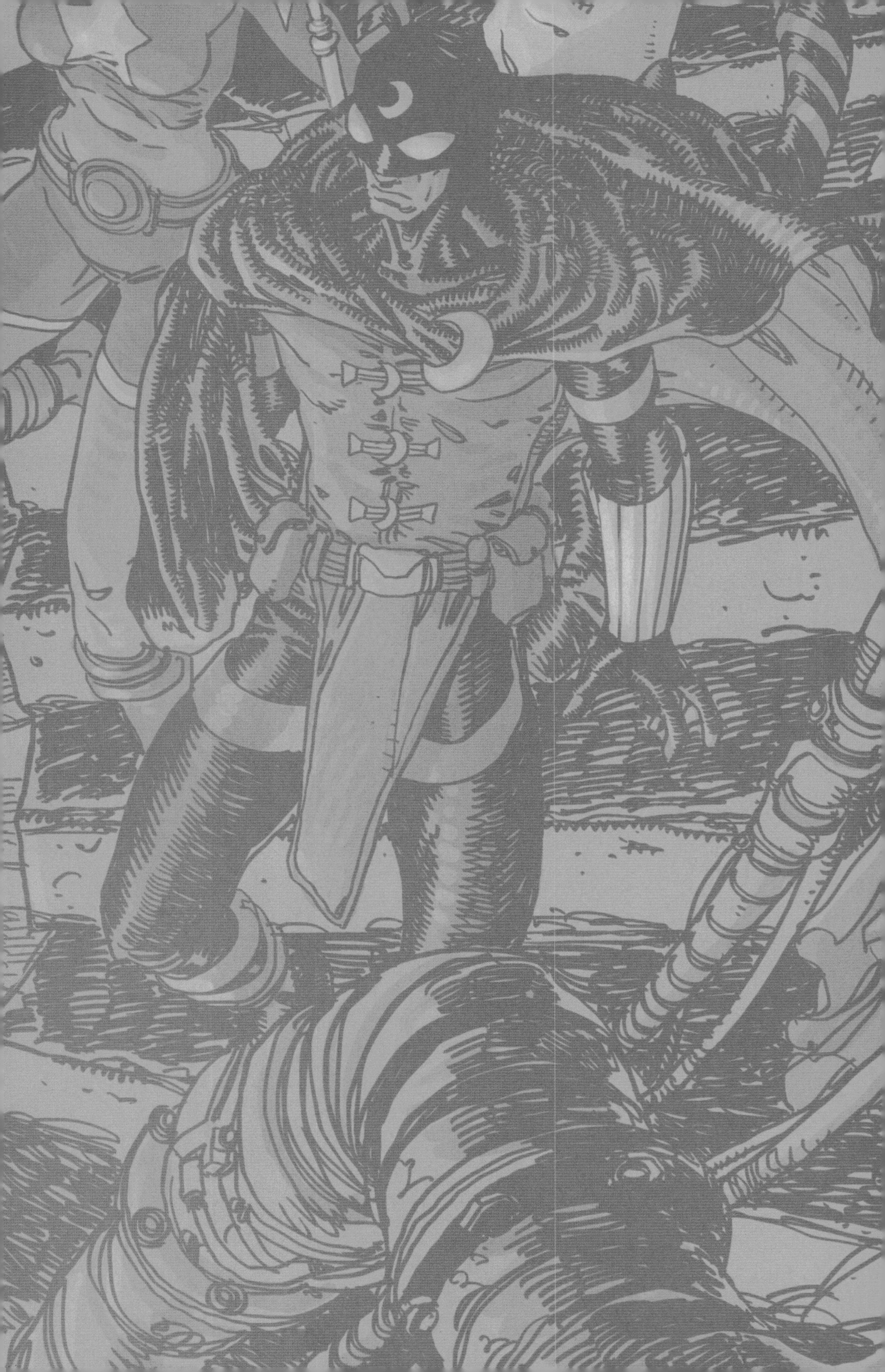

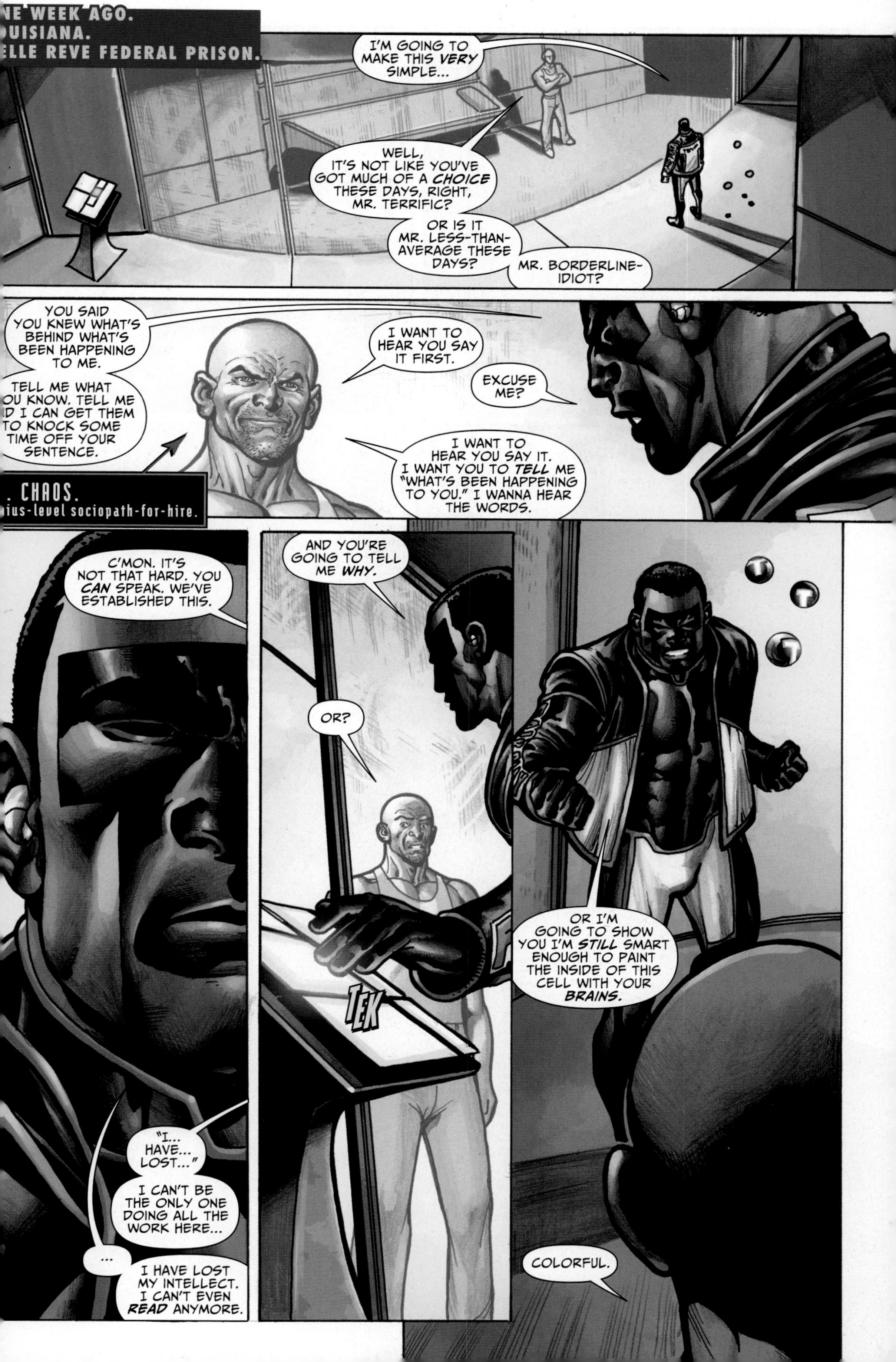
NE WEEK AGO.
UISIANA.
ELLE REVE FEDERAL PRISON.
I'M GOING TO MAKE THIS VERY SIMPLE...
WELL, IT'S NOT LIKE YOU'VE GOT MUCH OF A CHOICE THESE DAYS, RIGHT, MR. TERRIFIC?
OR IS IT MR. LESS-THAN-AVERAGE THESE DAYS?
MR. BORDERLINE-IDIOT?
YOU SAID YOU KNEW WHAT'S BEHIND WHAT'S BEEN HAPPENING TO ME.
TELL ME WHAT OU KNOW. TELL ME D I CAN GET THEM TO KNOCK SOME TIME OFF YOUR SENTENCE.
I WANT TO HEAR YOU SAY IT FIRST.
EXCUSE ME?
I WANT TO HEAR YOU SAY IT. I WANT YOU TO TELL ME "WHAT'S BEEN HAPPENING TO YOU." I WANNA HEAR THE WORDS.
. CHAOS.
ius-level sociopath-for-hire.
C'MON. IT'S NOT THAT HARD. YOU CAN SPEAK. WE'VE ESTABLISHED THIS.
"I... HAVE... LOST..."
I CAN'T BE THE ONLY ONE DOING ALL THE WORK HERE...
...
I HAVE LOST MY INTELLECT. I CAN'T EVEN READ ANYMORE.
AND YOU'RE GOING TO TELL ME WHY.
OR?
TEK
OR I'M GOING TO SHOW YOU I'M STILL SMART ENOUGH TO PAINT THE INSIDE OF THIS CELL WITH YOUR BRAINS.
COLORFUL.

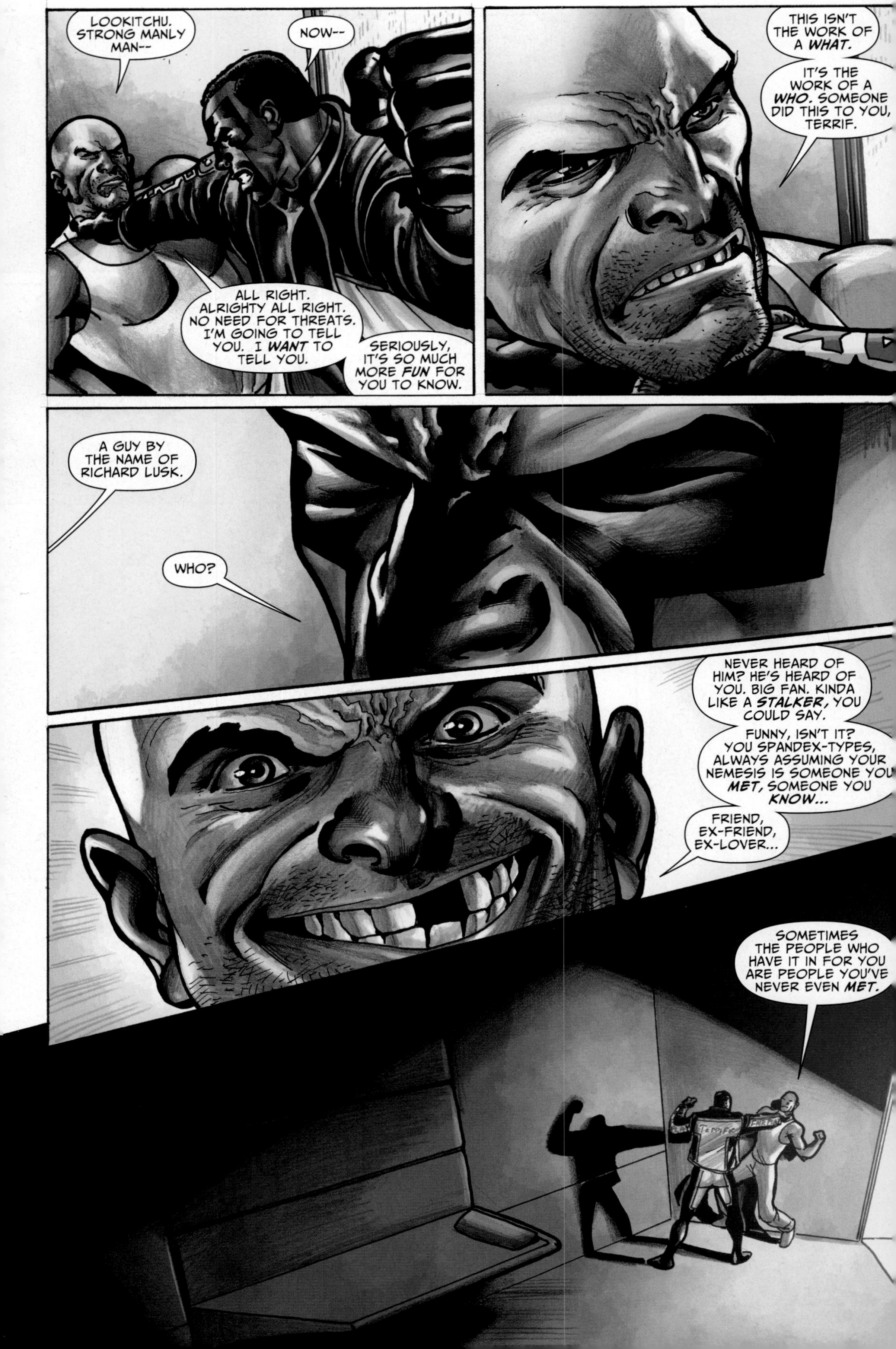
LOOKITCHU. STRONG MANLY MAN--
NOW--
ALL RIGHT. ALRIGHTY ALL RIGHT. NO NEED FOR THREATS. I'M GOING TO TELL YOU. I *WANT* TO TELL YOU.
SERIOUSLY, IT'S SO MUCH MORE *FUN* FOR YOU TO KNOW.
THIS ISN'T THE WORK OF A *WHAT.*
IT'S THE WORK OF A *WHO.* SOMEONE DID THIS TO YOU, TERRIF.
A GUY BY THE NAME OF RICHARD LUSK.
WHO?
NEVER HEARD OF HIM? HE'S HEARD OF YOU. BIG FAN. KINDA LIKE A *STALKER,* YOU COULD SAY.
FUNNY, ISN'T IT? YOU SPANDEX-TYPES, ALWAYS ASSUMING YOUR NEMESIS IS SOMEONE YOU *MET,* SOMEONE YOU *KNOW...*
FRIEND, EX-FRIEND, EX-LOVER...
SOMETIMES THE PEOPLE WHO HAVE IT IN FOR YOU ARE PEOPLE YOU'VE NEVER EVEN *MET.*

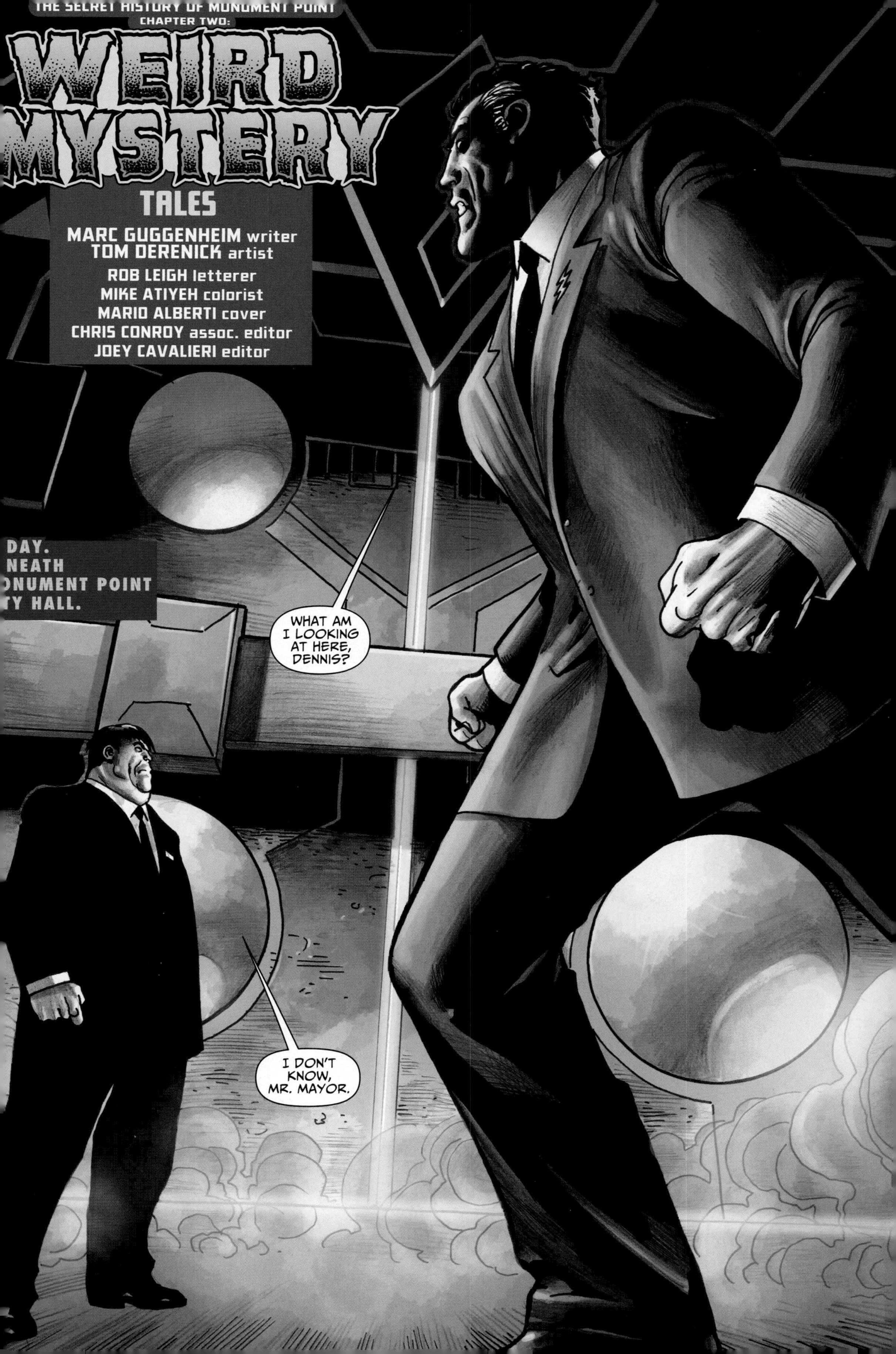
THE SECRET HISTORY OF MONUMENT POINT
CHAPTER TWO:
WEIRD MYSTERY TALES
MARC GUGGENHEIM writer
TOM DERENICK artist
ROB LEIGH letterer
MIKE ATIYEH colorist
MARIO ALBERTI cover
CHRIS CONROY assoc. editor
JOEY CAVALIERI editor
DAY. NEATH ONUMENT POINT TY HALL.
WHAT AM I LOOKING AT HERE, DENNIS?
I DON'T KNOW, MR. MAYOR.

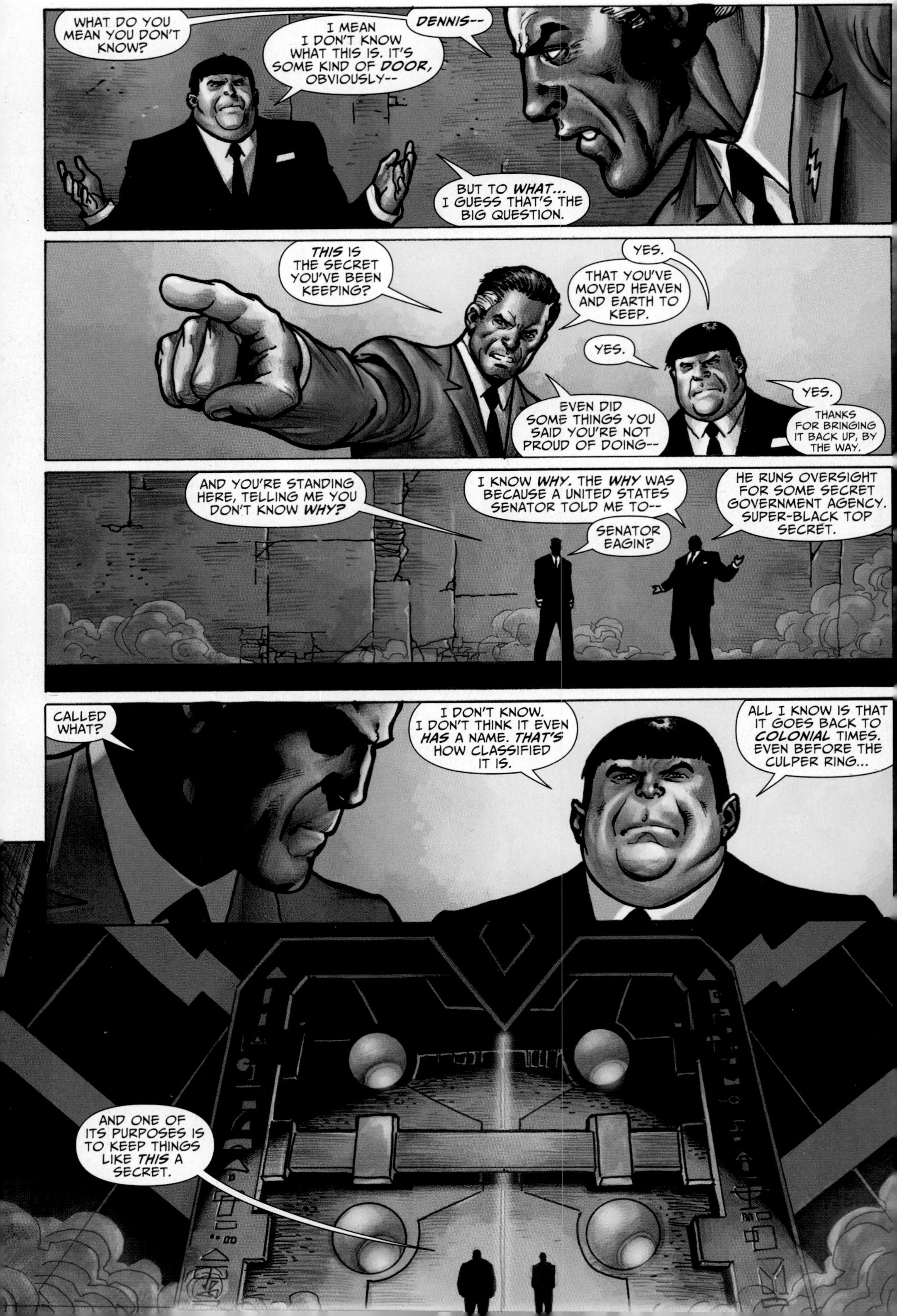
WHAT DO YOU MEAN YOU DON'T KNOW?
DENNIS--
I MEAN I DON'T KNOW WHAT THIS IS. IT'S SOME KIND OF DOOR, OBVIOUSLY--
BUT TO WHAT... I GUESS THAT'S THE BIG QUESTION.
THIS IS THE SECRET YOU'VE BEEN KEEPING?
YES.
THAT YOU'VE MOVED HEAVEN AND EARTH TO KEEP.
YES.
EVEN DID SOME THINGS YOU SAID YOU'RE NOT PROUD OF DOING--
YES.
THANKS FOR BRINGING IT BACK UP, BY THE WAY.
AND YOU'RE STANDING HERE, TELLING ME YOU DON'T KNOW WHY?
I KNOW WHY. THE WHY WAS BECAUSE A UNITED STATES SENATOR TOLD ME TO--
SENATOR EAGIN?
HE RUNS OVERSIGHT FOR SOME SECRET GOVERNMENT AGENCY. SUPER-BLACK TOP SECRET.
CALLED WHAT?
I DON'T KNOW. I DON'T THINK IT EVEN HAS A NAME. THAT'S HOW CLASSIFIED IT IS.
ALL I KNOW IS THAT IT GOES BACK TO COLONIAL TIMES. EVEN BEFORE THE CULPER RING...
AND ONE OF ITS PURPOSES IS TO KEEP THINGS LIKE THIS A SECRET.

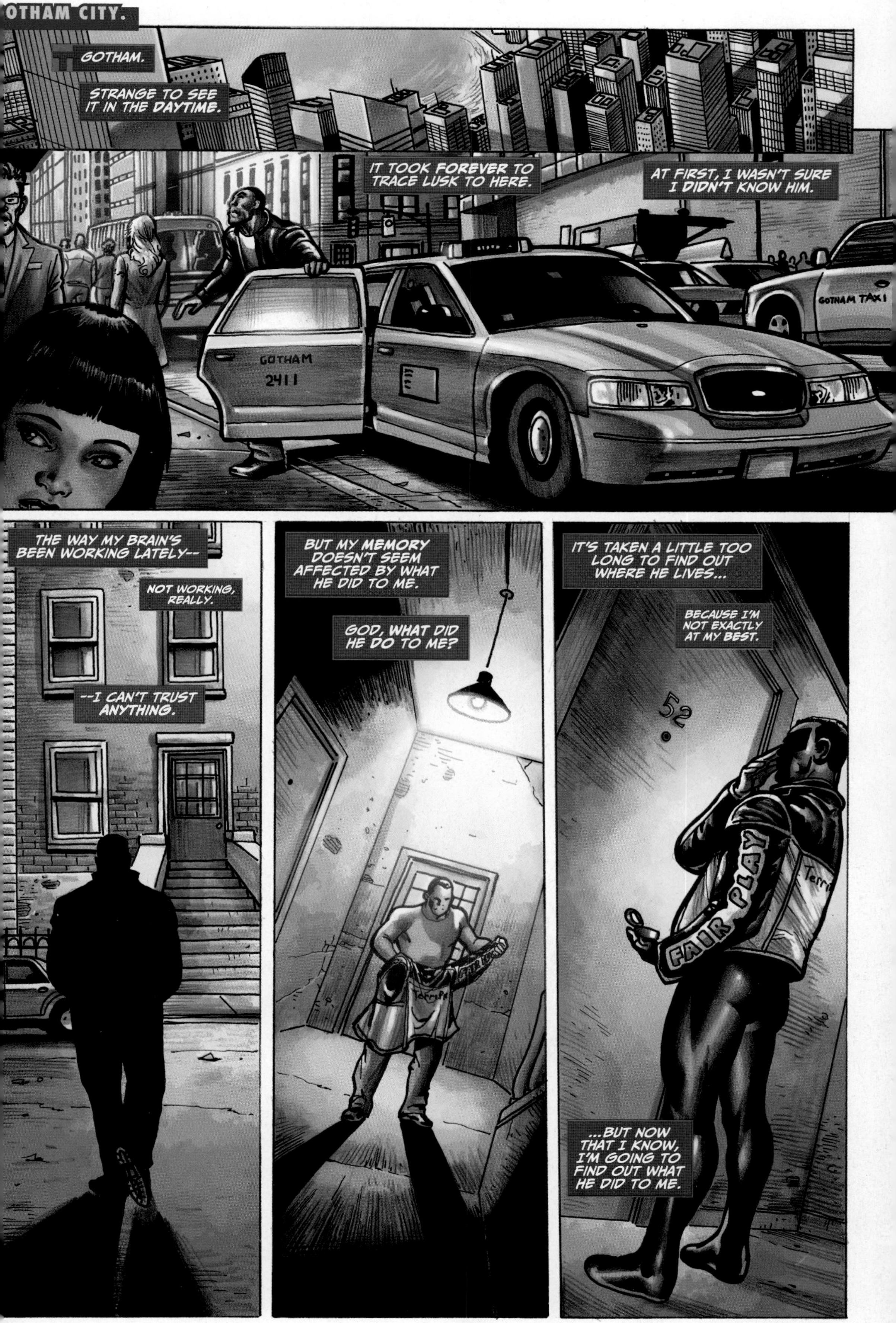
OTHAM CITY.
GOTHAM.
STRANGE TO SEE IT IN THE DAYTIME.
IT TOOK FOREVER TO TRACE LUSK TO HERE.
AT FIRST, I WASN'T SURE I DIDN'T KNOW HIM.
GOTHAM 2411
GOTHAM TAXI
THE WAY MY BRAIN'S BEEN WORKING LATELY--
NOT WORKING, REALLY.
--I CAN'T TRUST ANYTHING.
BUT MY MEMORY DOESN'T SEEM AFFECTED BY WHAT HE DID TO ME.
GOD, WHAT DID HE DO TO ME?
IT'S TAKEN A LITTLE TOO LONG TO FIND OUT WHERE HE LIVES...
BECAUSE I'M NOT EXACTLY AT MY BEST.
52
FAIR PLAY
...BUT NOW THAT I KNOW, I'M GOING TO FIND OUT WHAT HE DID TO ME.

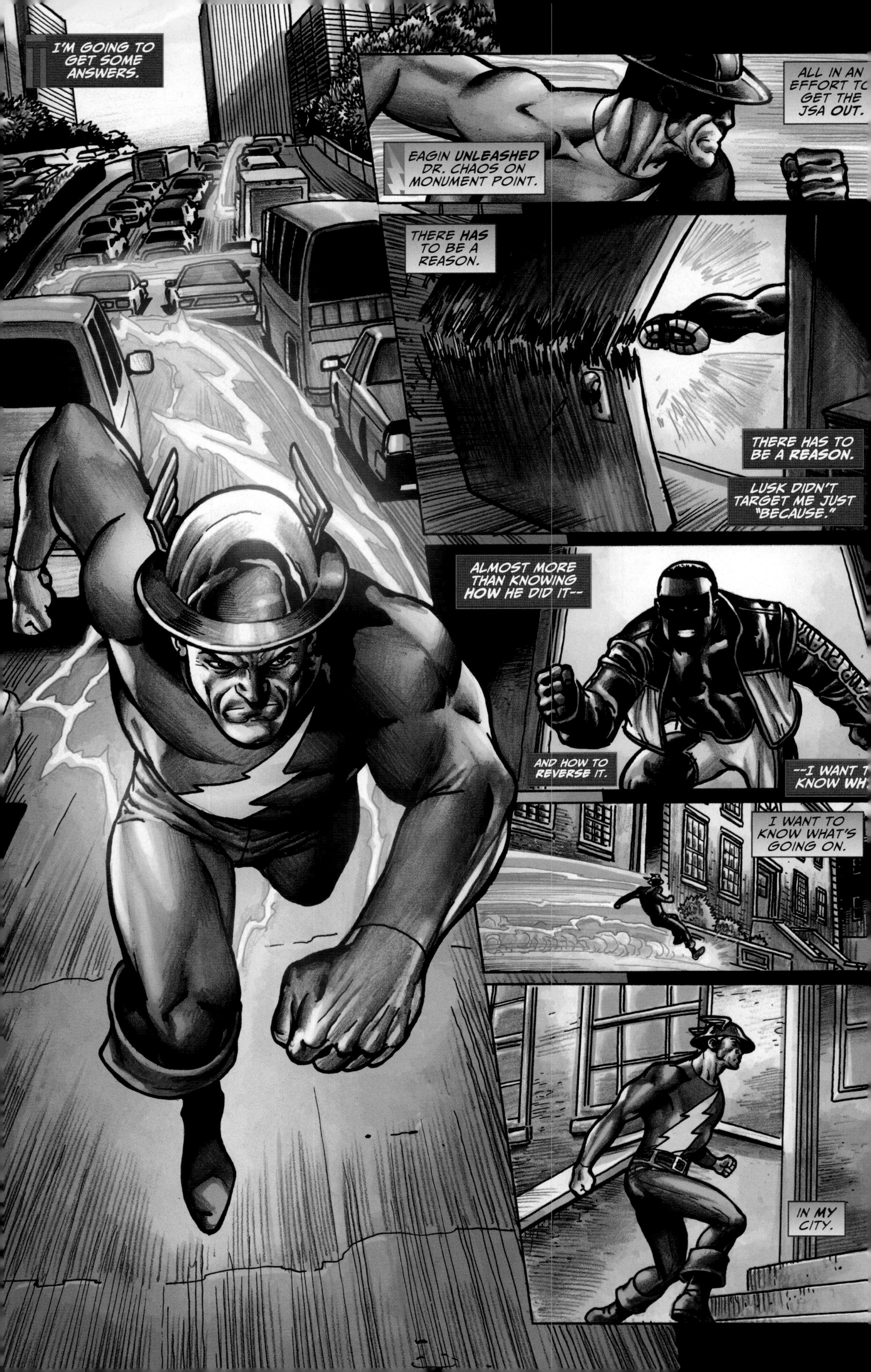
I'M GOING TO GET SOME ANSWERS.
EAGIN UNLEASHED DR. CHAOS ON MONUMENT POINT.
ALL IN AN EFFORT TO GET THE JSA OUT.
THERE HAS TO BE A REASON.
THERE HAS TO BE A REASON.
LUSK DIDN'T TARGET ME JUST "BECAUSE."
ALMOST MORE THAN KNOWING HOW HE DID IT--
AND HOW TO REVERSE IT.
--I WANT T KNOW WH
I WANT TO KNOW WHAT'S GOING ON.
IN MY CITY.

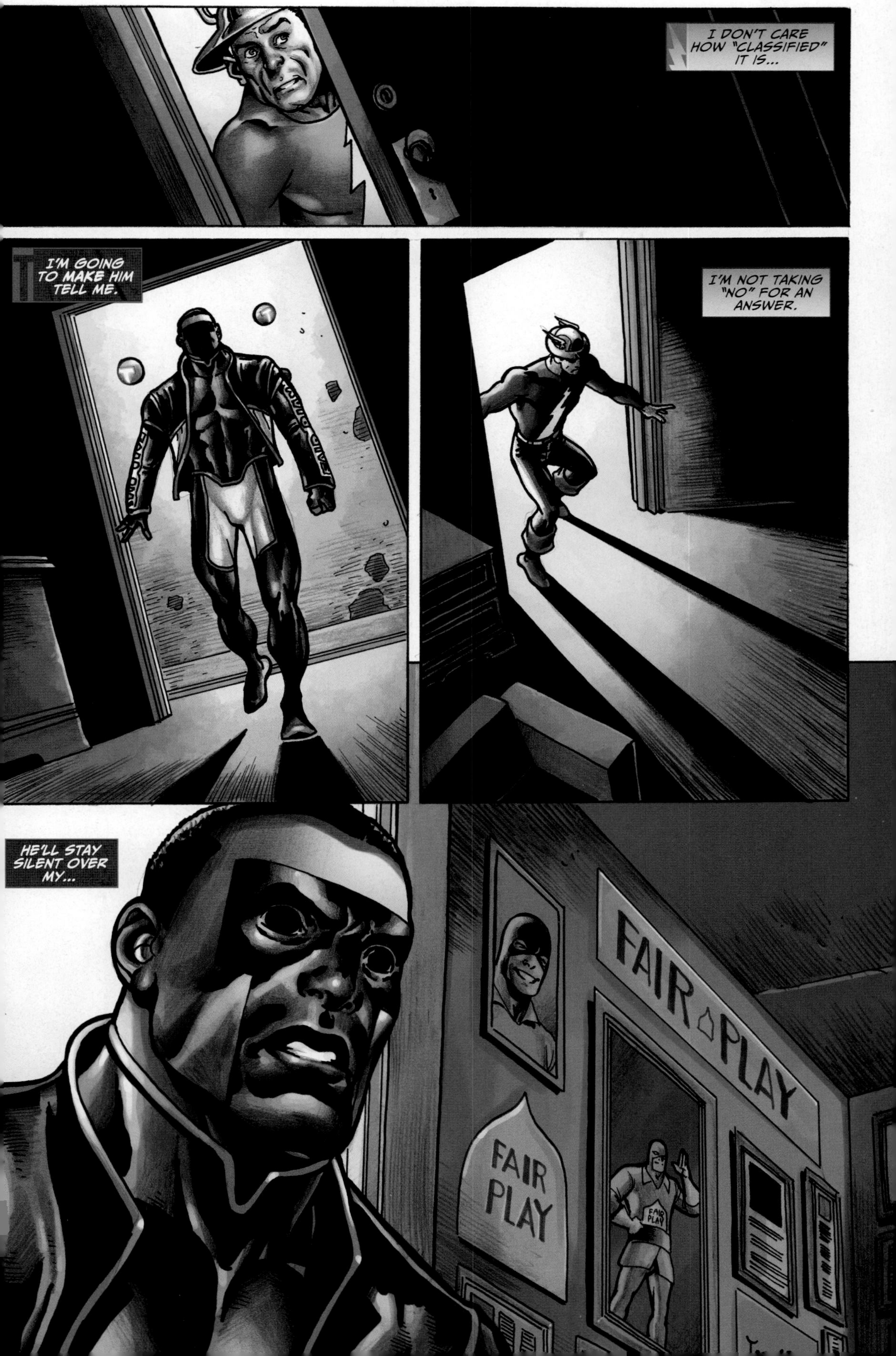
I DON'T CARE HOW "CLASSIFIED" IT IS...
I'M GOING TO MAKE HIM TELL ME.
I'M NOT TAKING "NO" FOR AN ANSWER.
HE'LL STAY SILENT OVER MY...
FAIR PLAY
FAIR PLAY

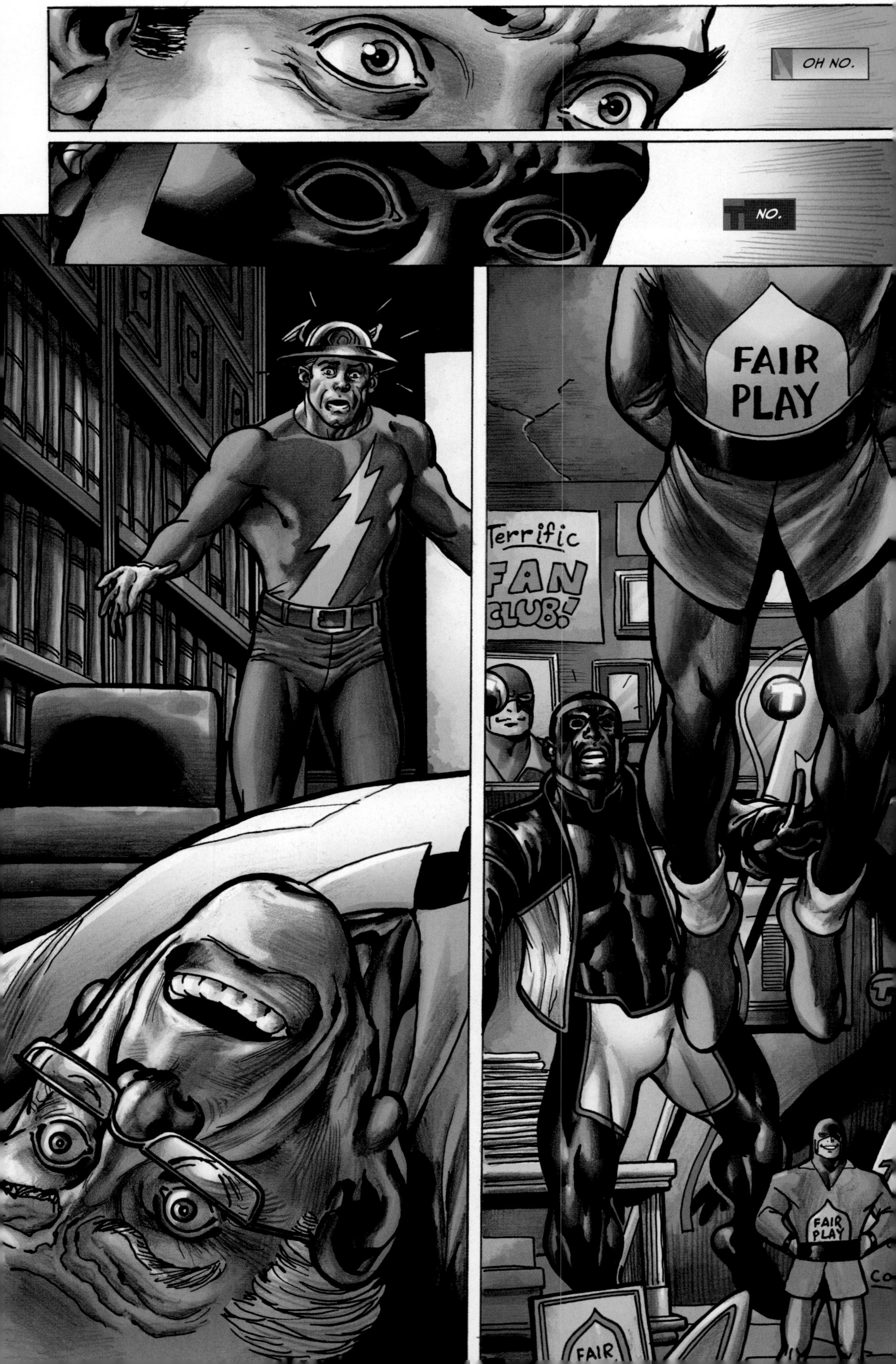
OH NO.
NO.
FAIR PLAY
Terrific FAN CLUB!
FAIR PLAY
FAIR

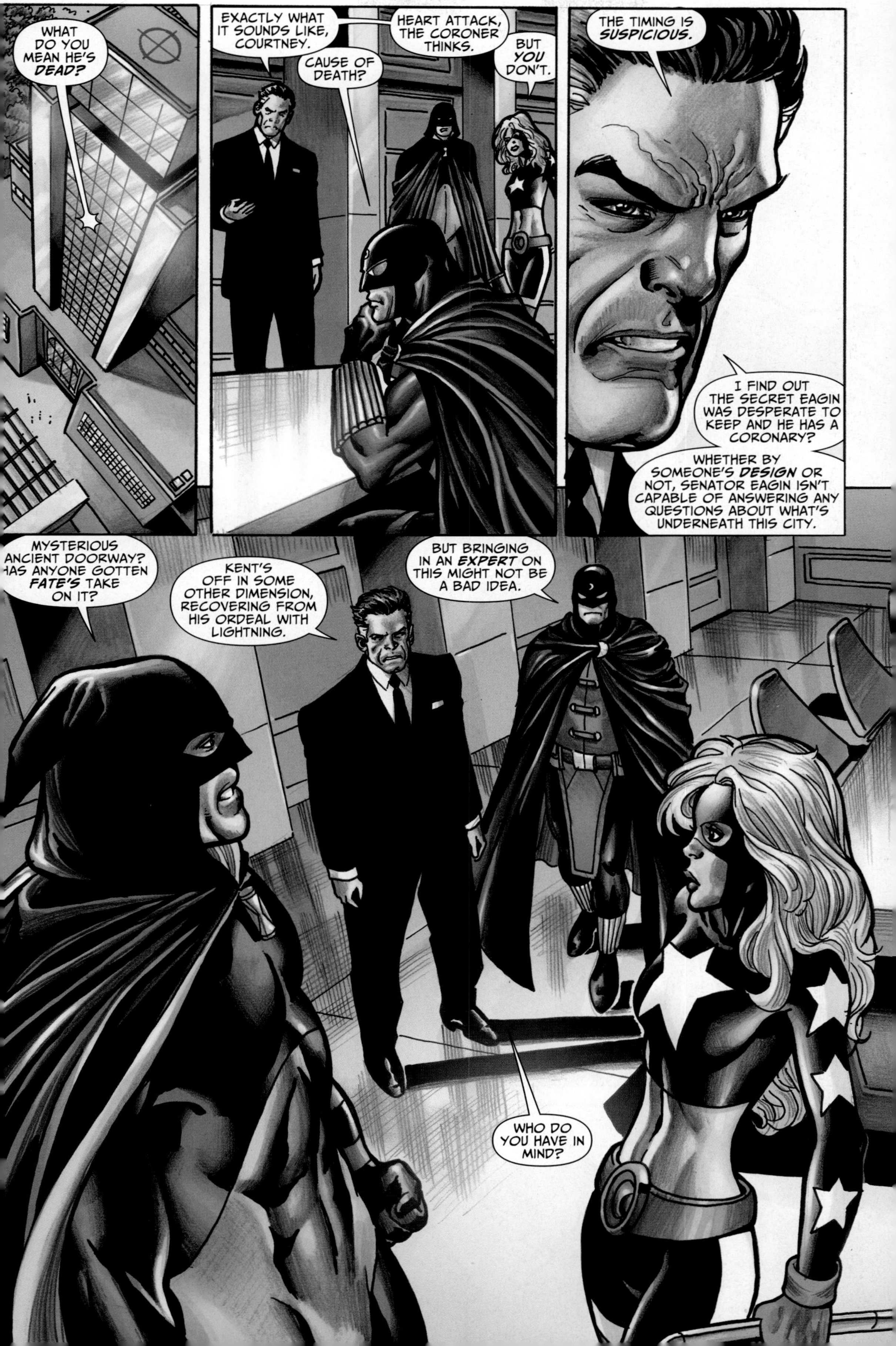

WHAT DO YOU MEAN HE'S *DEAD?*
EXACTLY WHAT IT SOUNDS LIKE, COURTNEY.
HEART ATTACK, THE CORONER THINKS.
CAUSE OF DEATH?
BUT *YOU* DON'T.
THE TIMING IS *SUSPICIOUS.*
I FIND OUT THE SECRET EAGIN WAS DESPERATE TO KEEP AND HE HAS A CORONARY?
WHETHER BY SOMEONE'S *DESIGN* OR NOT, SENATOR EAGIN ISN'T CAPABLE OF ANSWERING ANY QUESTIONS ABOUT WHAT'S UNDERNEATH THIS CITY.
MYSTERIOUS ANCIENT DOORWAY? HAS ANYONE GOTTEN *FATE'S* TAKE ON IT?
KENT'S OFF IN SOME OTHER DIMENSION, RECOVERING FROM HIS ORDEAL WITH LIGHTNING.
BUT BRINGING IN AN *EXPERT* ON THIS MIGHT NOT BE A BAD IDEA.
WHO DO YOU HAVE IN MIND?

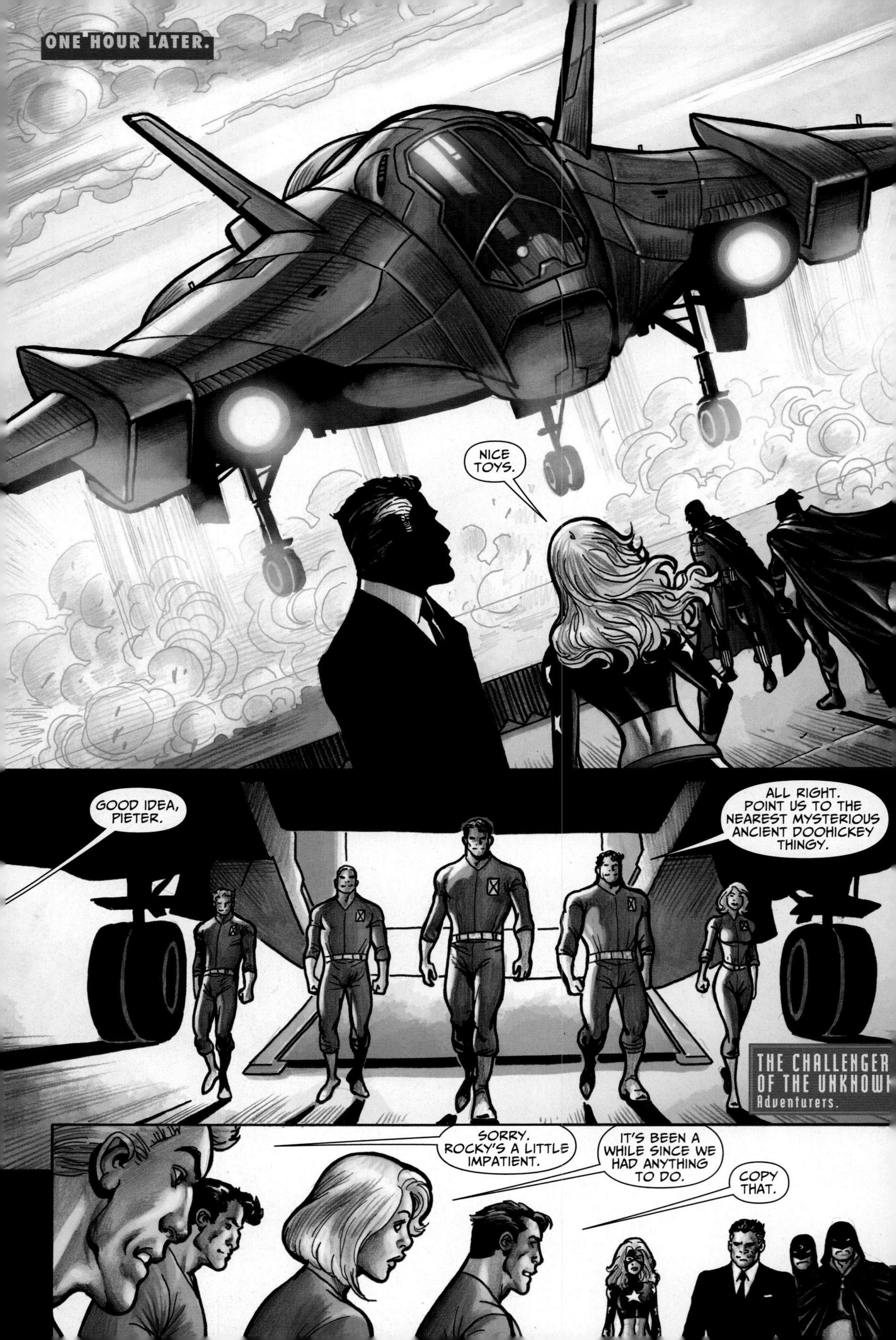
ONE HOUR LATER.
NICE TOYS.
GOOD IDEA, PIETER.
ALL RIGHT. POINT US TO THE NEAREST MYSTERIOUS ANCIENT DOOHICKEY THINGY.
THE CHALLENGER OF THE UNKNOWI
Adventurers.
SORRY. ROCKY'S A LITTLE IMPATIENT.
IT'S BEEN A WHILE SINCE WE HAD ANYTHING TO DO.
COPY THAT.

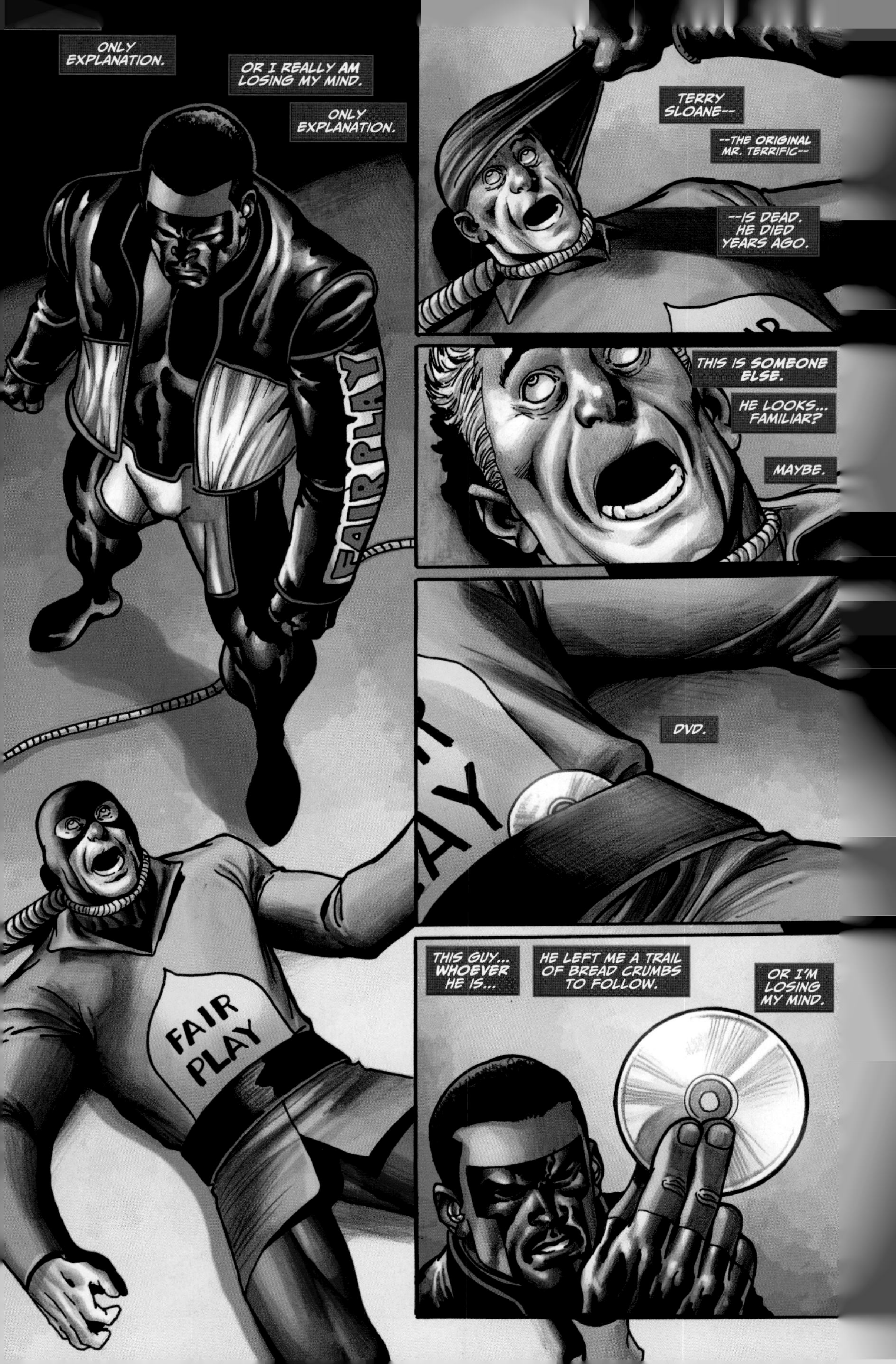
ONLY EXPLANATION.
OR I REALLY AM LOSING MY MIND.
ONLY EXPLANATION.
FAIR PLAY
FAIR PLAY
TERRY SLOANE--
--THE ORIGINAL MR. TERRIFIC--
--IS DEAD. HE DIED YEARS AGO.
THIS IS SOMEONE ELSE.
HE LOOKS... FAMILIAR?
MAYBE.
DVD.
THIS GUY... WHOEVER HE IS...
HE LEFT ME A TRAIL OF BREAD CRUMBS TO FOLLOW.
OR I'M LOSING MY MIND.

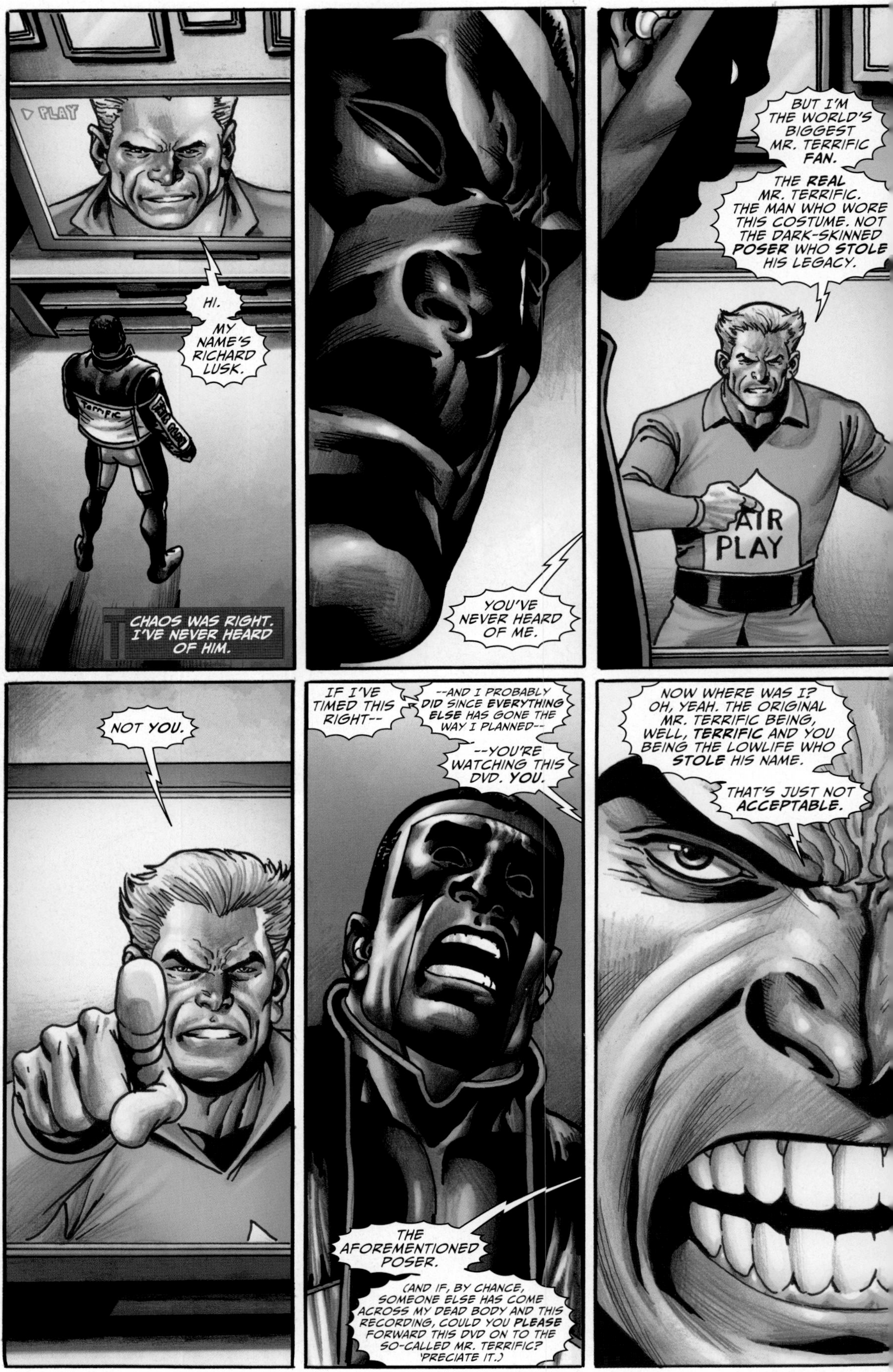
▷ PLAY
HI. MY NAME'S RICHARD LUSK.
CHAOS WAS RIGHT. I'VE NEVER HEARD OF HIM.
YOU'VE NEVER HEARD OF ME.
BUT I'M THE WORLD'S BIGGEST MR. TERRIFIC FAN.
THE REAL MR. TERRIFIC. THE MAN WHO WORE THIS COSTUME. NOT THE DARK-SKINNED POSER WHO STOLE HIS LEGACY.
AIR PLAY
NOT YOU.
IF I'VE TIMED THIS RIGHT--
--AND I PROBABLY DID SINCE EVERYTHING ELSE HAS GONE THE WAY I PLANNED--
--YOU'RE WATCHING THIS DVD. YOU.
THE AFOREMENTIONED POSER.
(AND IF, BY CHANCE, SOMEONE ELSE HAS COME ACROSS MY DEAD BODY AND THIS RECORDING, COULD YOU PLEASE FORWARD THIS DVD ON TO THE SO-CALLED MR. TERRIFIC? 'PRECIATE IT.)
NOW WHERE WAS I? OH, YEAH. THE ORIGINAL MR. TERRIFIC BEING, WELL, TERRIFIC AND YOU BEING THE LOWLIFE WHO STOLE HIS NAME.
THAT'S JUST NOT ACCEPTABLE.

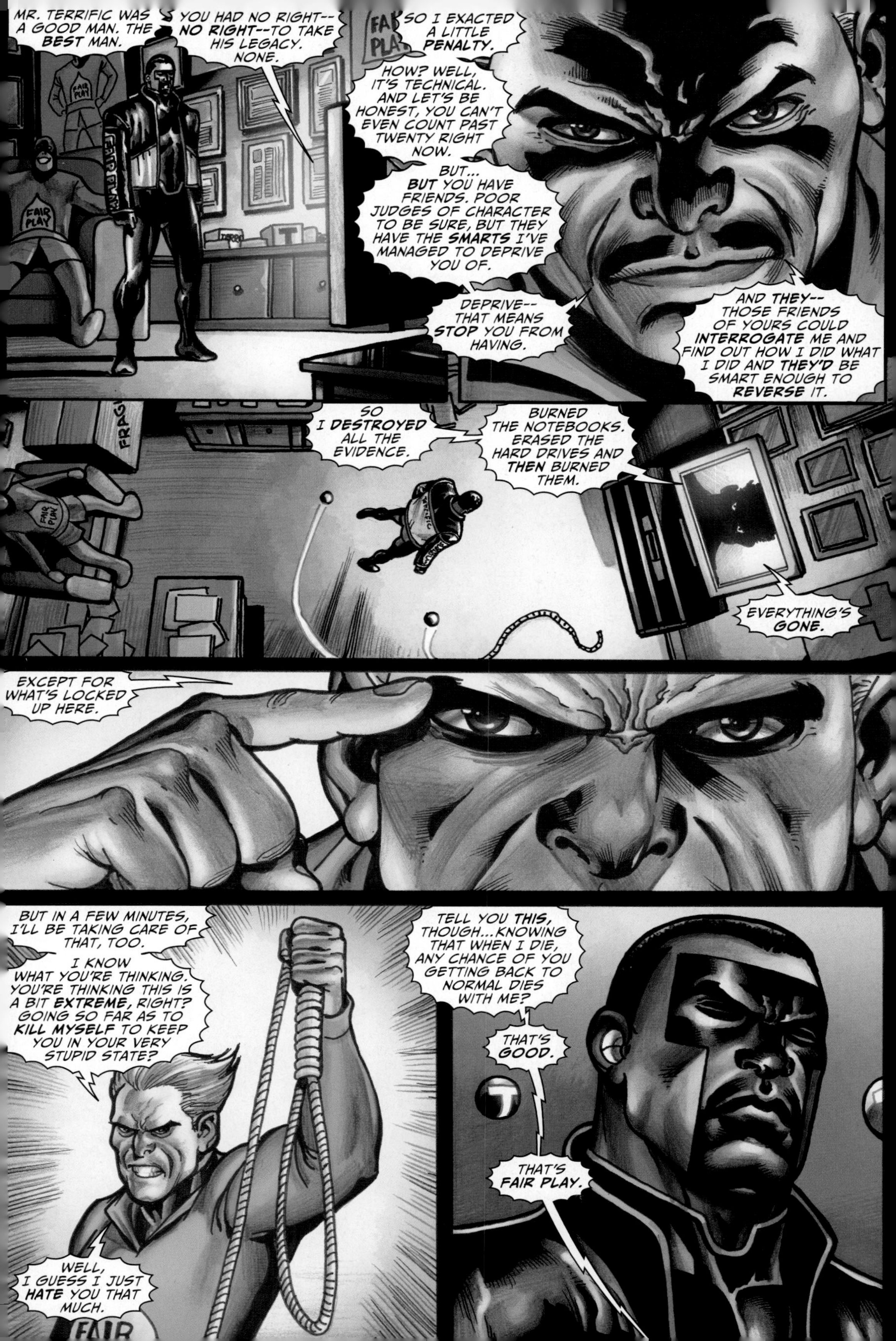
MR. TERRIFIC WAS A GOOD MAN. THE BEST MAN.
YOU HAD NO RIGHT-- NO RIGHT--TO TAKE HIS LEGACY. NONE.
FAIR PLAY
SO I EXACTED A LITTLE PENALTY.
HOW? WELL, IT'S TECHNICAL. AND LET'S BE HONEST, YOU CAN'T EVEN COUNT PAST TWENTY RIGHT NOW.
BUT... BUT YOU HAVE FRIENDS. POOR JUDGES OF CHARACTER TO BE SURE, BUT THEY HAVE THE SMARTS I'VE MANAGED TO DEPRIVE YOU OF.
DEPRIVE-- THAT MEANS STOP YOU FROM HAVING.
AND THEY-- THOSE FRIENDS OF YOURS COULD INTERROGATE ME AND FIND OUT HOW I DID WHAT I DID AND THEY'D BE SMART ENOUGH TO REVERSE IT.
SO I DESTROYED ALL THE EVIDENCE.
BURNED THE NOTEBOOKS. ERASED THE HARD DRIVES AND THEN BURNED THEM.
EVERYTHING'S GONE.
EXCEPT FOR WHAT'S LOCKED UP HERE.
BUT IN A FEW MINUTES, I'LL BE TAKING CARE OF THAT, TOO.
I KNOW WHAT YOU'RE THINKING. YOU'RE THINKING THIS IS A BIT EXTREME, RIGHT? GOING SO FAR AS TO KILL MYSELF TO KEEP YOU IN YOUR VERY STUPID STATE?
WELL, I GUESS I JUST HATE YOU THAT MUCH.
TELL YOU THIS, THOUGH...KNOWING THAT WHEN I DIE, ANY CHANCE OF YOU GETTING BACK TO NORMAL DIES WITH ME?
THAT'S GOOD.
THAT'S FAIR PLAY.

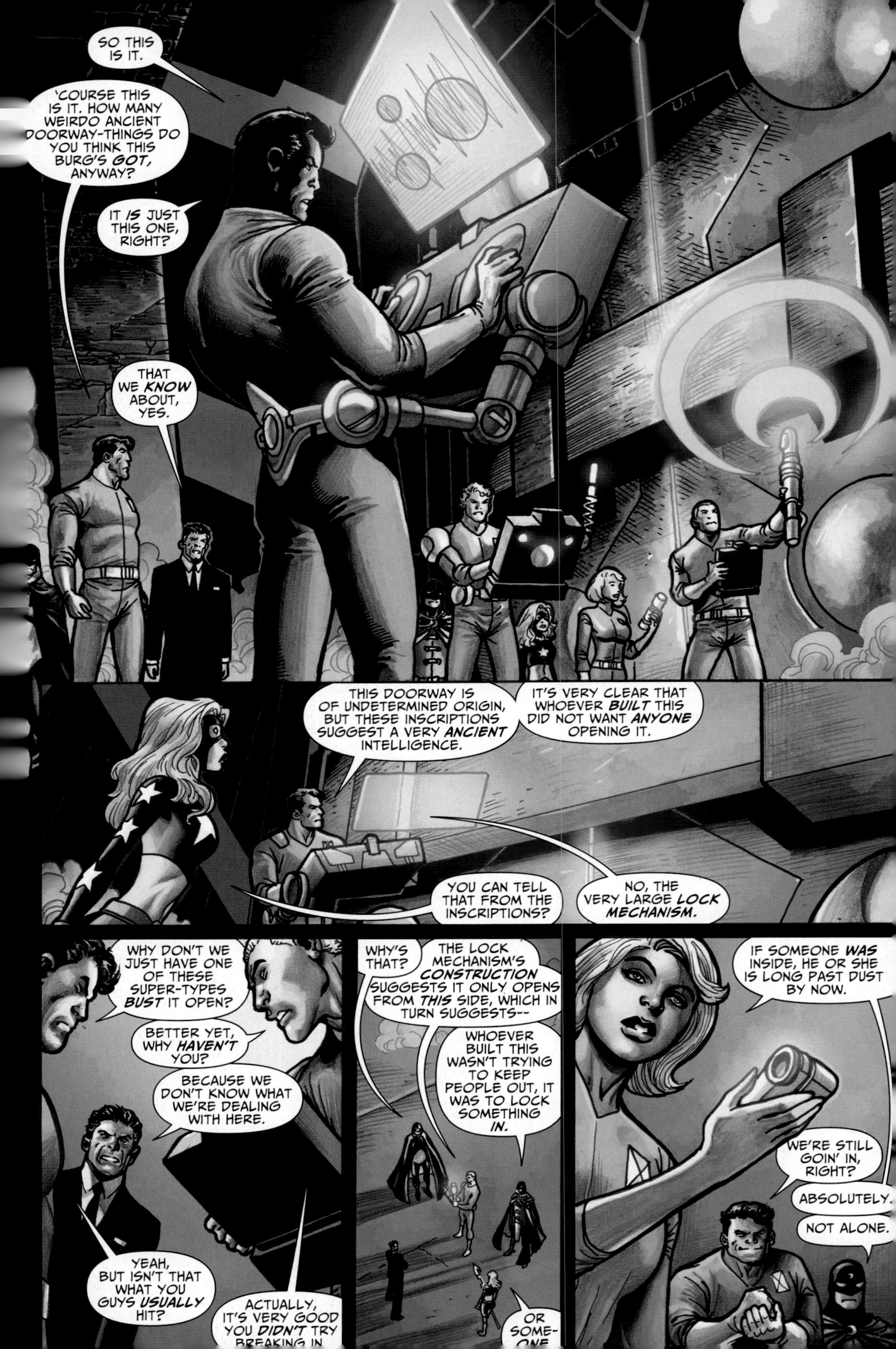
SO THIS IS IT.
'COURSE THIS IS IT. HOW MANY WEIRDO ANCIENT DOORWAY-THINGS DO YOU THINK THIS BURG'S GOT, ANYWAY?
IT IS JUST THIS ONE, RIGHT?
THAT WE KNOW ABOUT, YES.
THIS DOORWAY IS OF UNDETERMINED ORIGIN, BUT THESE INSCRIPTIONS SUGGEST A VERY ANCIENT INTELLIGENCE.
IT'S VERY CLEAR THAT WHOEVER BUILT THIS DID NOT WANT ANYONE OPENING IT.
YOU CAN TELL THAT FROM THE INSCRIPTIONS?
NO, THE VERY LARGE LOCK MECHANISM.
WHY DON'T WE JUST HAVE ONE OF THESE SUPER-TYPES BUST IT OPEN?
BETTER YET, WHY HAVEN'T YOU?
BECAUSE WE DON'T KNOW WHAT WE'RE DEALING WITH HERE.
YEAH, BUT ISN'T THAT WHAT YOU GUYS USUALLY HIT?
ACTUALLY, IT'S VERY GOOD YOU DIDN'T TRY
WHY'S THAT?
THE LOCK MECHANISM'S CONSTRUCTION SUGGESTS IT ONLY OPENS FROM THIS SIDE, WHICH IN TURN SUGGESTS--
WHOEVER BUILT THIS WASN'T TRYING TO KEEP PEOPLE OUT, IT WAS TO LOCK SOMETHING IN.
OR SOME-
IF SOMEONE WAS INSIDE, HE OR SHE IS LONG PAST DUST BY NOW.
WE'RE STILL GOIN' IN, RIGHT?
ABSOLUTELY.
NOT ALONE.

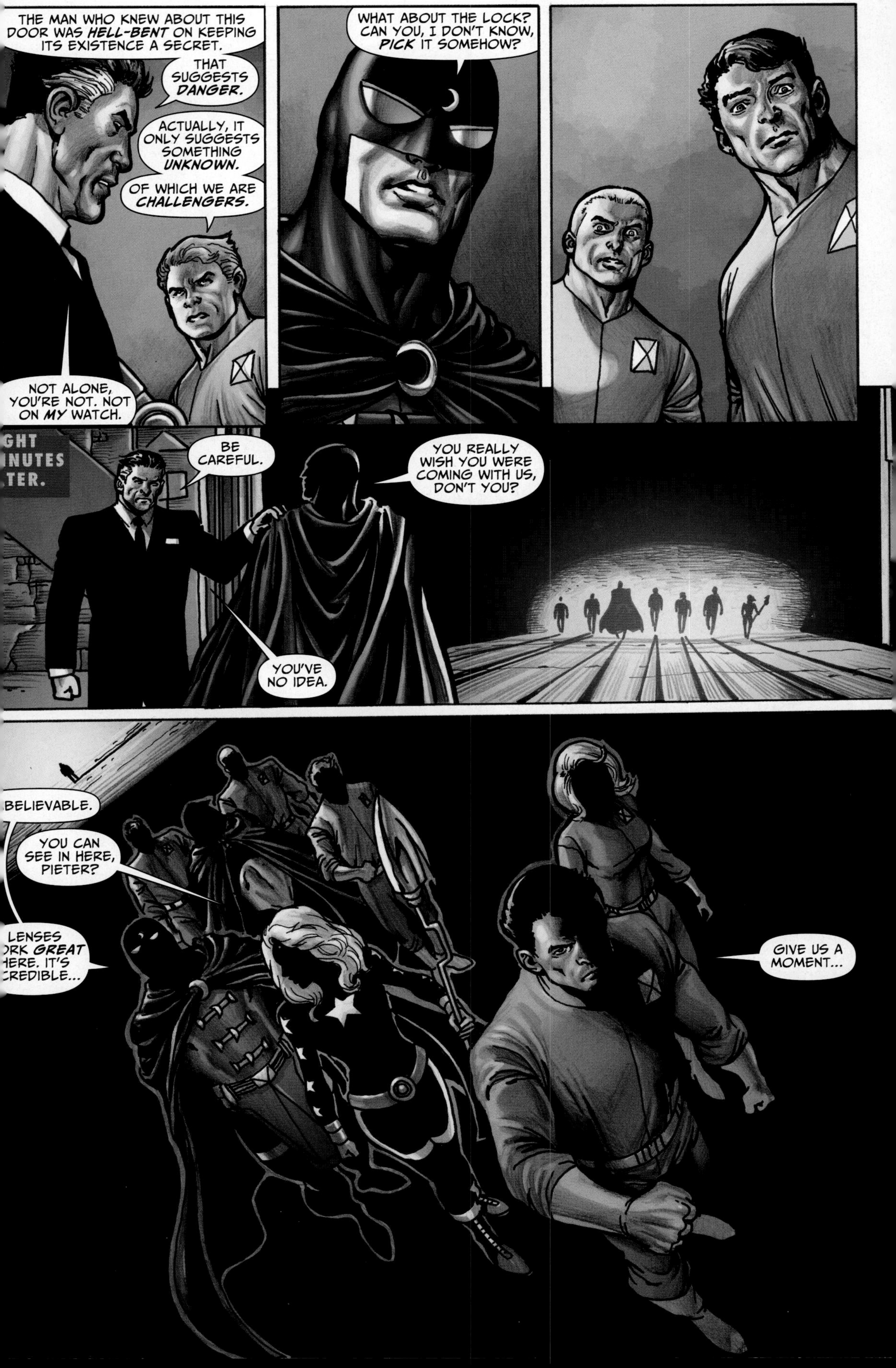
THE MAN WHO KNEW ABOUT THIS DOOR WAS HELL-BENT ON KEEPING ITS EXISTENCE A SECRET.
THAT SUGGESTS DANGER.
ACTUALLY, IT ONLY SUGGESTS SOMETHING UNKNOWN.
OF WHICH WE ARE CHALLENGERS.
NOT ALONE, YOU'RE NOT. NOT ON MY WATCH.
WHAT ABOUT THE LOCK? CAN YOU, I DON'T KNOW, PICK IT SOMEHOW?
GHT
NUTES
TER.
BE CAREFUL.
YOU REALLY WISH YOU WERE COMING WITH US, DON'T YOU?
YOU'VE NO IDEA.
BELIEVABLE.
YOU CAN SEE IN HERE, PIETER?
LENSES
ORK GREAT
HERE. IT'S
CREDIBLE...
GIVE US A MOMENT...

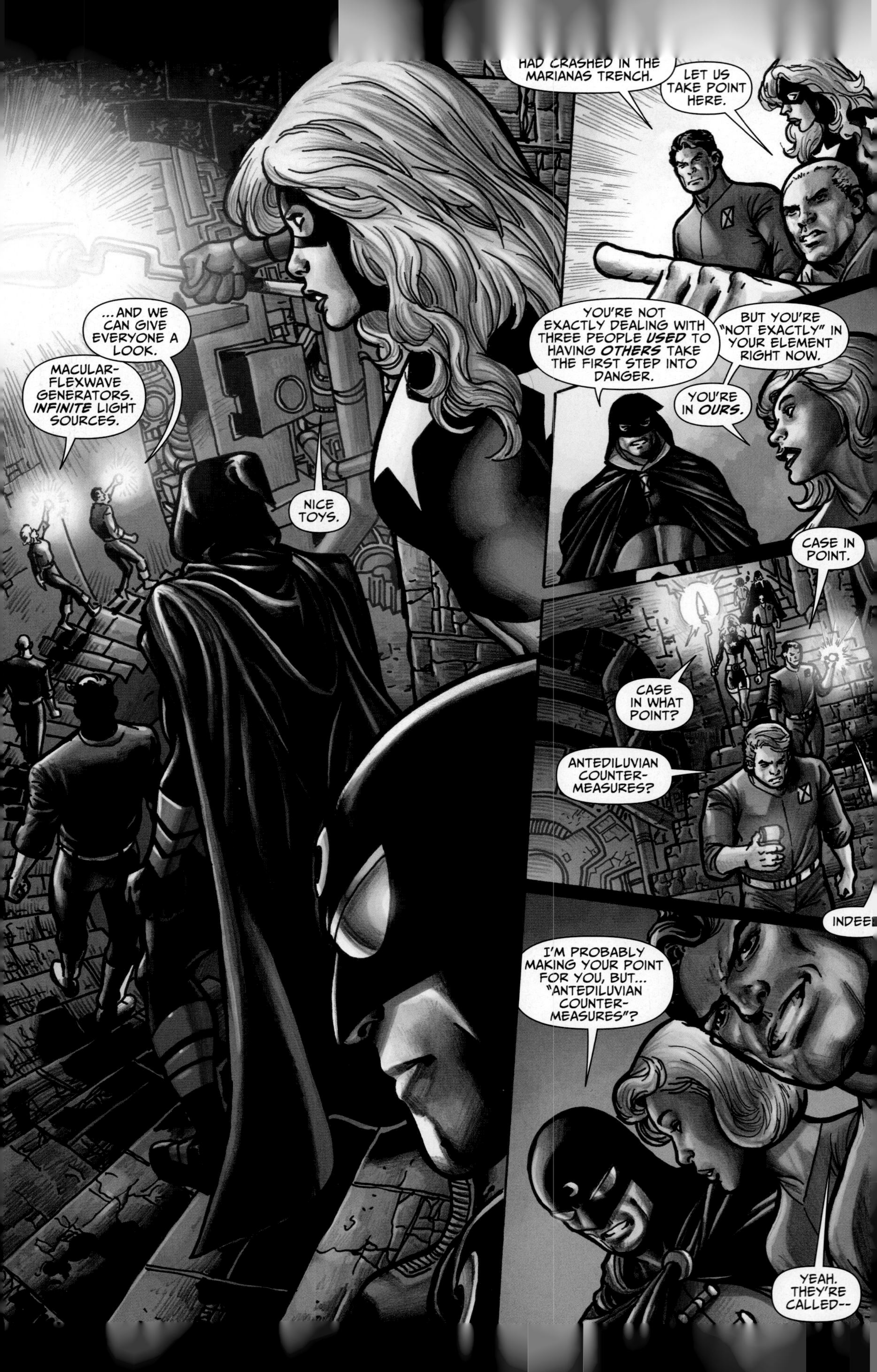

...AND WE CAN GIVE EVERYONE A LOOK.
MACULAR-FLEXWAVE GENERATORS. INFINITE LIGHT SOURCES.
NICE TOYS.
HAD CRASHED IN THE MARIANAS TRENCH.
LET US TAKE POINT HERE.
YOU'RE NOT EXACTLY DEALING WITH THREE PEOPLE USED TO HAVING OTHERS TAKE THE FIRST STEP INTO DANGER.
BUT YOU'RE "NOT EXACTLY" IN YOUR ELEMENT RIGHT NOW.
YOU'RE IN OURS.
CASE IN POINT.
CASE IN WHAT POINT?
ANTEDILUVIAN COUNTER-MEASURES?
INDEE
I'M PROBABLY MAKING YOUR POINT FOR YOU, BUT... "ANTEDILUVIAN COUNTER-MEASURES"?
YEAH. THEY'RE CALLED--

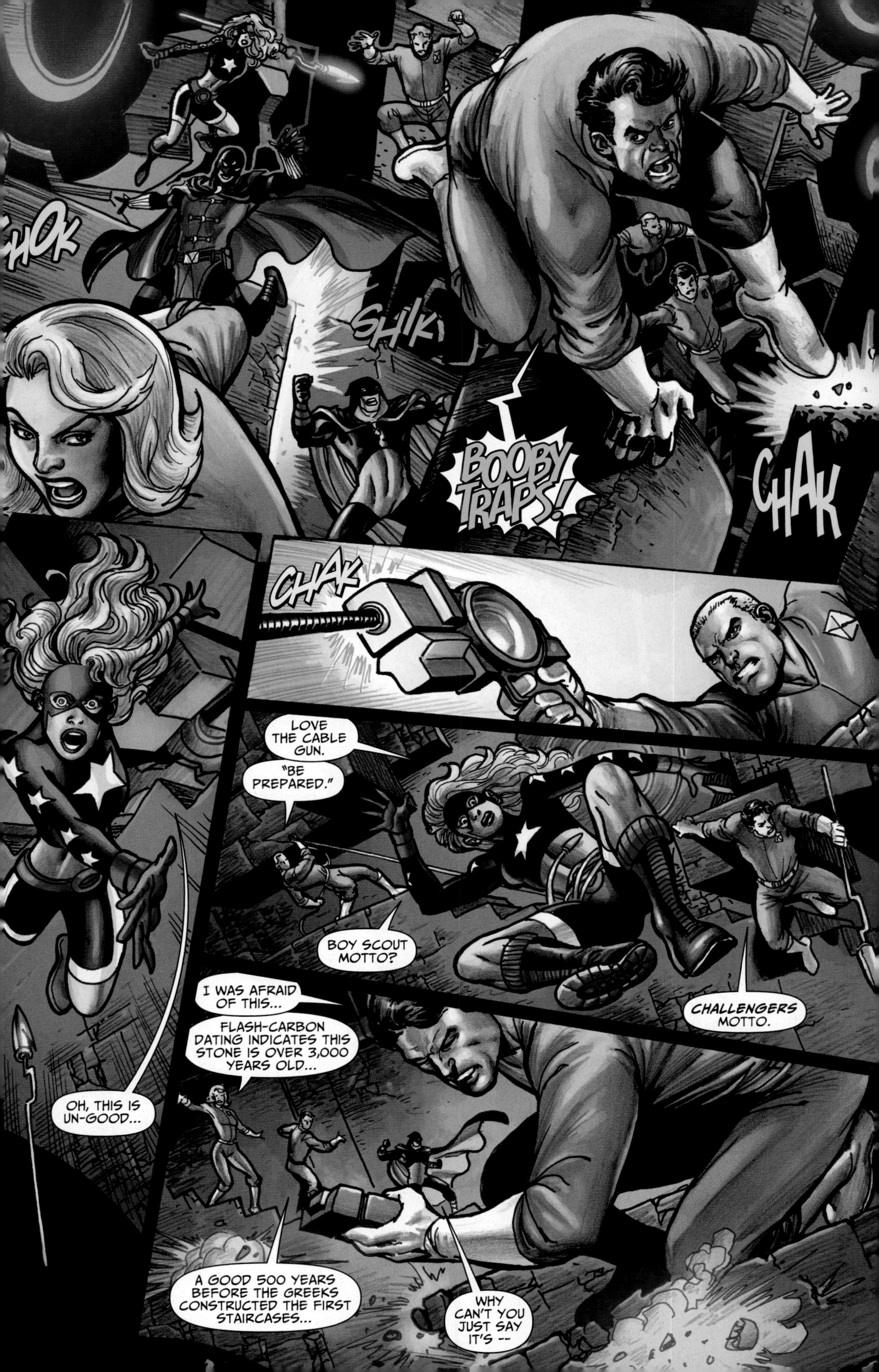

CHOK
SHIK
BOOBY TRAPS!
CHAK
CHAK
LOVE THE CABLE GUN.
"BE PREPARED."
BOY SCOUT MOTTO?
CHALLENGERS MOTTO.
OH, THIS IS UN-GOOD...
I WAS AFRAID OF THIS...
FLASH-CARBON DATING INDICATES THIS STONE IS OVER 3,000 YEARS OLD...
A GOOD 500 YEARS BEFORE THE GREEKS CONSTRUCTED THE FIRST STAIRCASES...
WHY CAN'T YOU JUST SAY IT'S --

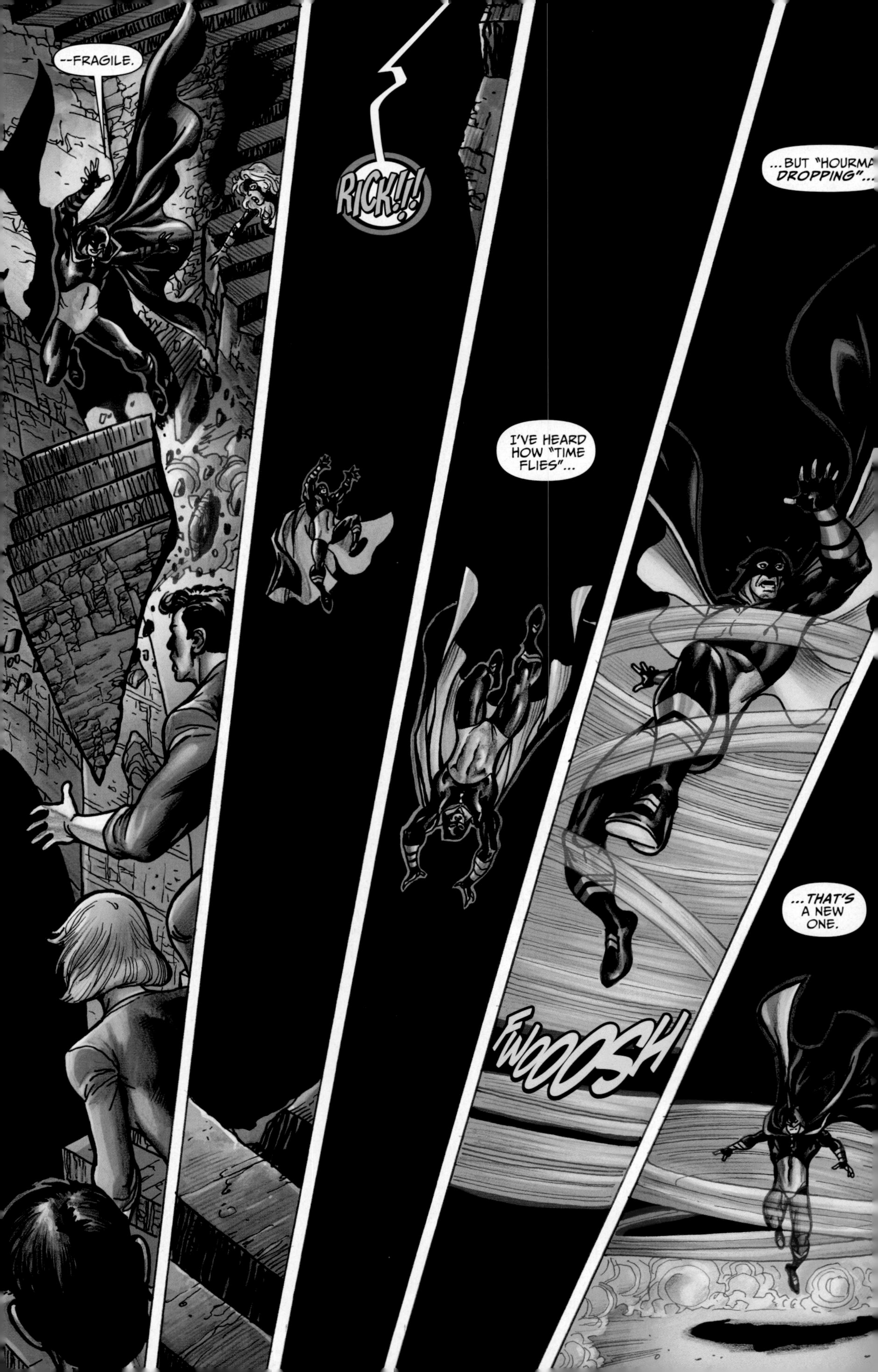
--FRAGILE.
RICK!!!
I'VE HEARD HOW "TIME FLIES"...
...BUT "HOURMA
DROPPING"...
FWOOOSH
...THAT'S A NEW ONE.

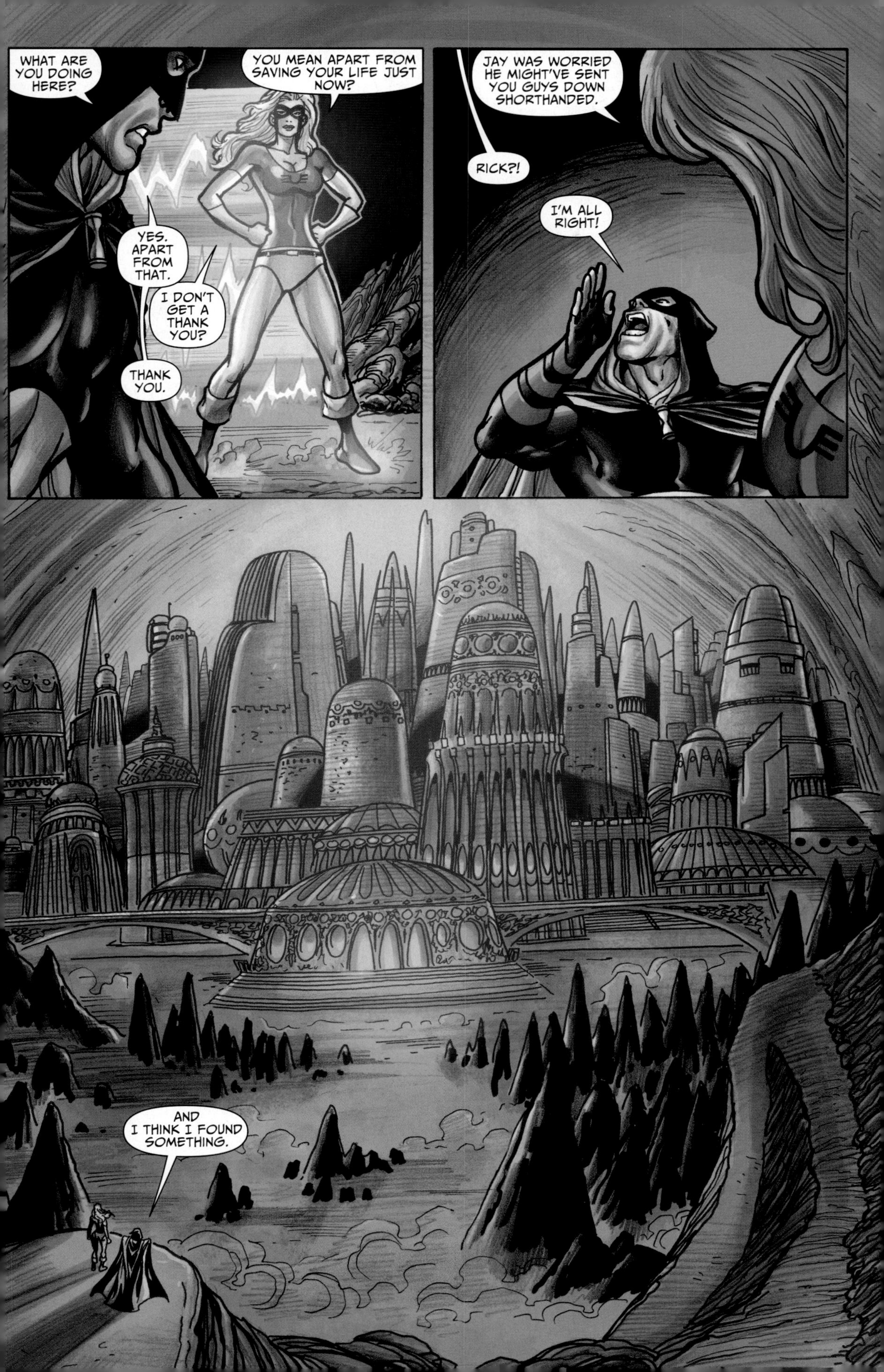
WHAT ARE YOU DOING HERE?
YOU MEAN APART FROM SAVING YOUR LIFE JUST NOW?
YES. APART FROM THAT.
I DON'T GET A THANK YOU?
THANK YOU.
JAY WAS WORRIED HE MIGHT'VE SENT YOU GUYS DOWN SHORTHANDED.
RICK?!
I'M ALL RIGHT!
AND I THINK I FOUND SOMETHING.

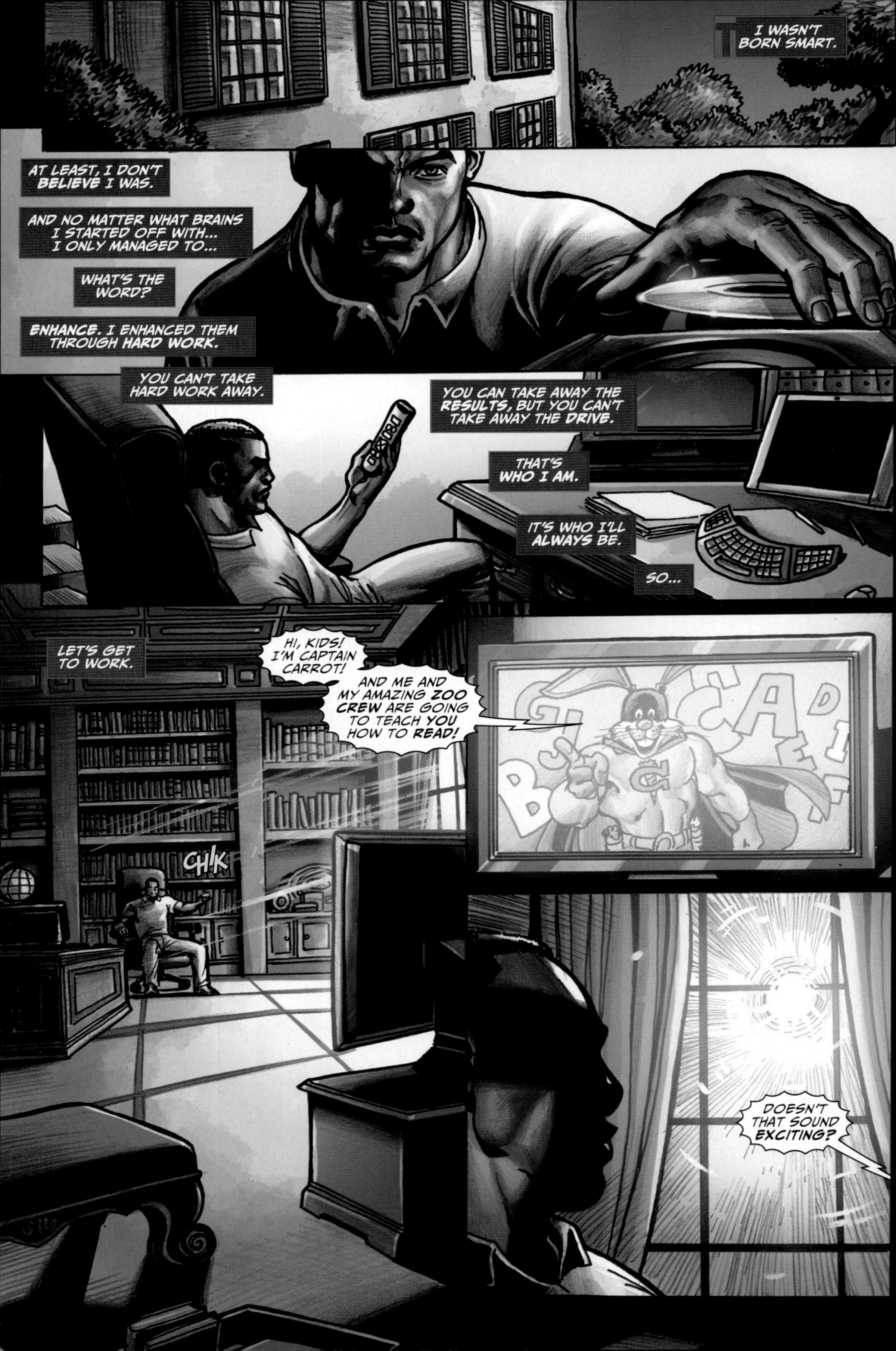
I WASN'T BORN SMART.
AT LEAST, I DON'T BELIEVE I WAS.
AND NO MATTER WHAT BRAINS I STARTED OFF WITH... I ONLY MANAGED TO...
WHAT'S THE WORD?
ENHANCE. I ENHANCED THEM THROUGH HARD WORK.
YOU CAN'T TAKE HARD WORK AWAY.
YOU CAN TAKE AWAY THE RESULTS, BUT YOU CAN'T TAKE AWAY THE DRIVE.
THAT'S WHO I AM.
IT'S WHO I'LL ALWAYS BE.
SO...
LET'S GET TO WORK.
HI, KIDS! I'M CAPTAIN CARROT!
AND ME AND MY AMAZING ZOO CREW ARE GOING TO TEACH YOU HOW TO READ!
CHIK
DOESN'T THAT SOUND EXCITING?

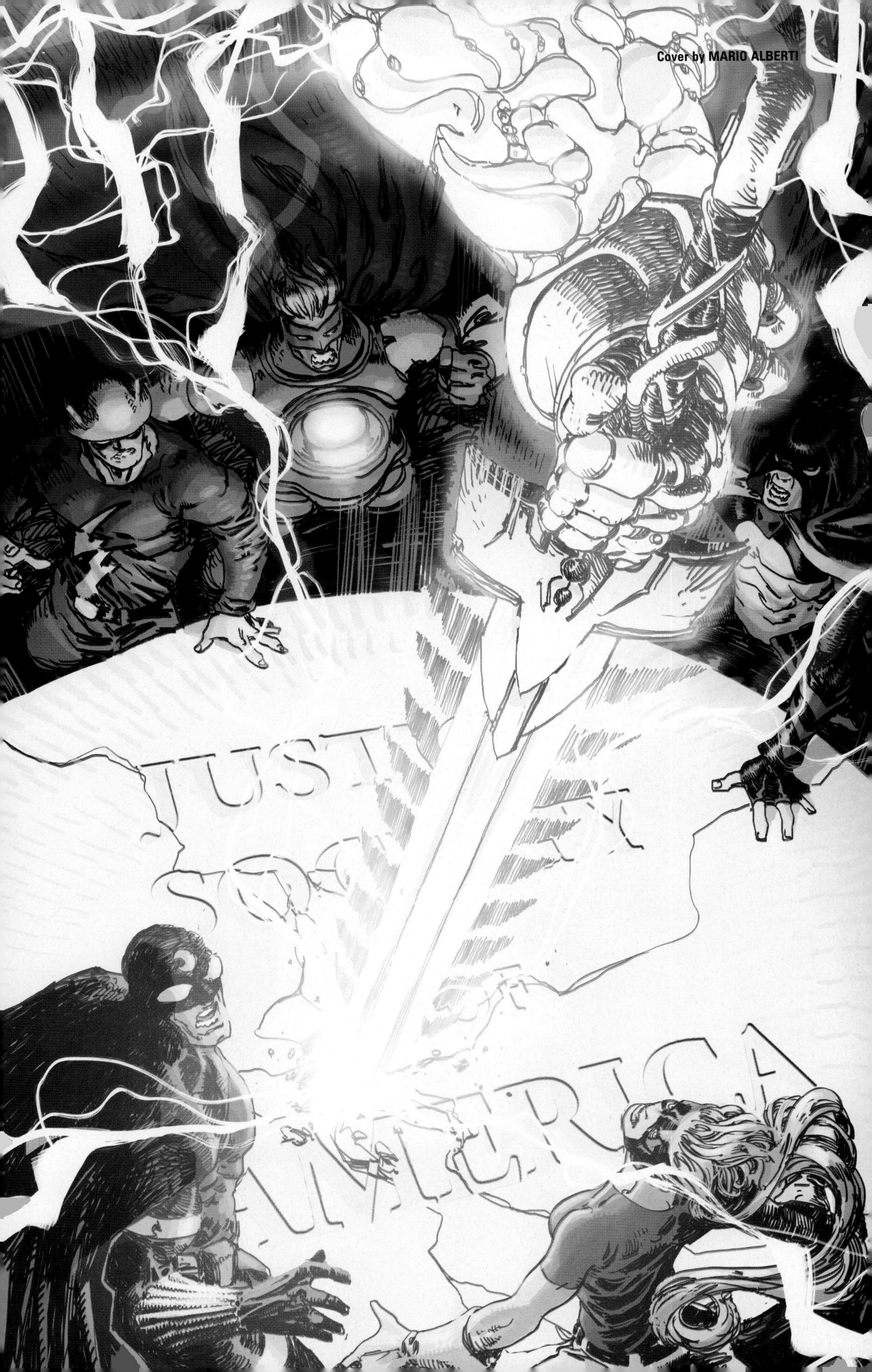

Cover by MARIO ALBERTI

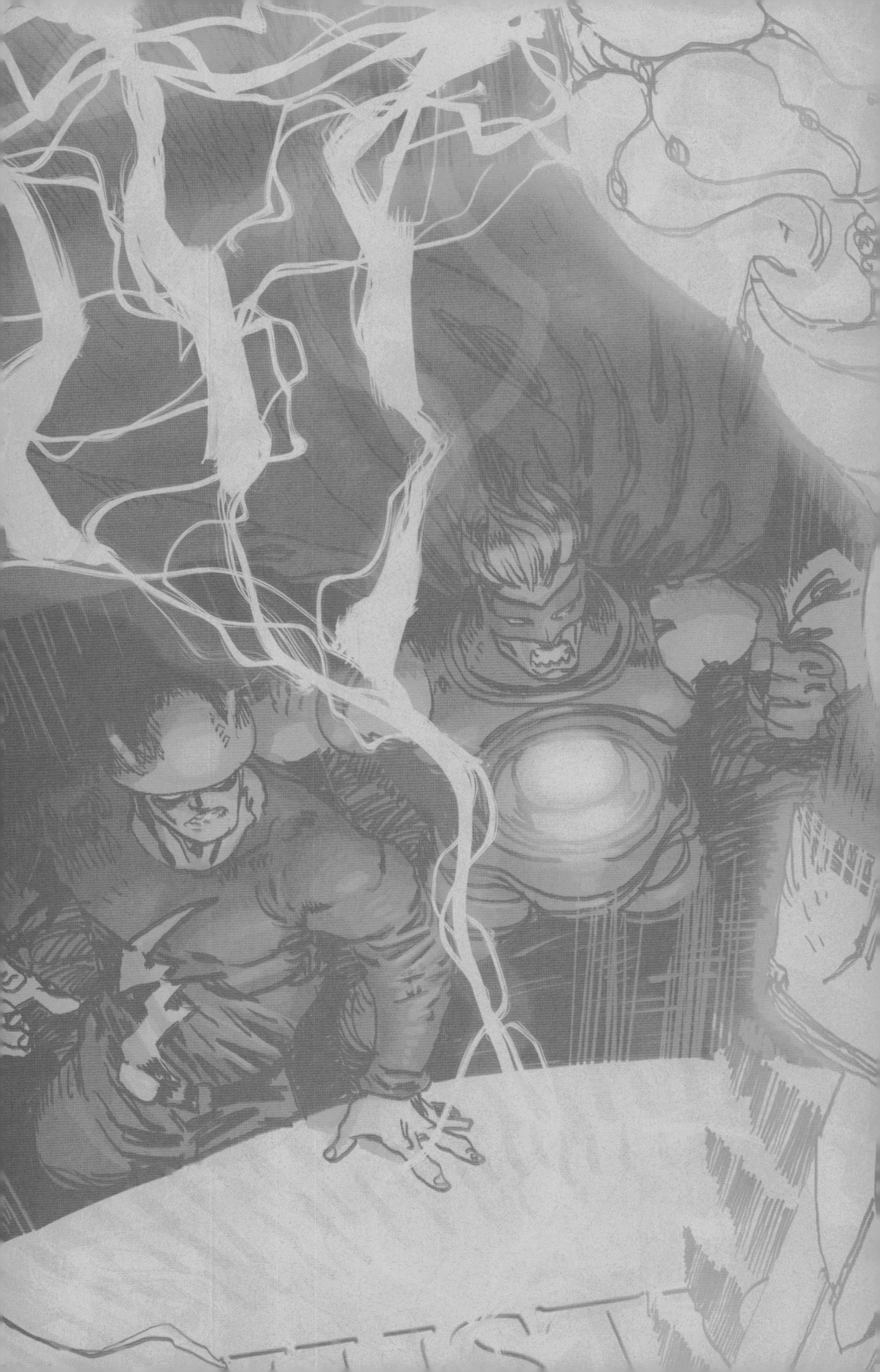

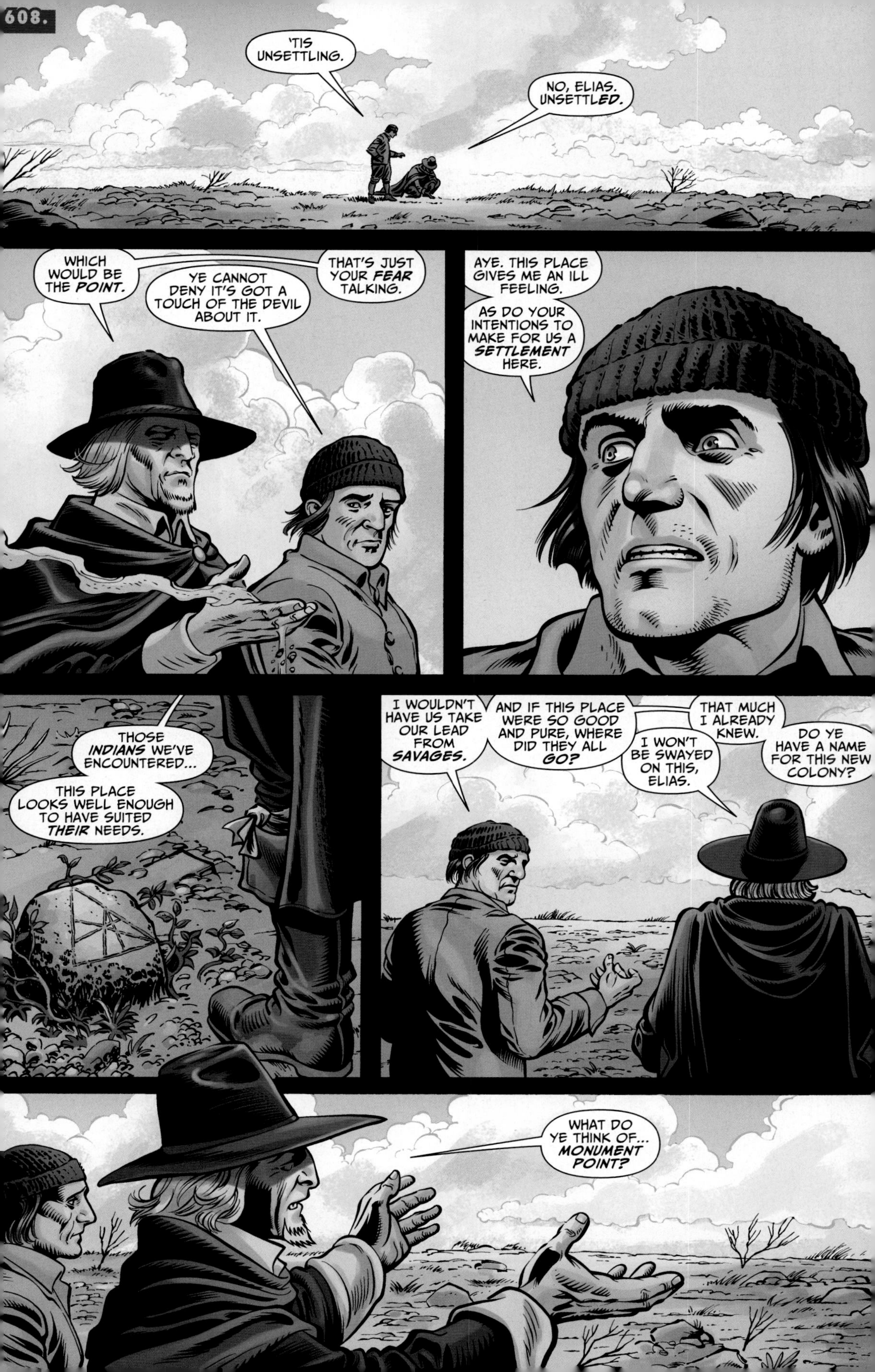
'TIS UNSETTLING.
NO, ELIAS. UNSETTLED.
WHICH WOULD BE THE POINT.
YE CANNOT DENY IT'S GOT A TOUCH OF THE DEVIL ABOUT IT.
THAT'S JUST YOUR FEAR TALKING.
AYE. THIS PLACE GIVES ME AN ILL FEELING.
AS DO YOUR INTENTIONS TO MAKE FOR US A SETTLEMENT HERE.
THOSE INDIANS WE'VE ENCOUNTERED...
THIS PLACE LOOKS WELL ENOUGH TO HAVE SUITED THEIR NEEDS.
I WOULDN'T HAVE US TAKE OUR LEAD FROM SAVAGES.
AND IF THIS PLACE WERE SO GOOD AND PURE, WHERE DID THEY ALL GO?
THAT MUCH I ALREADY KNEW.
I WON'T BE SWAYED ON THIS, ELIAS.
DO YE HAVE A NAME FOR THIS NEW COLONY?
WHAT DO YE THINK OF... MONUMENT POINT?

TODAY.
1.2 MILES BENEATH
MONUMENT POINT.

THE SECRET HISTORY OF MONUMENT POINT
CHAPTER THREE:

STRANGE
ADVENTURES

MARC GUGGENHEIM writer · JERRY ORDWAY penciller
SEAN PARSONS inker
ROB LEIGH letterer · MIKE ATIYEH colorist · MARIO ALBERTI co
CHRIS CONROY assoc. editor · JOEY CAVALIERI editor

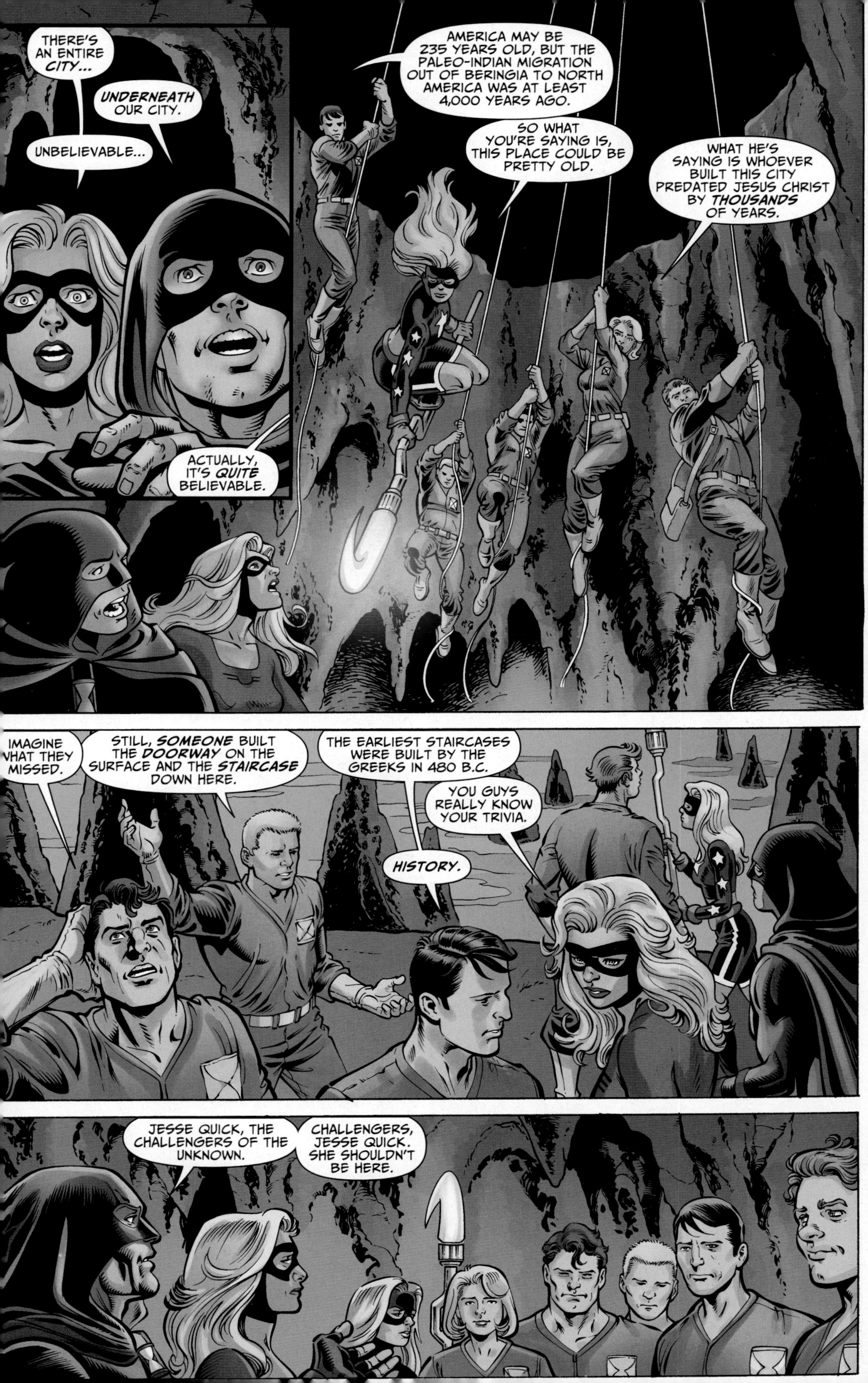

THERE'S AN ENTIRE CITY...
UNDERNEATH OUR CITY.
UNBELIEVABLE...
AMERICA MAY BE 235 YEARS OLD, BUT THE PALEO-INDIAN MIGRATION OUT OF BERINGIA TO NORTH AMERICA WAS AT LEAST 4,000 YEARS AGO.
SO WHAT YOU'RE SAYING IS, THIS PLACE COULD BE PRETTY OLD.
WHAT HE'S SAYING IS WHOEVER BUILT THIS CITY PREDATED JESUS CHRIST BY THOUSANDS OF YEARS.
ACTUALLY, IT'S QUITE BELIEVABLE.
IMAGINE WHAT THEY MISSED.
STILL, SOMEONE BUILT THE DOORWAY ON THE SURFACE AND THE STAIRCASE DOWN HERE.
THE EARLIEST STAIRCASES WERE BUILT BY THE GREEKS IN 480 B.C.
YOU GUYS REALLY KNOW YOUR TRIVIA.
HISTORY.
JESSE QUICK, THE CHALLENGERS OF THE UNKNOWN.
CHALLENGERS, JESSE QUICK. SHE SHOULDN'T BE HERE.

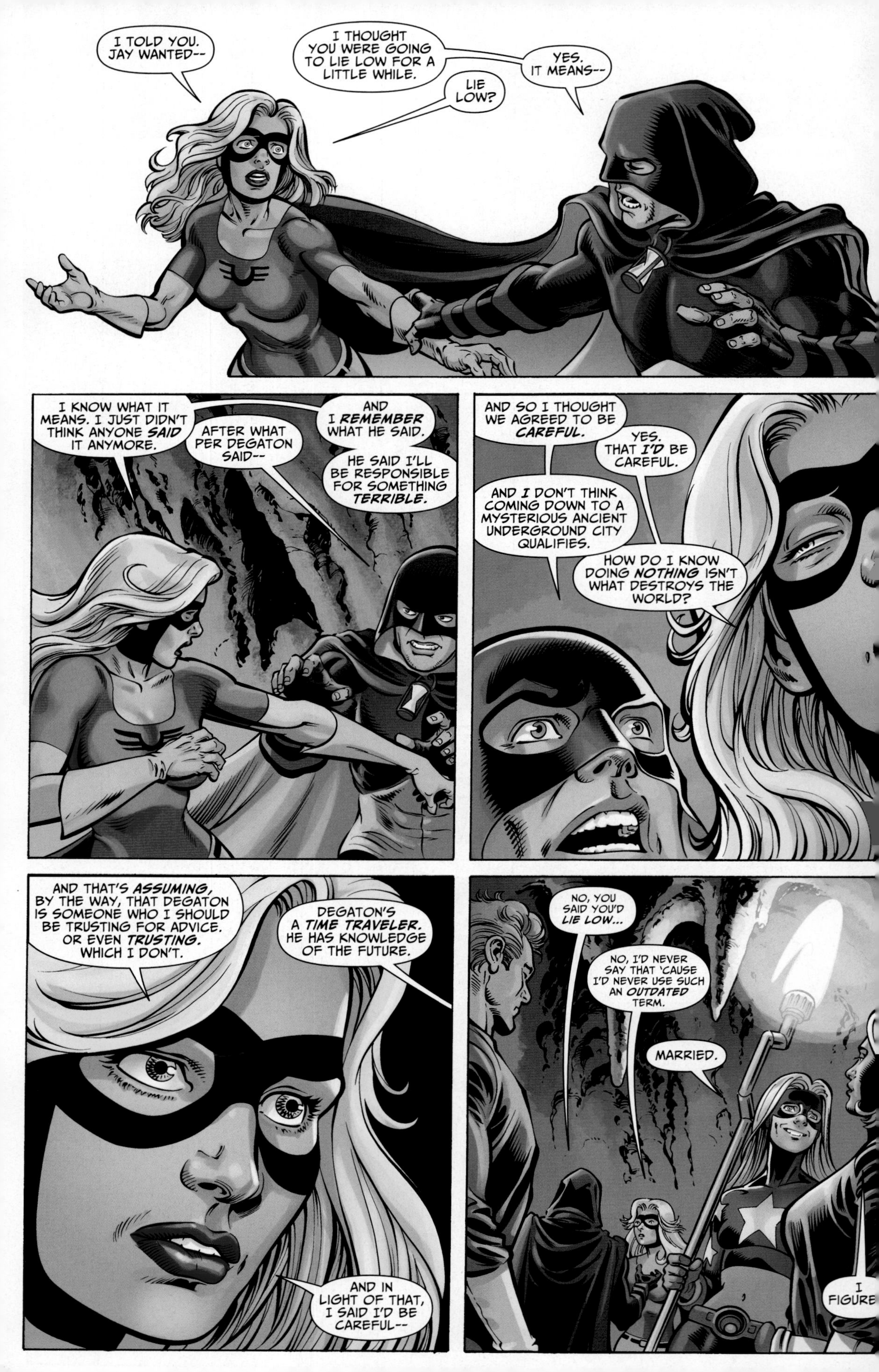
I TOLD YOU. JAY WANTED--
I THOUGHT YOU WERE GOING TO LIE LOW FOR A LITTLE WHILE.
LIE LOW?
YES. IT MEANS--
I KNOW WHAT IT MEANS. I JUST DIDN'T THINK ANYONE SAID IT ANYMORE.
AFTER WHAT PER DEGATON SAID--
AND I REMEMBER WHAT HE SAID.
HE SAID I'LL BE RESPONSIBLE FOR SOMETHING TERRIBLE.
AND SO I THOUGHT WE AGREED TO BE CAREFUL.
YES. THAT I'D BE CAREFUL.
AND I DON'T THINK COMING DOWN TO A MYSTERIOUS ANCIENT UNDERGROUND CITY QUALIFIES.
HOW DO I KNOW DOING NOTHING ISN'T WHAT DESTROYS THE WORLD?
AND THAT'S ASSUMING, BY THE WAY, THAT DEGATON IS SOMEONE WHO I SHOULD BE TRUSTING FOR ADVICE. OR EVEN TRUSTING. WHICH I DON'T.
DEGATON'S A TIME TRAVELER. HE HAS KNOWLEDGE OF THE FUTURE.
AND IN LIGHT OF THAT, I SAID I'D BE CAREFUL--
NO, YOU SAID YOU'D LIE LOW...
NO, I'D NEVER SAY THAT 'CAUSE I'D NEVER USE SUCH AN OUTDATED TERM.
MARRIED.
I FIGURE

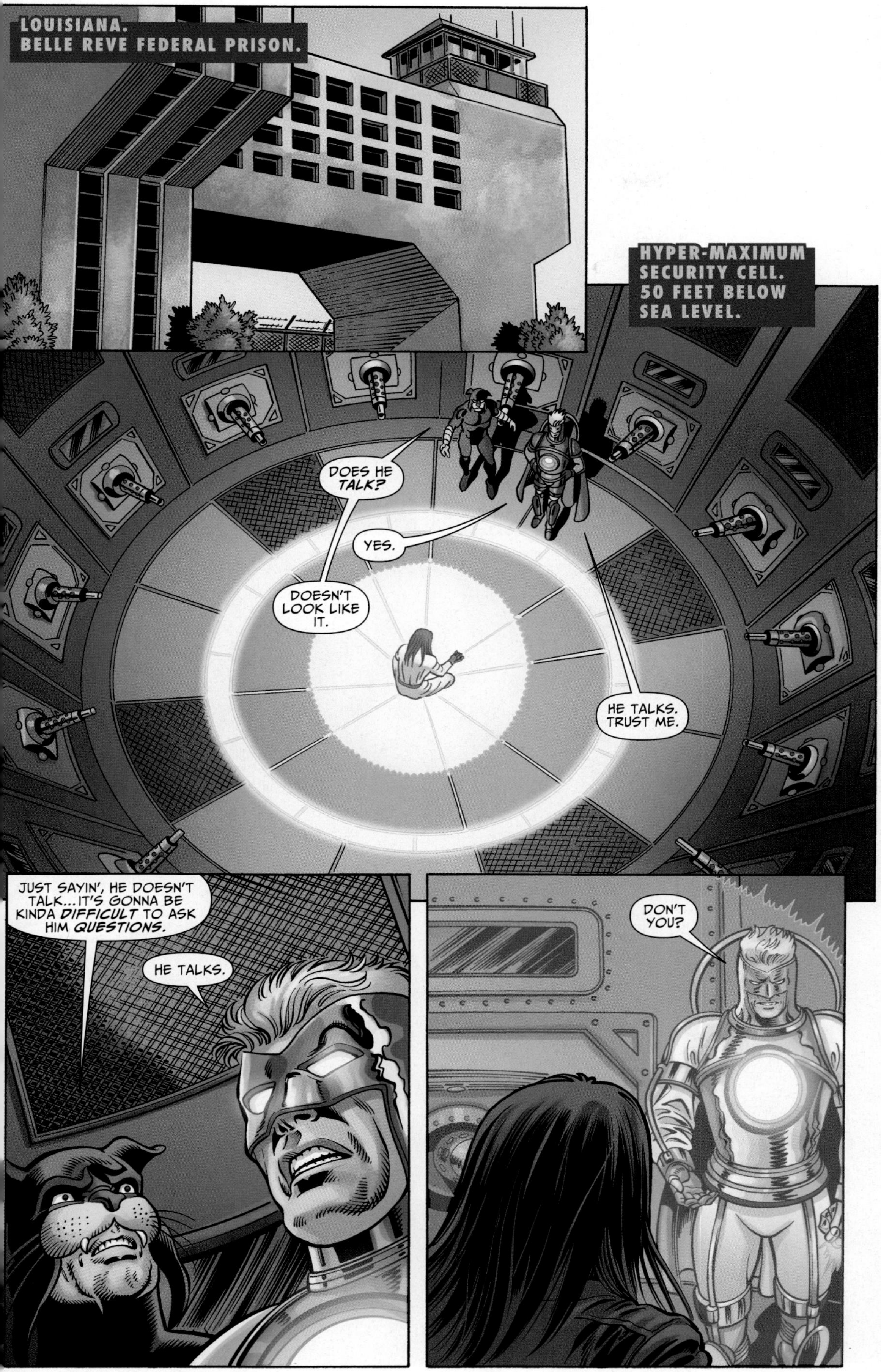
LOUISIANA.
BELLE REVE FEDERAL PRISON.
HYPER-MAXIMUM SECURITY CELL. 50 FEET BELOW SEA LEVEL.
DOES HE *TALK?*
YES.
DOESN'T LOOK LIKE IT.
HE TALKS. TRUST ME.
JUST SAYIN', HE DOESN'T TALK...IT'S GONNA BE KINDA *DIFFICULT* TO ASK HIM *QUESTIONS.*
HE TALKS.
DON'T YOU?

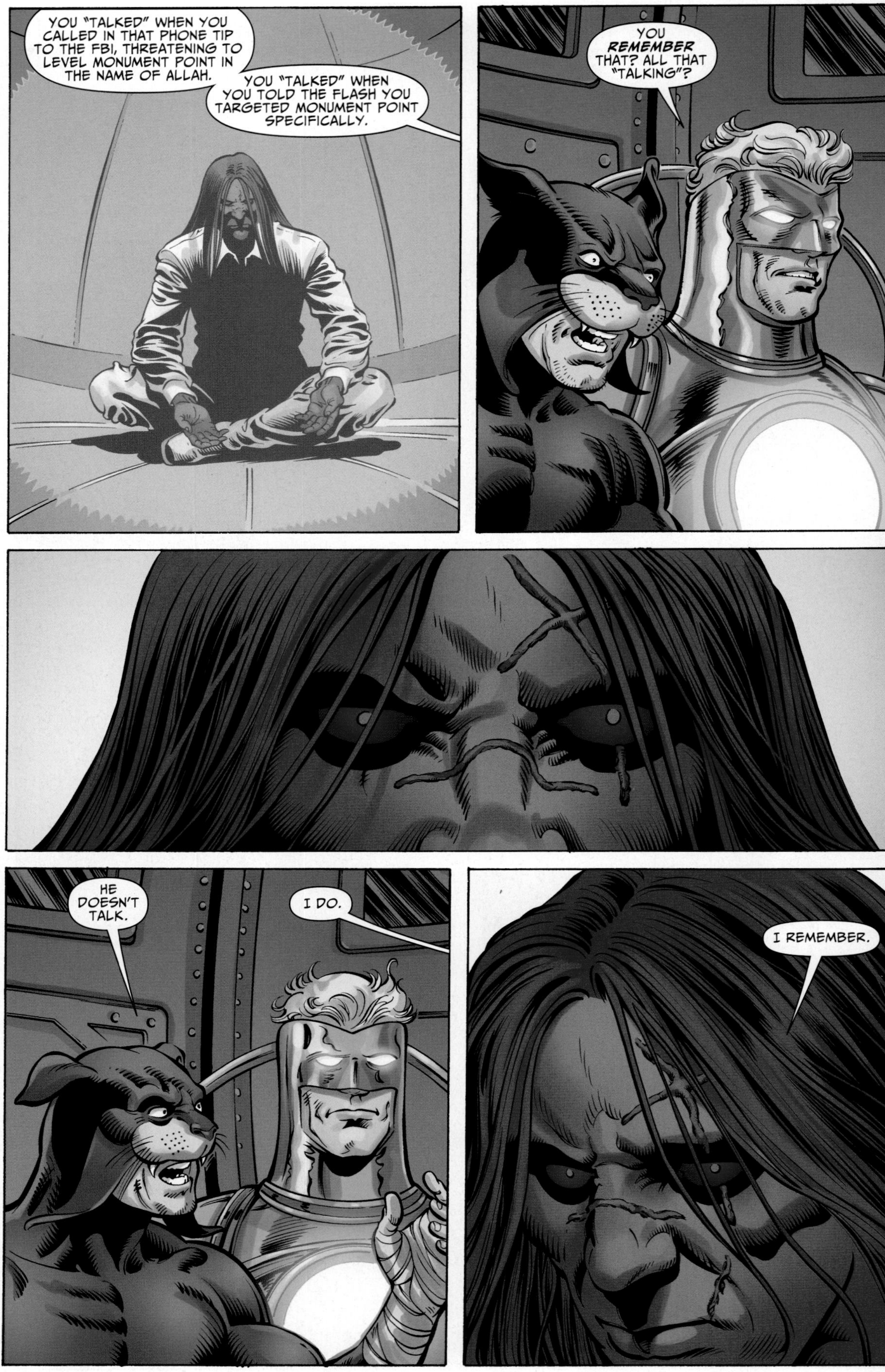
YOU "TALKED" WHEN YOU CALLED IN THAT PHONE TIP TO THE FBI, THREATENING TO LEVEL MONUMENT POINT IN THE NAME OF ALLAH.
YOU "TALKED" WHEN YOU TOLD THE FLASH YOU TARGETED MONUMENT POINT SPECIFICALLY.
YOU ***REMEMBER*** THAT? ALL THAT "TALKING"?
HE DOESN'T TALK.
I DO.
I REMEMBER.

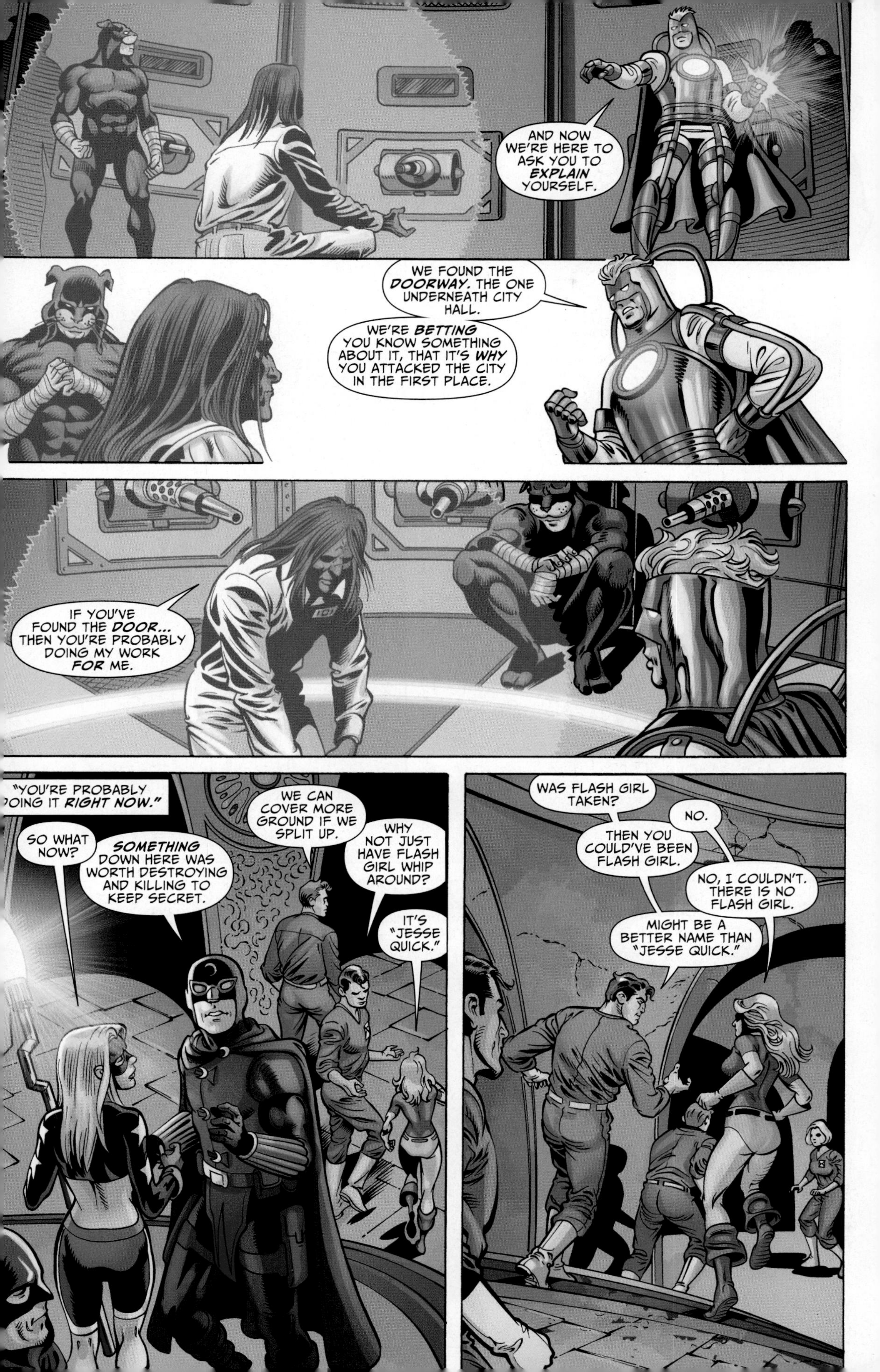
AND NOW WE'RE HERE TO ASK YOU TO EXPLAIN YOURSELF.
WE FOUND THE DOORWAY. THE ONE UNDERNEATH CITY HALL.
WE'RE BETTING YOU KNOW SOMETHING ABOUT IT, THAT IT'S WHY YOU ATTACKED THE CITY IN THE FIRST PLACE.
IF YOU'VE FOUND THE DOOR... THEN YOU'RE PROBABLY DOING MY WORK FOR ME.
"YOU'RE PROBABLY DOING IT RIGHT NOW."
SO WHAT NOW?
SOMETHING DOWN HERE WAS WORTH DESTROYING AND KILLING TO KEEP SECRET.
WE CAN COVER MORE GROUND IF WE SPLIT UP.
WHY NOT JUST HAVE FLASH GIRL WHIP AROUND?
IT'S "JESSE QUICK."
WAS FLASH GIRL TAKEN?
NO.
THEN YOU COULD'VE BEEN FLASH GIRL.
NO, I COULDN'T. THERE IS NO FLASH GIRL.
MIGHT BE A BETTER NAME THAN "JESSE QUICK."

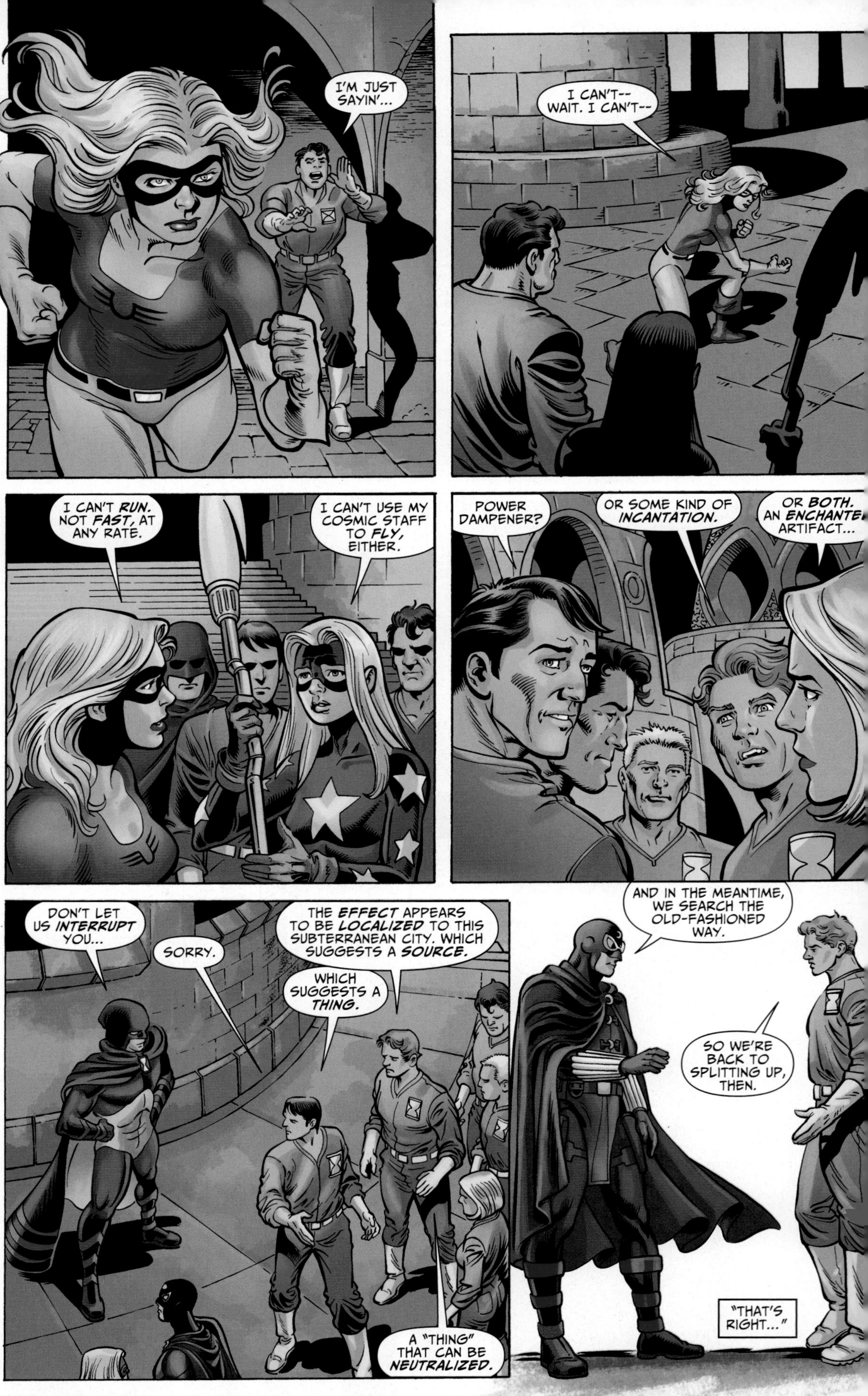

I'M JUST SAYIN'...
I CAN'T-- WAIT. I CAN'T--
I CAN'T *RUN.* NOT *FAST,* AT ANY RATE.
I CAN'T USE MY COSMIC STAFF TO *FLY,* EITHER.
POWER DAMPENER?
OR SOME KIND OF *INCANTATION.*
OR *BOTH.* AN *ENCHANTE*
ARTIFACT...
DON'T LET US *INTERRUPT* YOU...
SORRY.
THE *EFFECT* APPEARS TO BE *LOCALIZED* TO THIS SUBTERRANEAN CITY. WHICH SUGGESTS A *SOURCE.*
WHICH SUGGESTS A *THING.*
A "THING" THAT CAN BE *NEUTRALIZED.*
AND IN THE MEANTIME, WE SEARCH THE OLD-FASHIONED WAY.
SO WE'RE BACK TO SPLITTING UP, THEN.
"THAT'S RIGHT..."

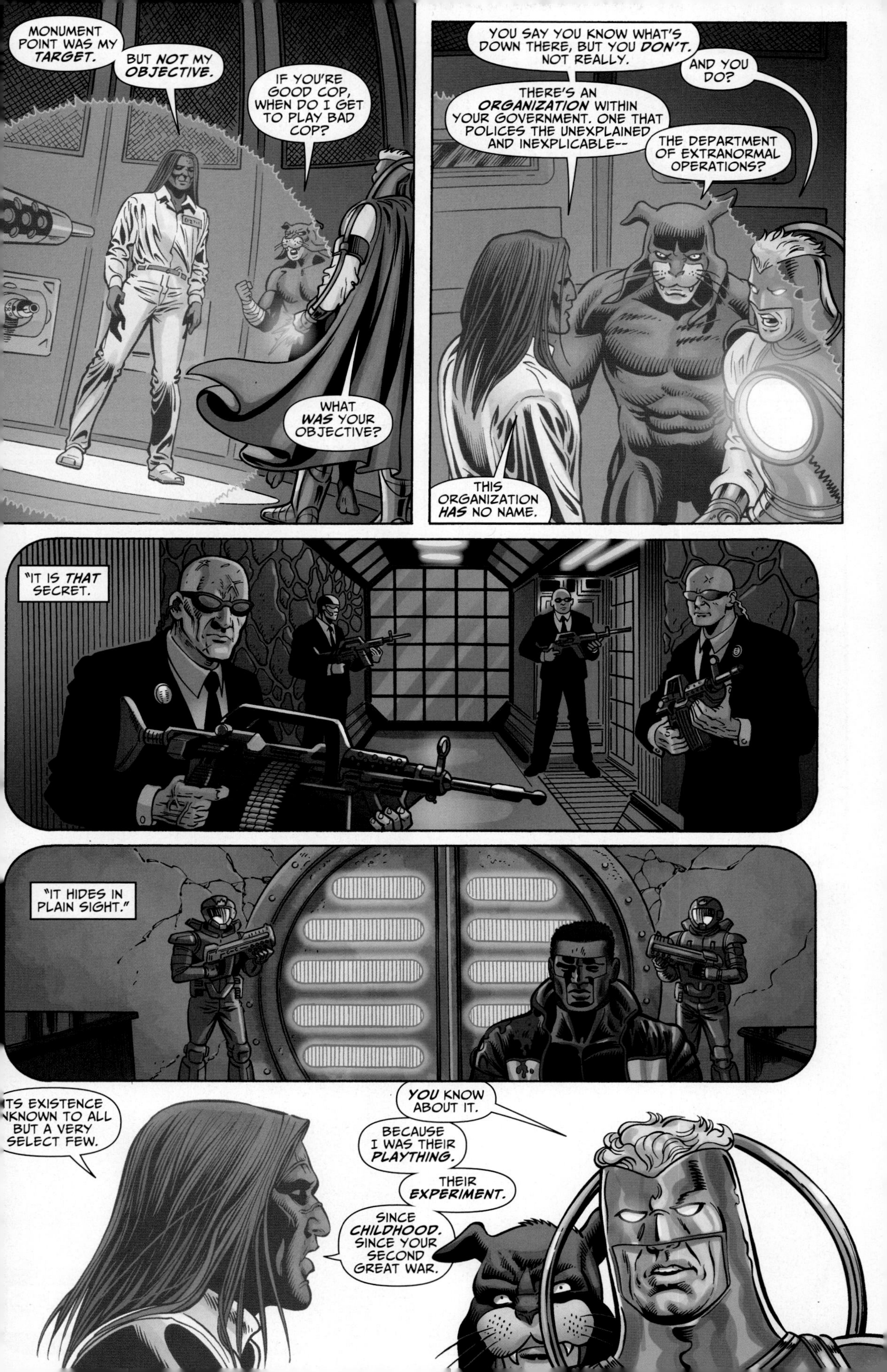
MONUMENT POINT WAS MY TARGET.
BUT NOT MY OBJECTIVE.
IF YOU'RE GOOD COP, WHEN DO I GET TO PLAY BAD COP?
WHAT WAS YOUR OBJECTIVE?
YOU SAY YOU KNOW WHAT'S DOWN THERE, BUT YOU DON'T. NOT REALLY.
AND YOU DO?
THERE'S AN ORGANIZATION WITHIN YOUR GOVERNMENT. ONE THAT POLICES THE UNEXPLAINED AND INEXPLICABLE--
THE DEPARTMENT OF EXTRANORMAL OPERATIONS?
THIS ORGANIZATION HAS NO NAME.
"IT IS THAT SECRET.
"IT HIDES IN PLAIN SIGHT."
TS EXISTENCE NKNOWN TO ALL BUT A VERY SELECT FEW.
YOU KNOW ABOUT IT.
BECAUSE I WAS THEIR PLAYTHING.
THEIR EXPERIMENT.
SINCE CHILDHOOD. SINCE YOUR SECOND GREAT WAR.

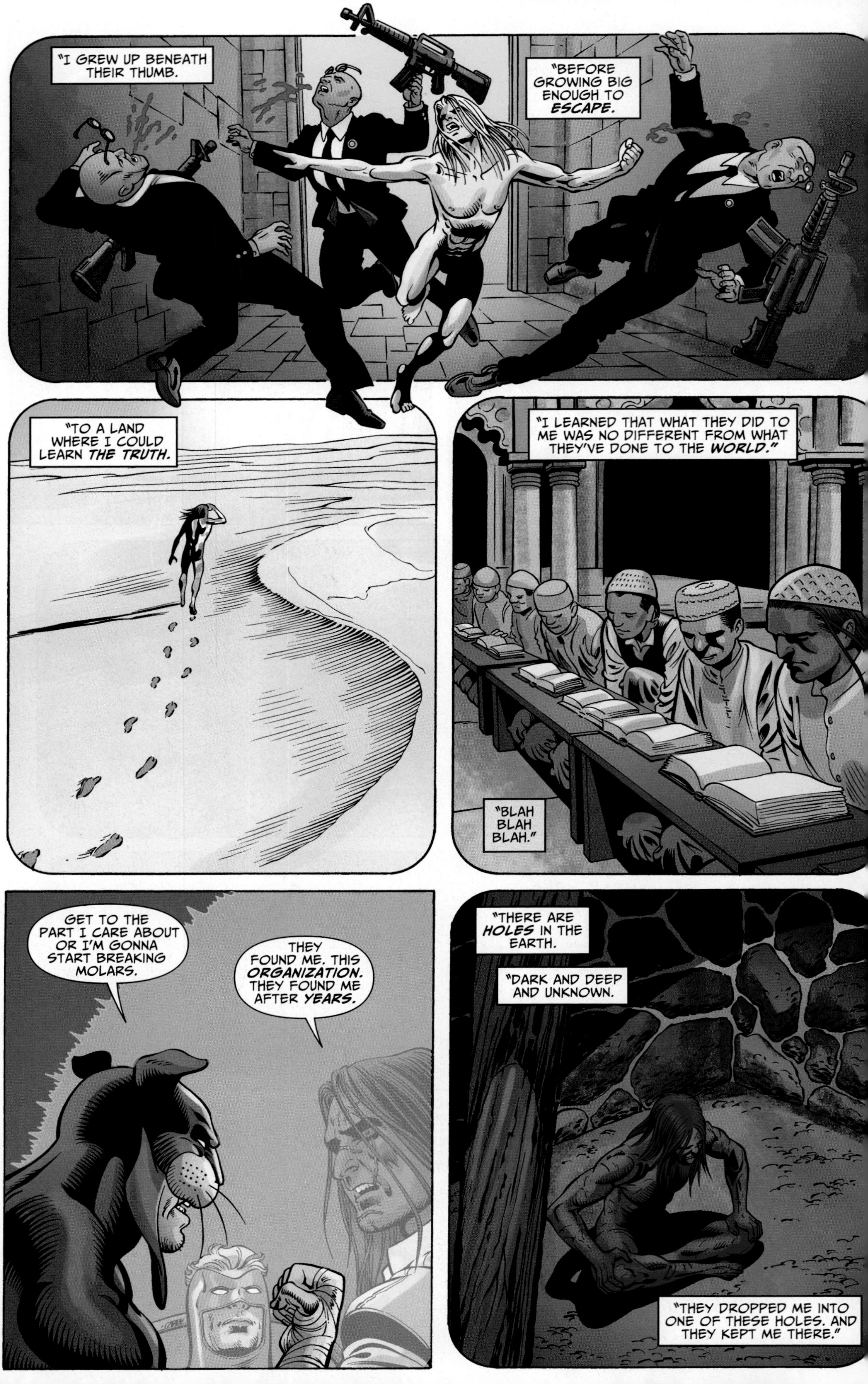
"I GREW UP BENEATH THEIR THUMB.
"BEFORE GROWING BIG ENOUGH TO ESCAPE.
"TO A LAND WHERE I COULD LEARN THE TRUTH.
"I LEARNED THAT WHAT THEY DID TO ME WAS NO DIFFERENT FROM WHAT THEY'VE DONE TO THE WORLD."
"BLAH BLAH BLAH."
GET TO THE PART I CARE ABOUT OR I'M GONNA START BREAKING MOLARS.
THEY FOUND ME. THIS ORGANIZATION. THEY FOUND ME AFTER YEARS.
"THERE ARE HOLES IN THE EARTH.
"DARK AND DEEP AND UNKNOWN.
"THEY DROPPED ME INTO ONE OF THESE HOLES. AND THEY KEPT ME THERE."

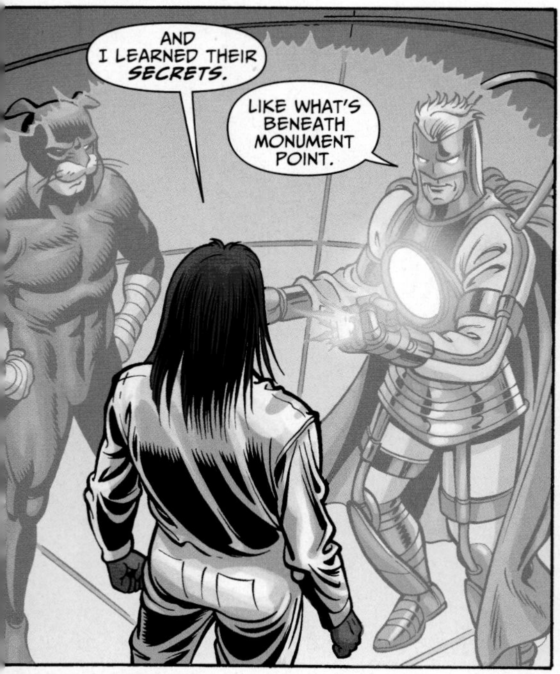
AND I LEARNED THEIR SECRETS.
LIKE WHAT'S BENEATH MONUMENT POINT.

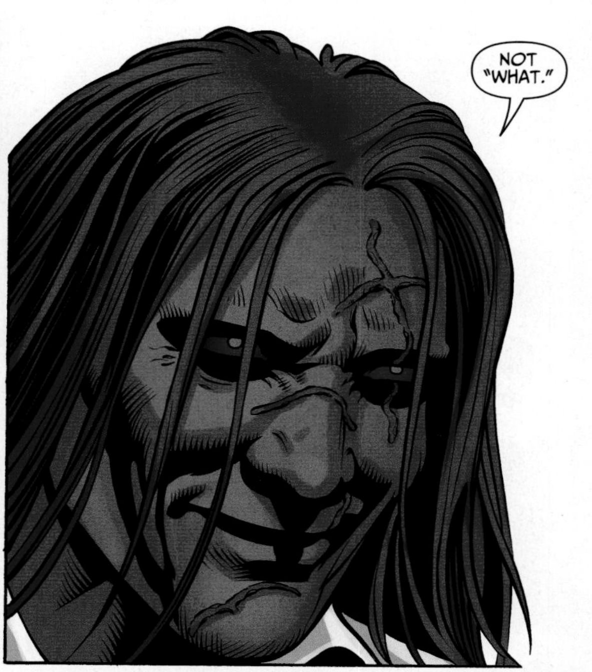
NOT "WHAT."

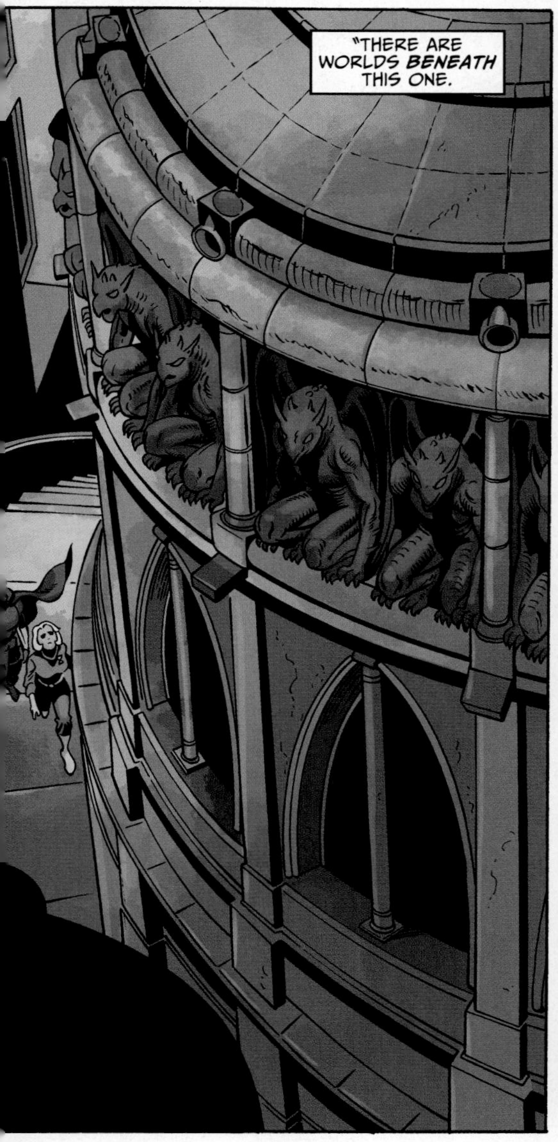
"THERE ARE WORLDS BENEATH THIS ONE.

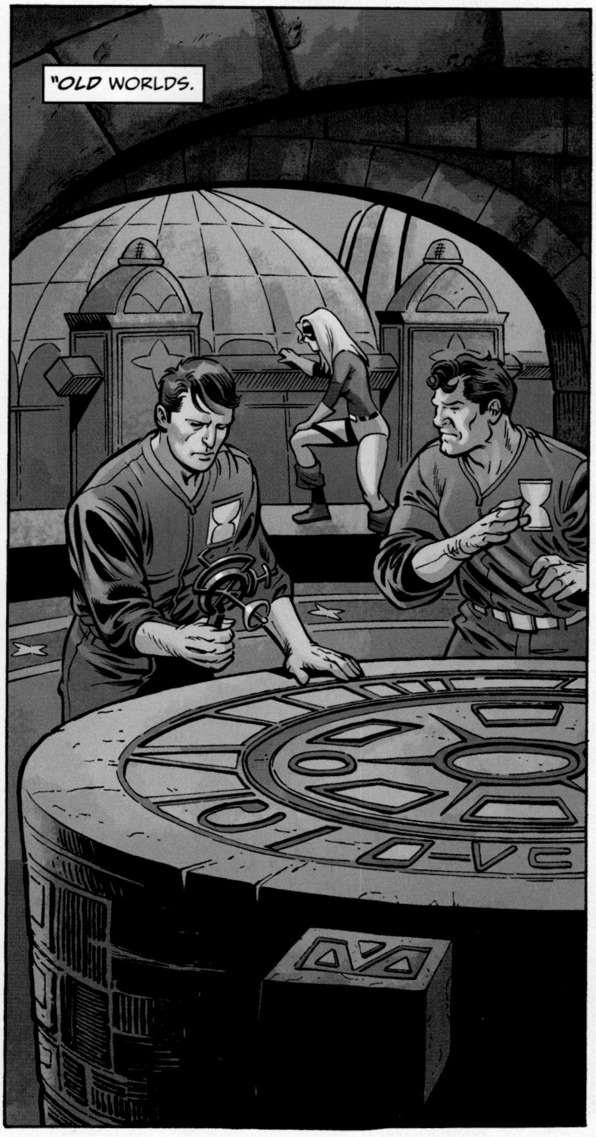
"OLD WORLDS.

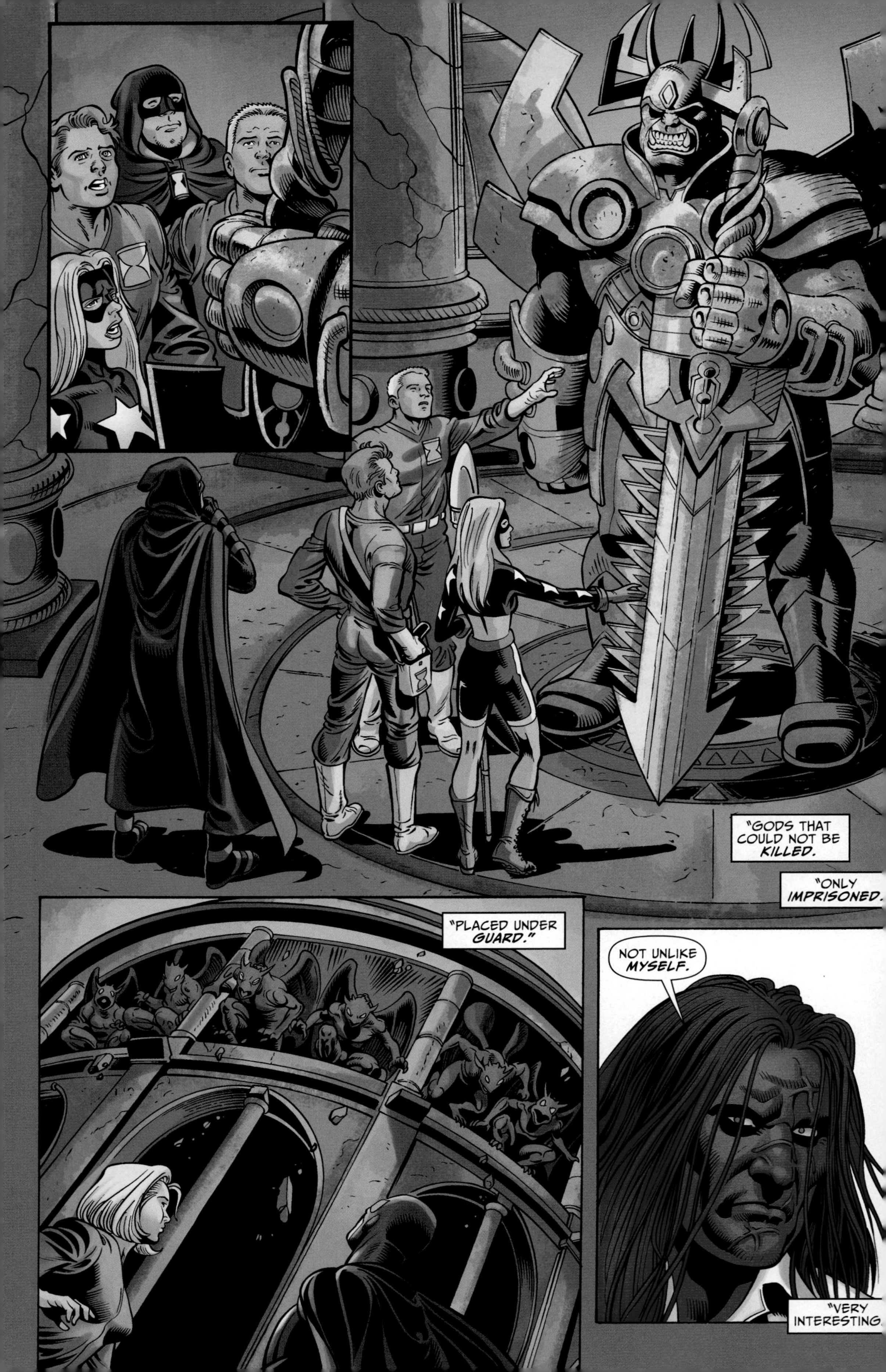
"GODS THAT COULD NOT BE KILLED.
"ONLY IMPRISONED.
"PLACED UNDER GUARD."
NOT UNLIKE MYSELF.
"VERY INTERESTING.

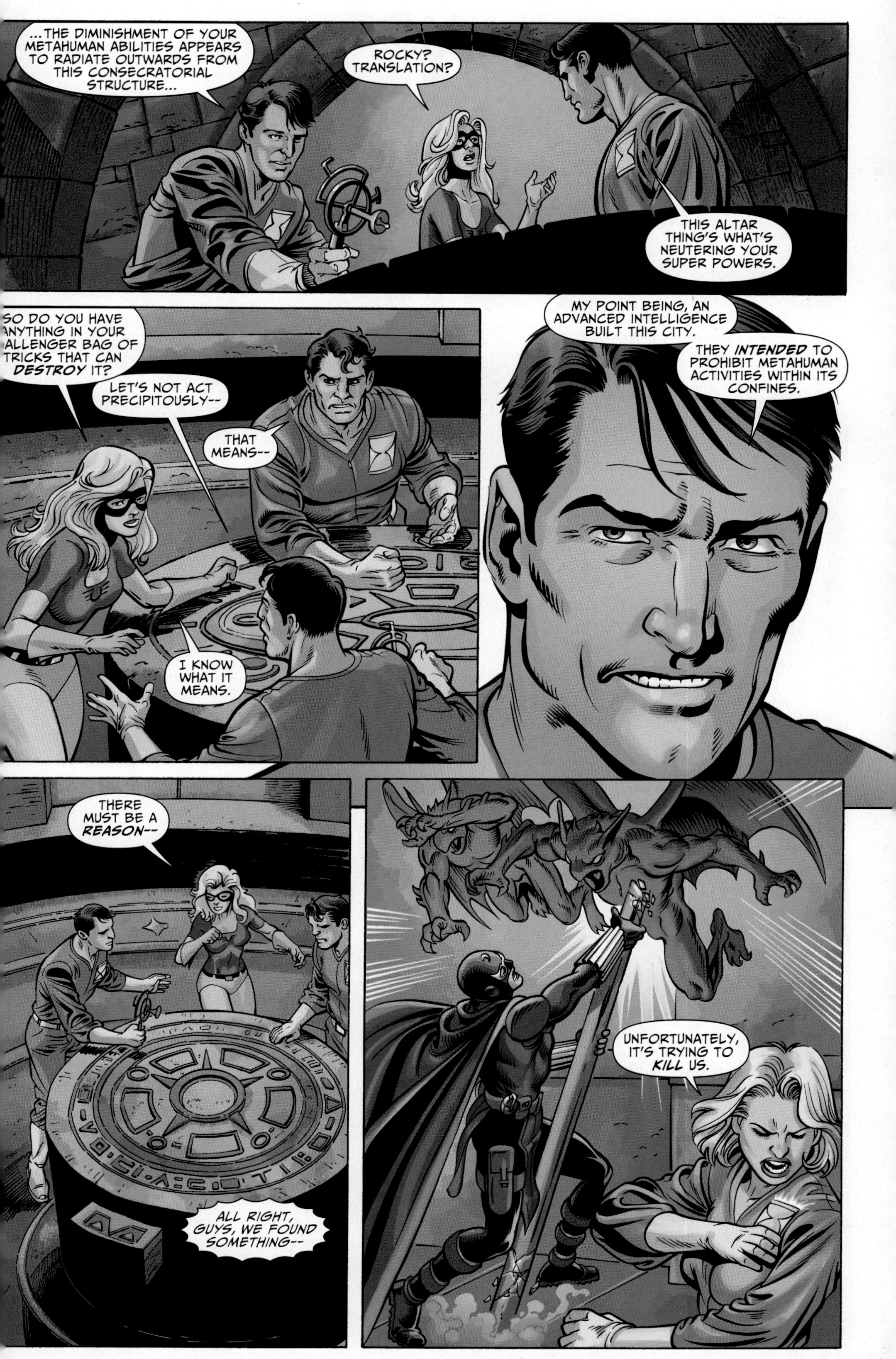
...THE DIMINISHMENT OF YOUR METAHUMAN ABILITIES APPEARS TO RADIATE OUTWARDS FROM THIS CONSECRATORIAL STRUCTURE...
ROCKY? TRANSLATION?
THIS ALTAR THING'S WHAT'S NEUTERING YOUR SUPER POWERS.
SO DO YOU HAVE ANYTHING IN YOUR ALLENGER BAG OF TRICKS THAT CAN DESTROY IT?
LET'S NOT ACT PRECIPITOUSLY--
THAT MEANS--
I KNOW WHAT IT MEANS.
MY POINT BEING, AN ADVANCED INTELLIGENCE BUILT THIS CITY.
THEY INTENDED TO PROHIBIT METAHUMAN ACTIVITIES WITHIN ITS CONFINES.
THERE MUST BE A REASON--
ALL RIGHT, GUYS, WE FOUND SOMETHING--
UNFORTUNATELY, IT'S TRYING TO KILL US.

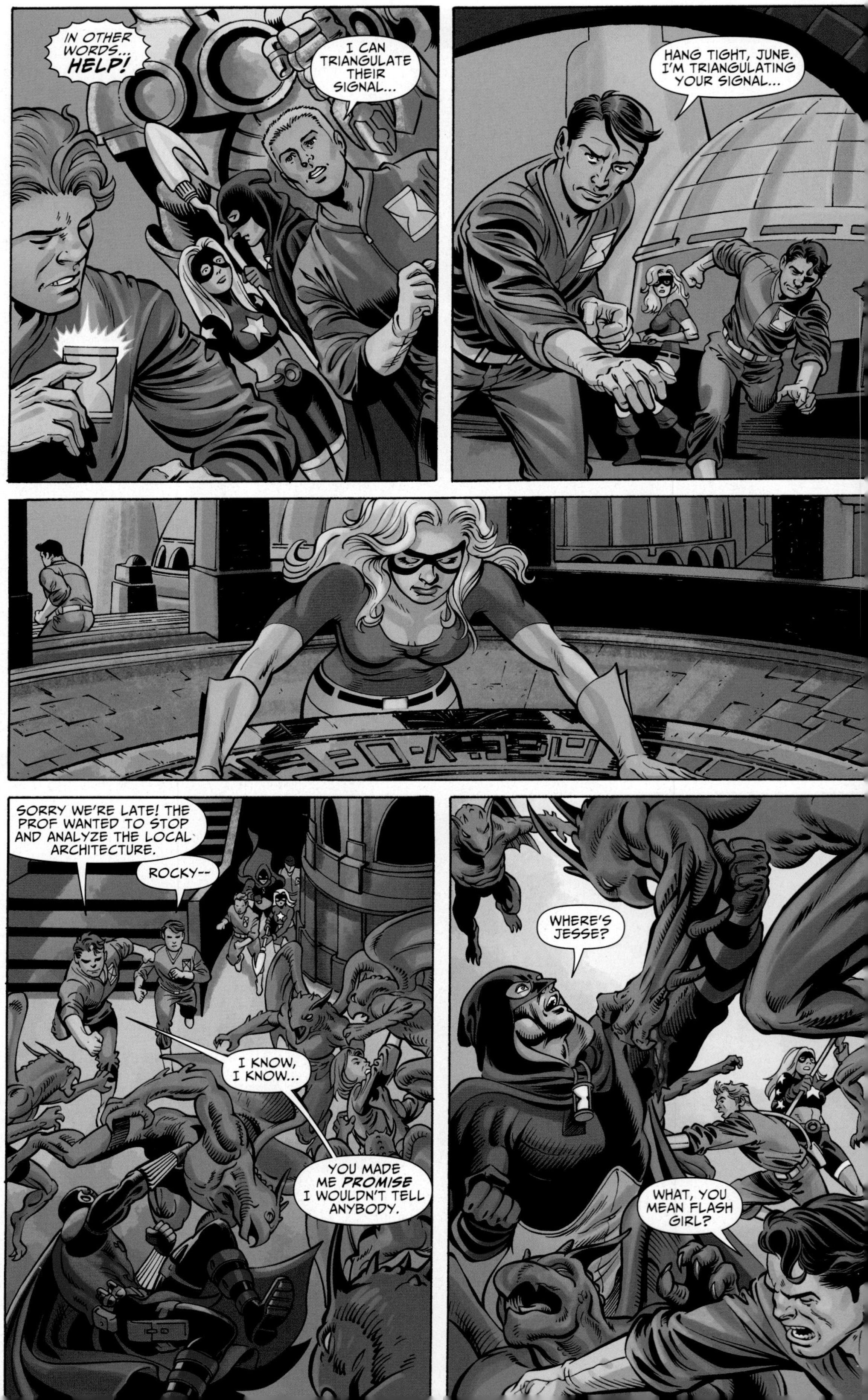
IN OTHER WORDS... **HELP!**
I CAN TRIANGULATE THEIR SIGNAL...
HANG TIGHT, JUNE. I'M TRIANGULATING YOUR SIGNAL...
SORRY WE'RE LATE! THE PROF WANTED TO STOP AND ANALYZE THE LOCAL ARCHITECTURE.
ROCKY--
I KNOW, I KNOW...
YOU MADE ME **PROMISE** I WOULDN'T TELL ANYBODY.
WHERE'S JESSE?
WHAT, YOU MEAN FLASH GIRL?

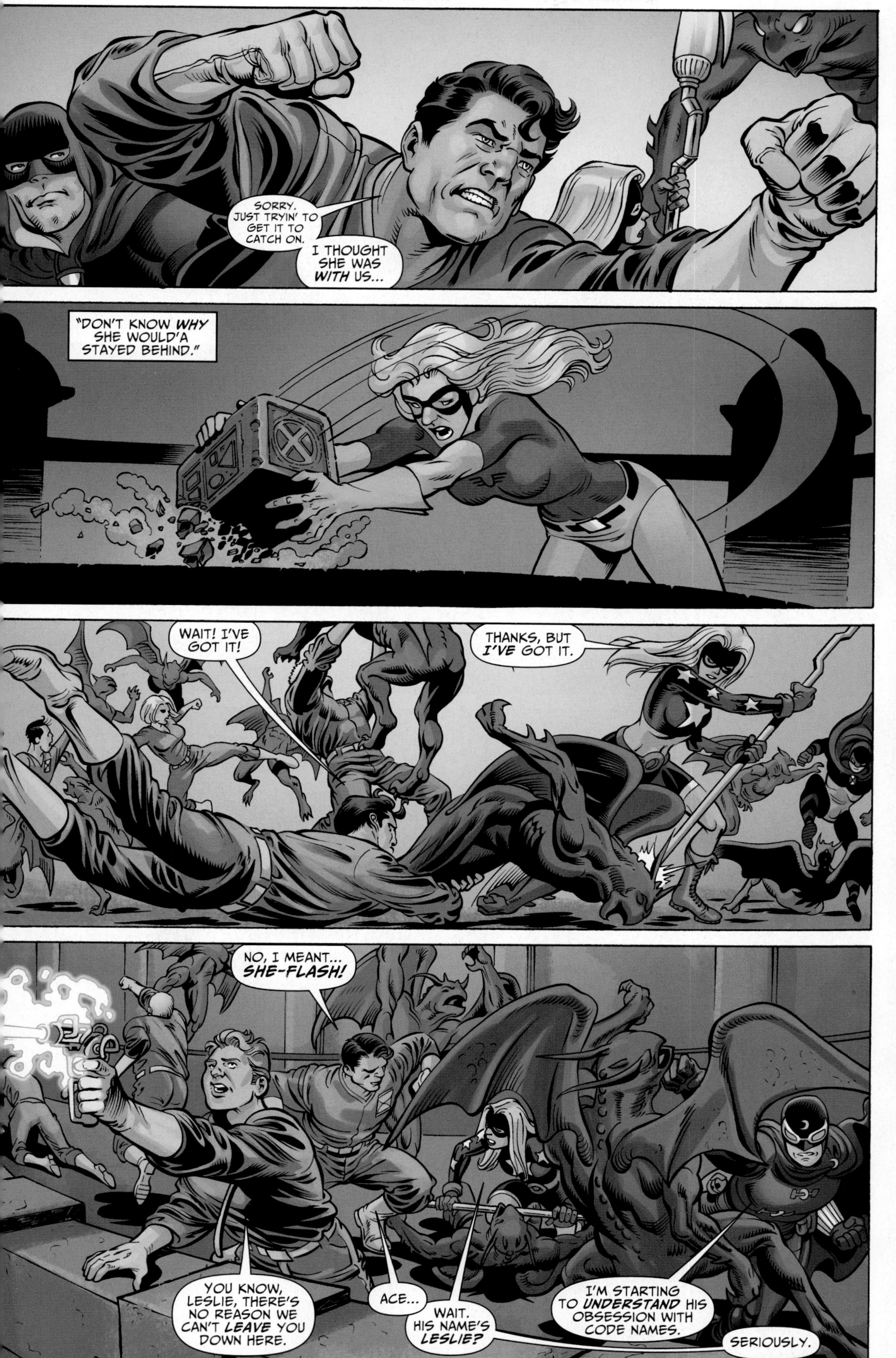
SORRY. JUST TRYIN' TO GET IT TO CATCH ON.
I THOUGHT SHE WAS WITH US...
"DON'T KNOW WHY SHE WOULD'A STAYED BEHIND."
WAIT! I'VE GOT IT!
THANKS, BUT I'VE GOT IT.
NO, I MEANT... SHE-FLASH!
YOU KNOW, LESLIE, THERE'S NO REASON WE CAN'T LEAVE YOU DOWN HERE.
ACE...
WAIT. HIS NAME'S LESLIE?
I'M STARTING TO UNDERSTAND HIS OBSESSION WITH CODE NAMES.
SERIOUSLY.

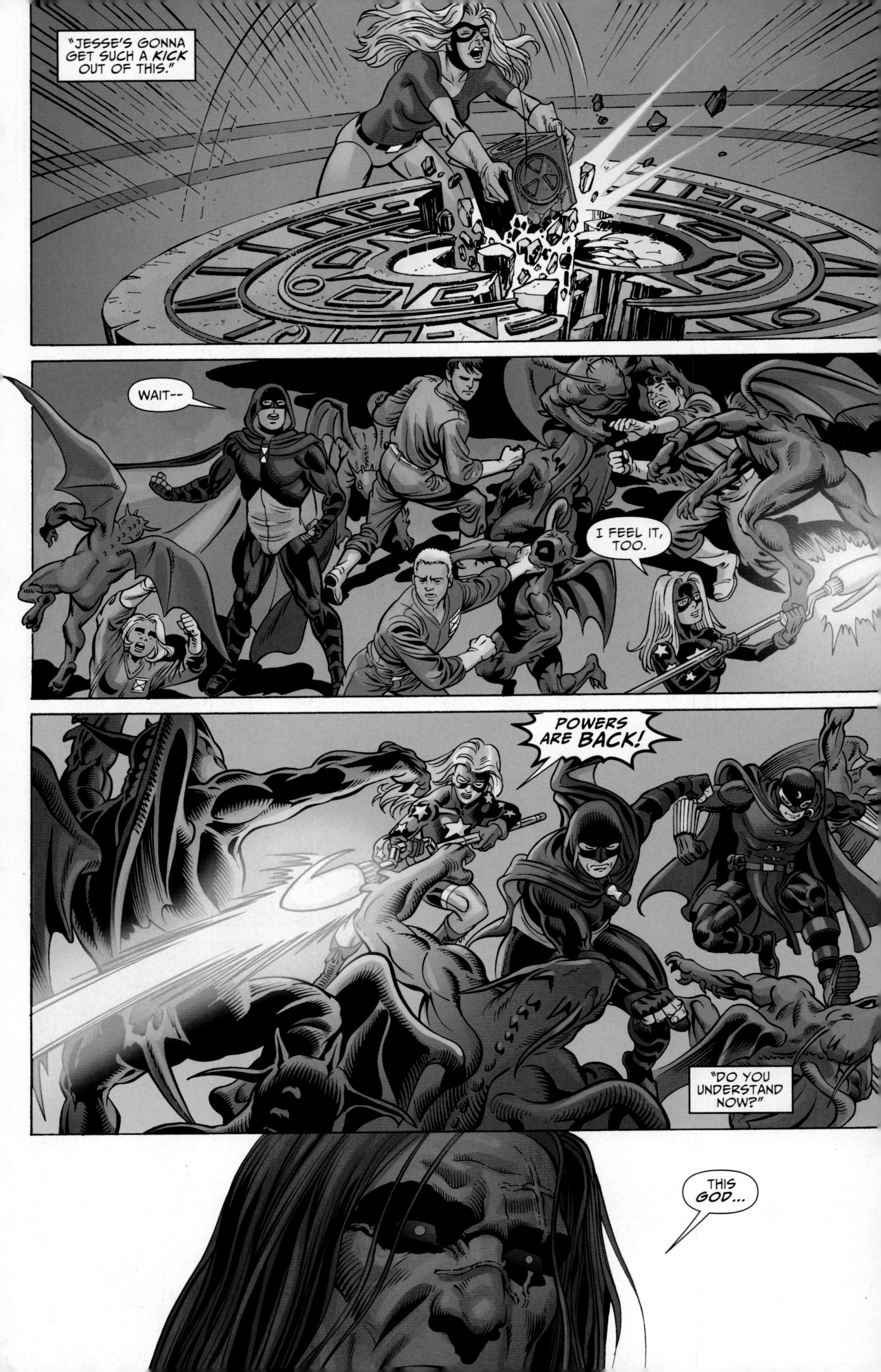
"JESSE'S GONNA GET SUCH A *KICK* OUT OF THIS."
WAIT--
I FEEL IT, TOO.
POWERS ARE *BACK!*
"DO YOU UNDERSTAND NOW?"
THIS *GOD*...

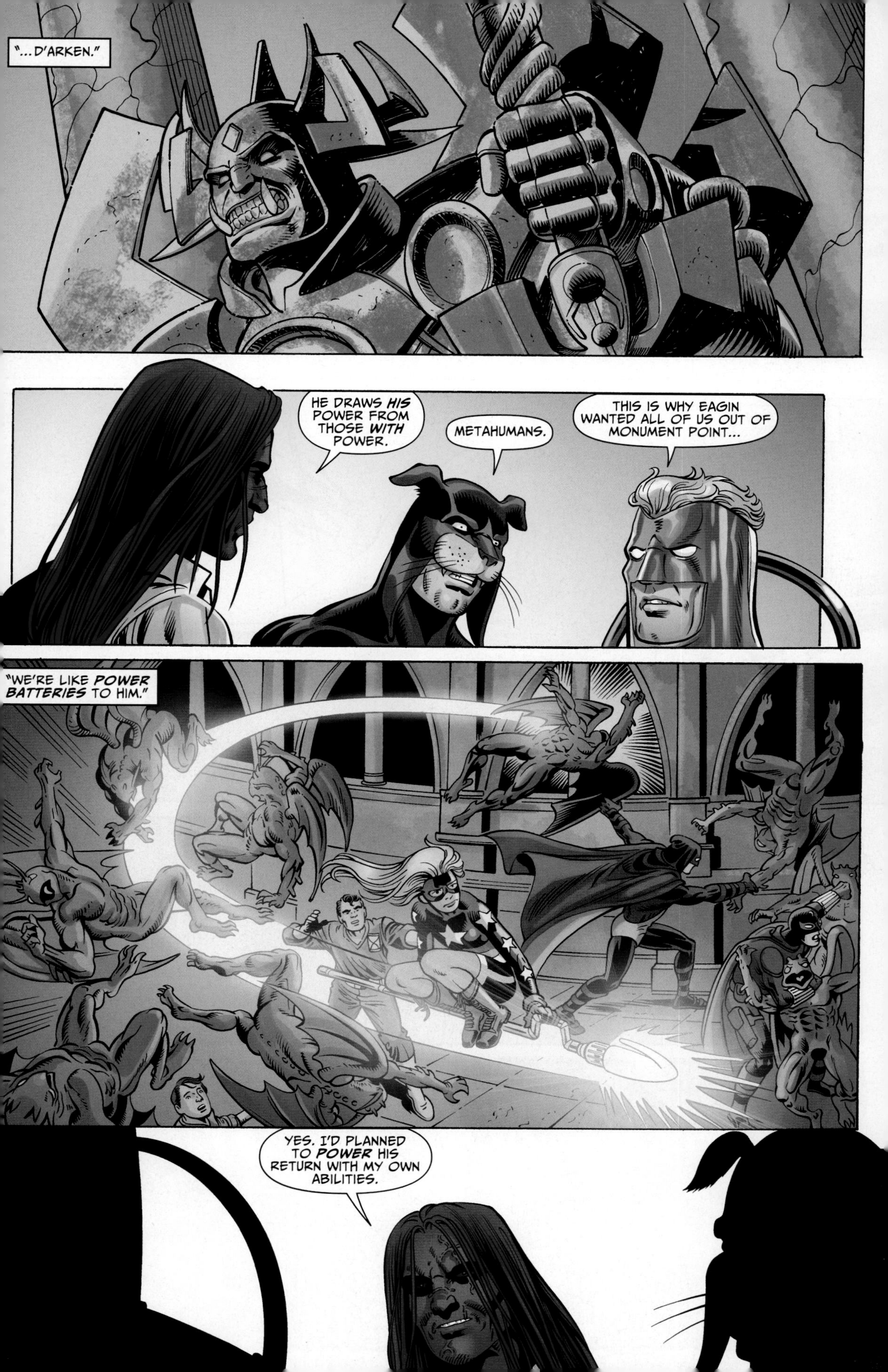
"...D'ARKEN."
HE DRAWS HIS POWER FROM THOSE WITH POWER.
METAHUMANS.
THIS IS WHY EAGIN WANTED ALL OF US OUT OF MONUMENT POINT...
"WE'RE LIKE POWER BATTERIES TO HIM."
YES. I'D PLANNED TO POWER HIS RETURN WITH MY OWN ABILITIES.

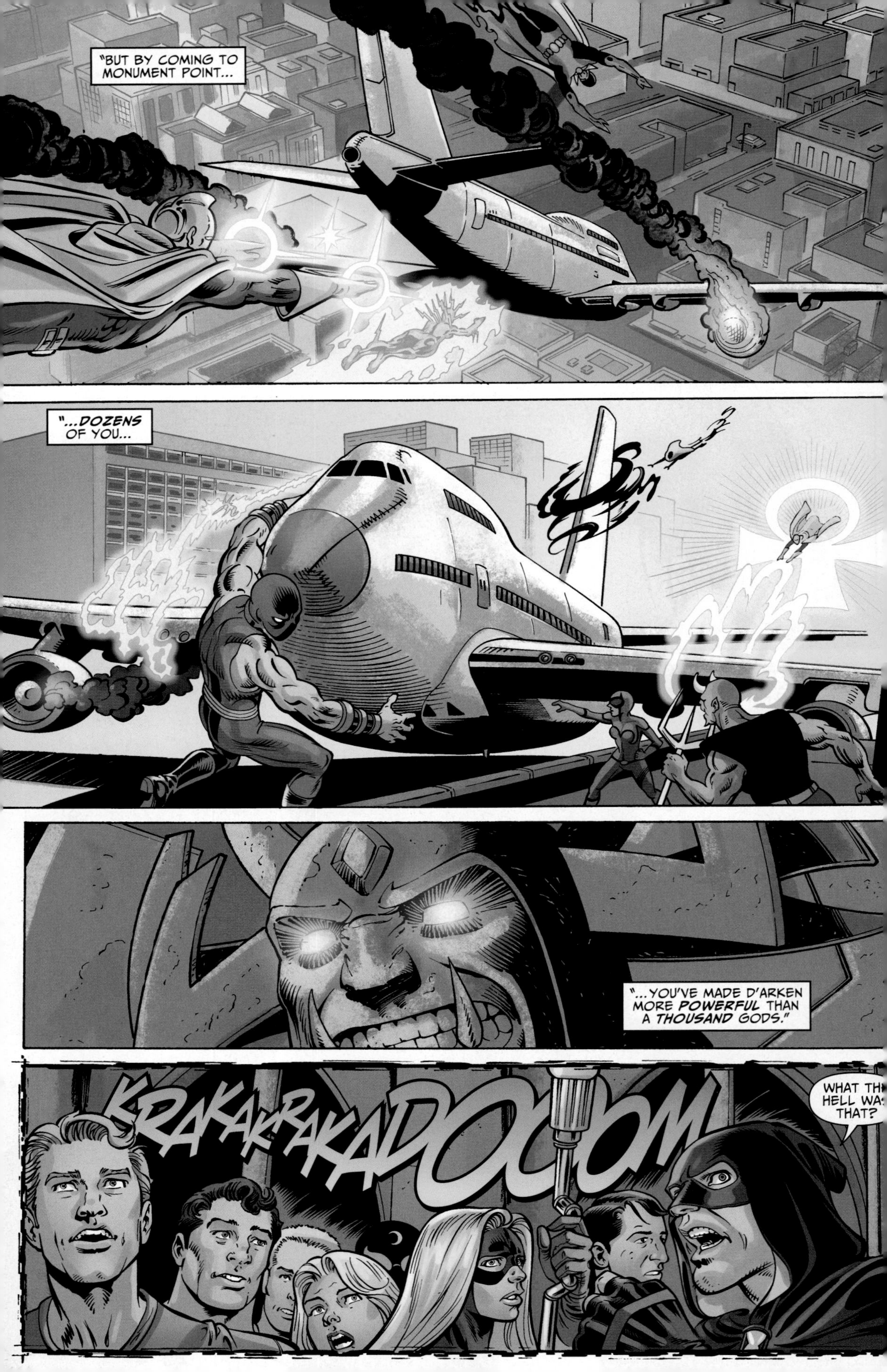
"BUT BY COMING TO MONUMENT POINT...
"...DOZENS OF YOU...
"...YOU'VE MADE D'ARKEN MORE POWERFUL THAN A THOUSAND GODS."
KRAKAKRAKADOOOOM
WHAT TH HELL WA THAT?

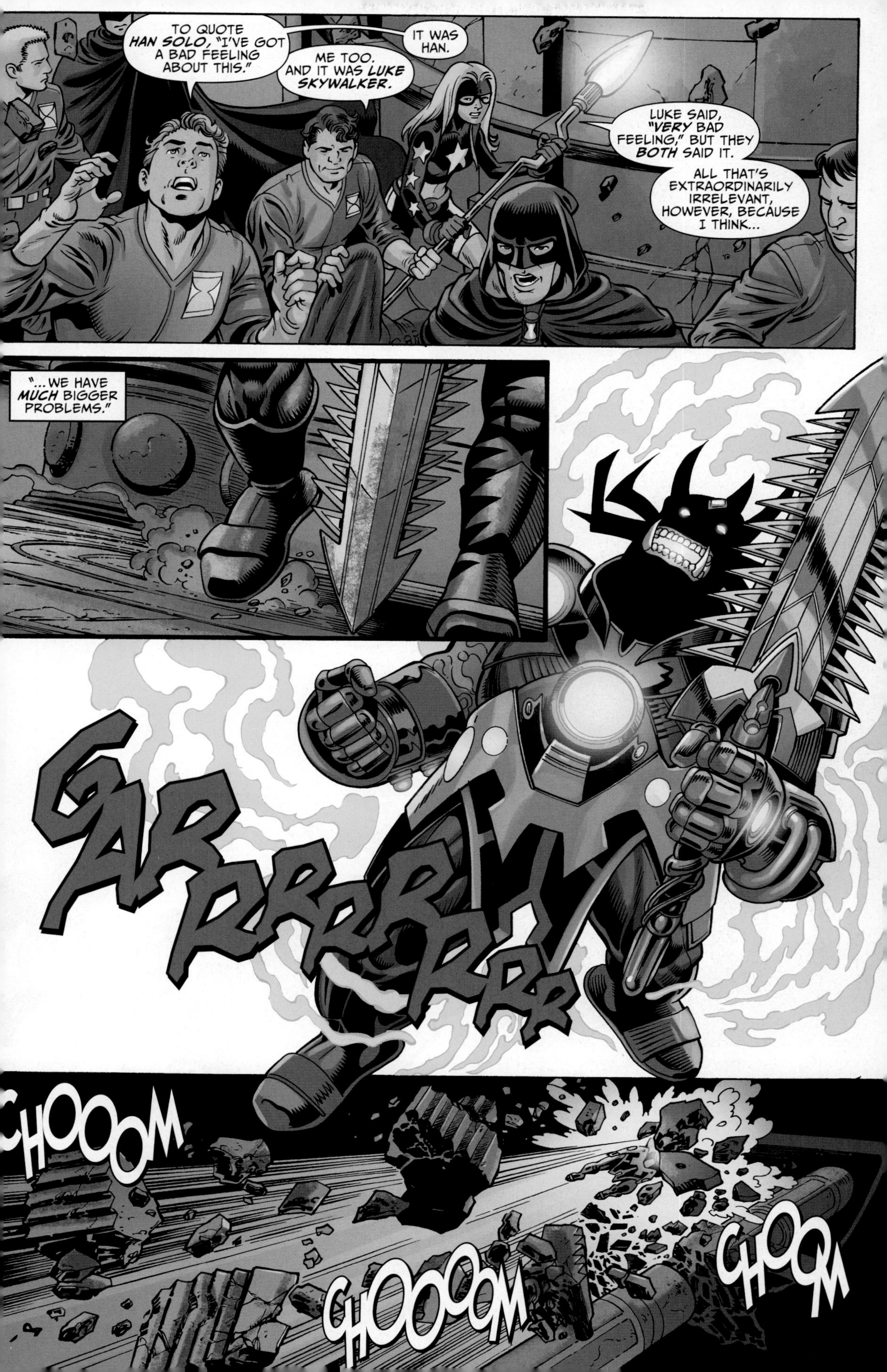
TO QUOTE HAN SOLO, "I'VE GOT A BAD FEELING ABOUT THIS."
ME TOO. AND IT WAS LUKE SKYWALKER.
IT WAS HAN.
LUKE SAID, "VERY BAD FEELING," BUT THEY BOTH SAID IT.
ALL THAT'S EXTRAORDINARILY IRRELEVANT, HOWEVER, BECAUSE I THINK...
"...WE HAVE MUCH BIGGER PROBLEMS."
GARRRRRRRRRR
CHOOOM
CHOOOOOM
CHOOM

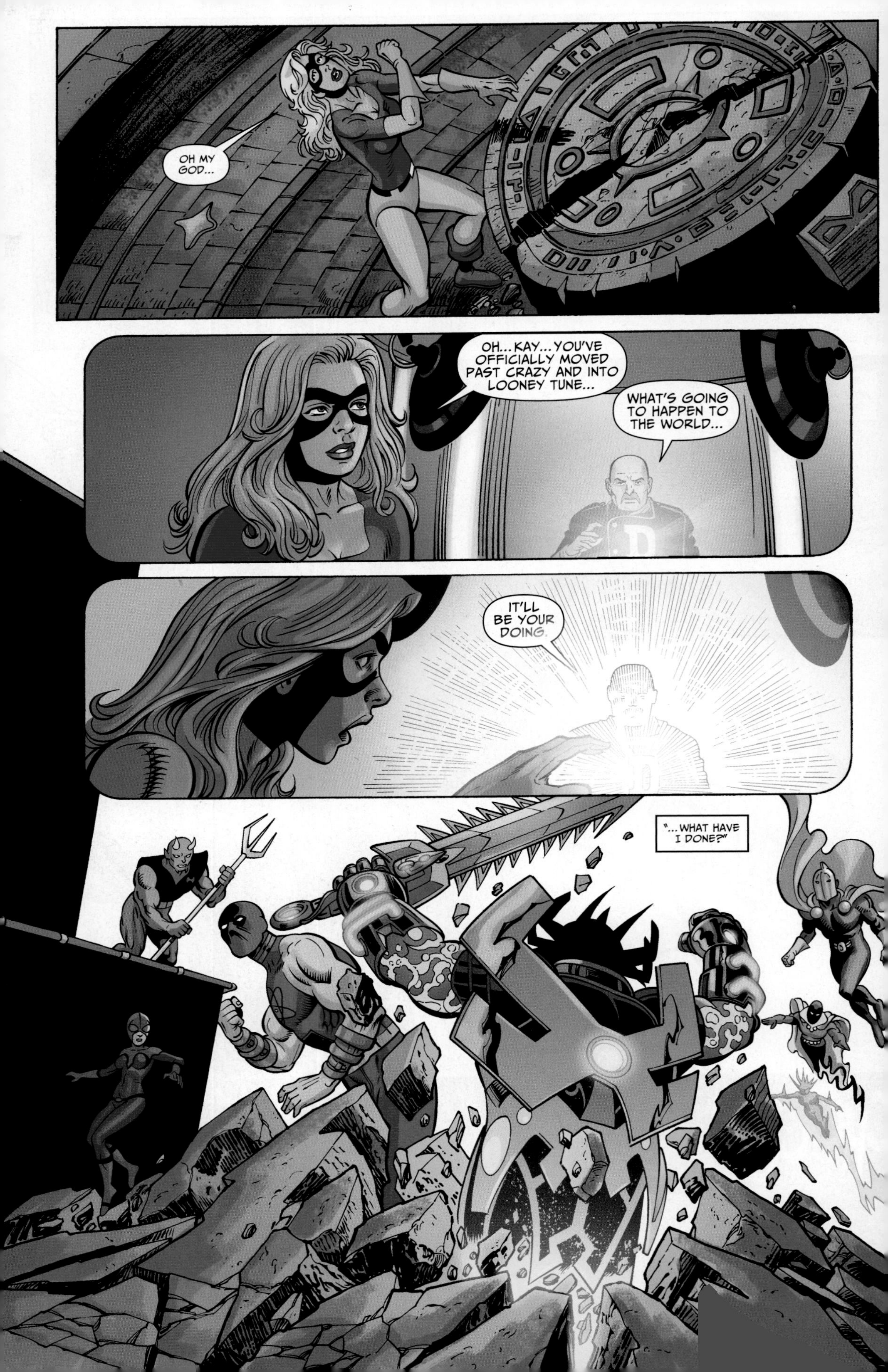
OH MY GOD...
OH...KAY...YOU'VE OFFICIALLY MOVED PAST CRAZY AND INTO LOONEY TUNE...
WHAT'S GOING TO HAPPEN TO THE WORLD...
IT'LL BE YOUR DOING.
"...WHAT HAVE I DONE?"

Cover by DARWYN COOKE

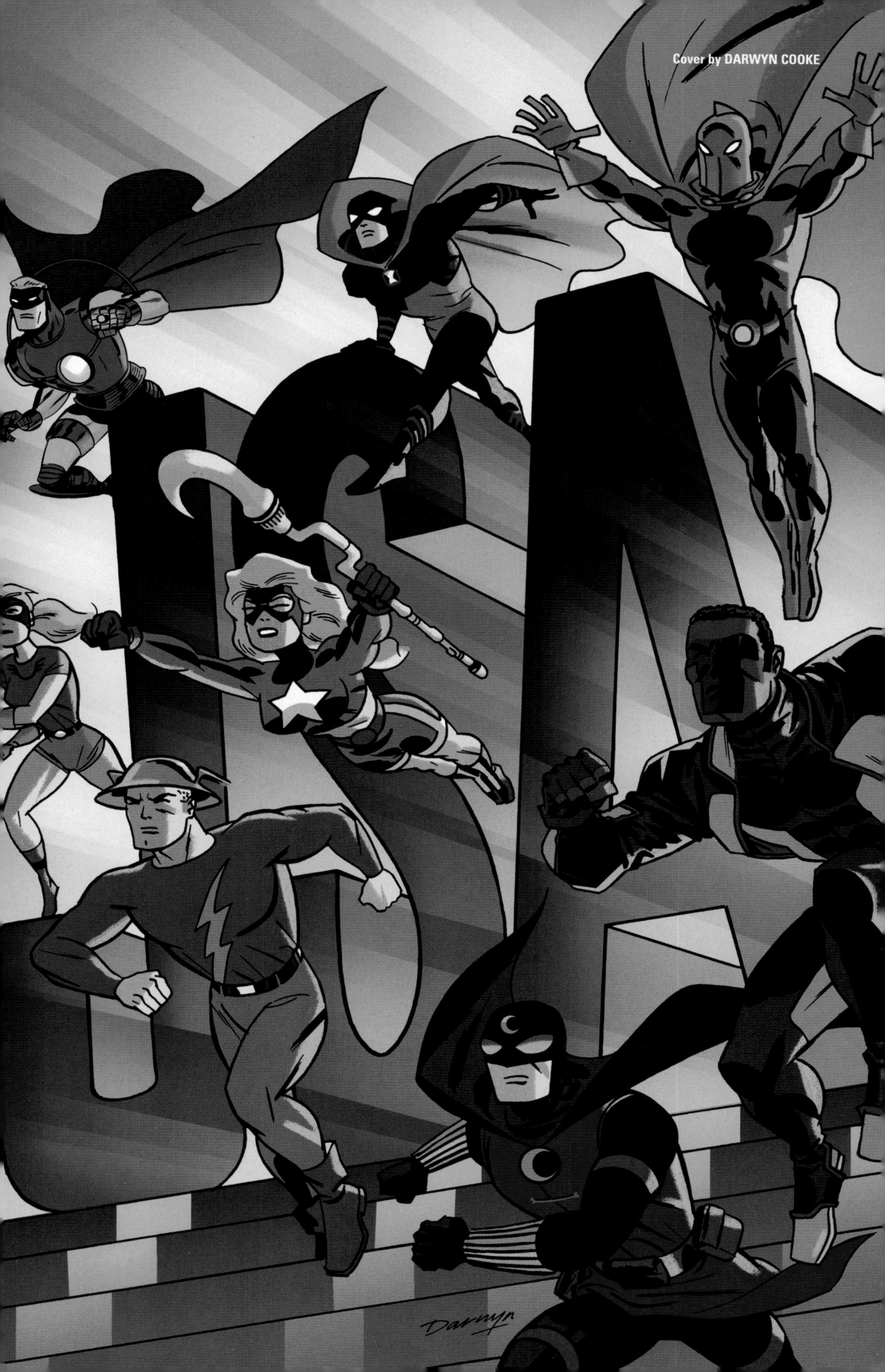
Darwyn

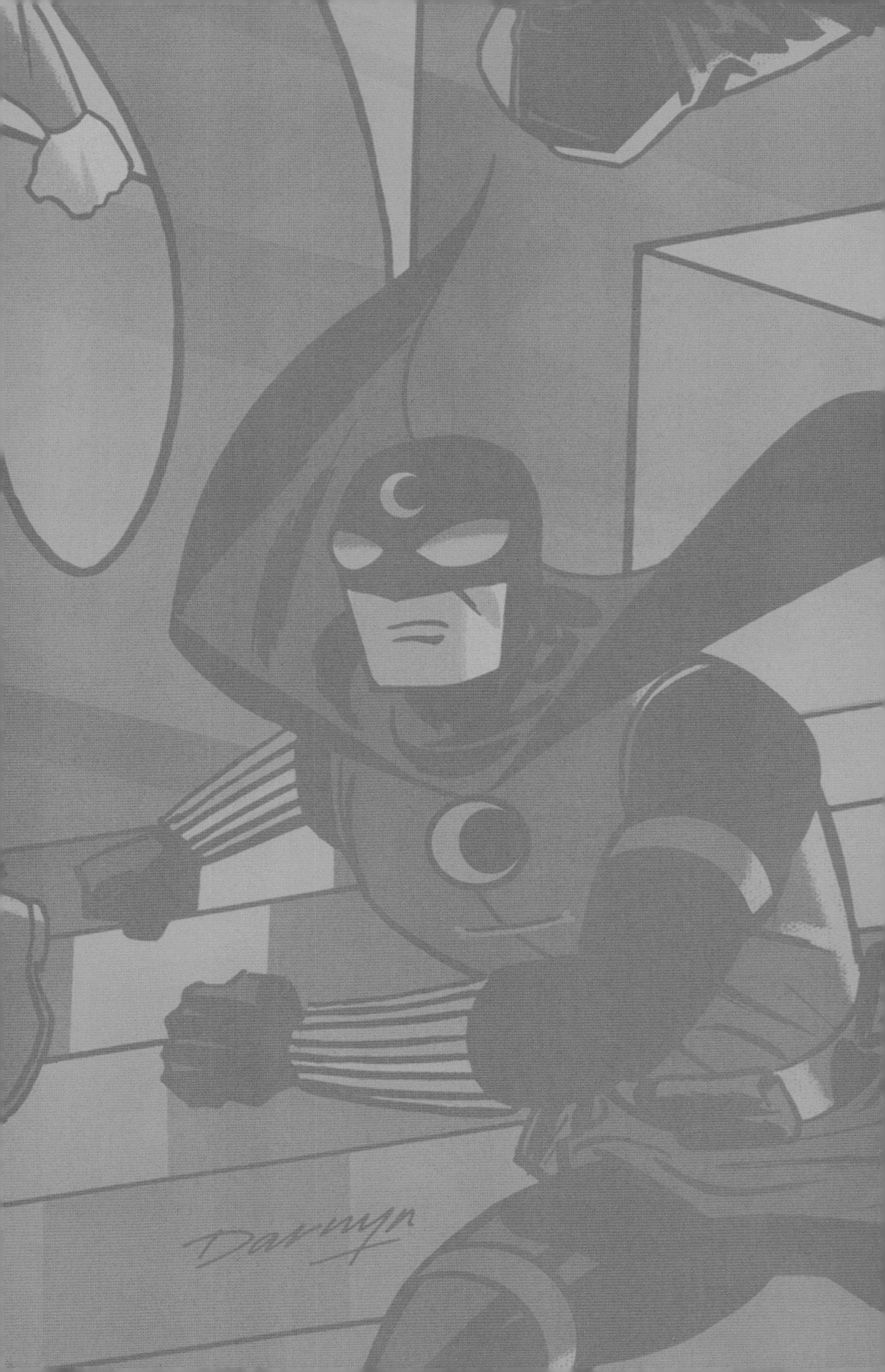
Darwyn

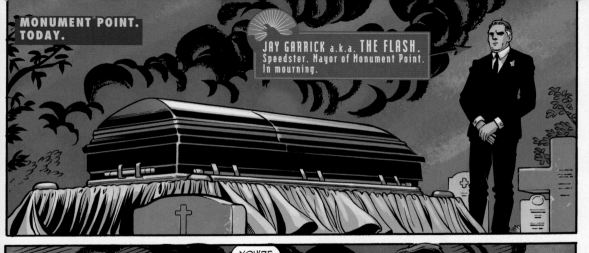

JAY GARRICK a.k.a. THE FLASH. Speedster. Mayor of Monument Point. In mourning.

YOU'RE HERE.

I GUESS I SHOULDN'T BE SURPRISED.

BUT IT ALL ENDED SIX HOURS AGO...

SO IF YOU'RE HERE TO SOW SOME CHAOS OF YOUR OWN, YOU'RE A LITTLE LATE.

I'M PRIME DEGATON.

I'M ALWAYS ON TIME.

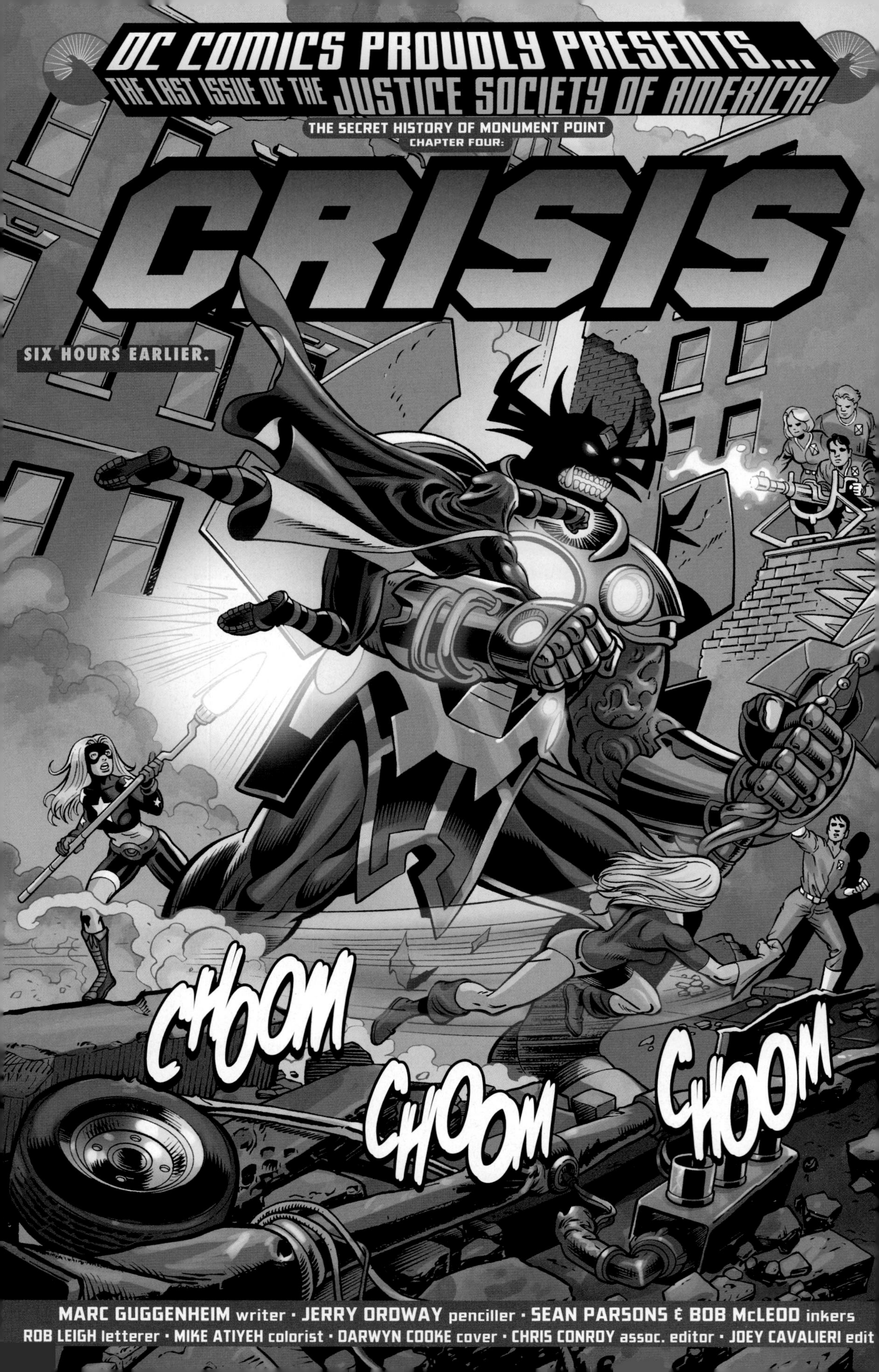
DC COMICS PROUDLY PRESENTS...
THE LAST ISSUE OF THE JUSTICE SOCIETY OF AMERICA!
THE SECRET HISTORY OF MONUMENT POINT
CHAPTER FOUR:
CRISIS
SIX HOURS EARLIER.
CHOOM
CHOOM
CHOOM
MARC GUGGENHEIM writer · JERRY ORDWAY penciller · SEAN PARSONS & BOB McLEOD inkers
ROB LEIGH letterer · MIKE ATIYEH colorist · DARWYN COOKE cover · CHRIS CONROY assoc. editor · JOEY CAVALIERI edit

CHOOM
CHOOM
CHOOM

NO. I FEAR...THIS IS SOMETHING ELSE...

IS THAT NOISE FROM THE AIRPLANE?

ALL RIGHT, WHAT'S WITH ALL THE CHOOMING?

DENNIS--

MR. MAYOR, WE HAVE A *PROBLEM*--

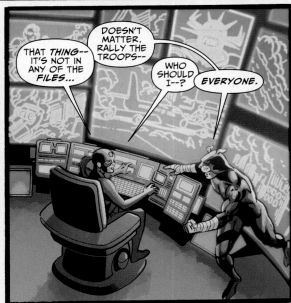

THAT *THING*-- IT'S NOT IN ANY OF THE *FILES*...

DOESN'T MATTER. RALLY THE TROOPS--

WHO SHOULD I--?

*EVERYONE.*

YOUR HONOR--

LET GO, DENNIS.

YOU'RE THE *MAYOR*, NOT THE FLASH, SIR. WE'VE DISCUSSED THIS. YOU CAN'T--

GODSPEED, SIR.

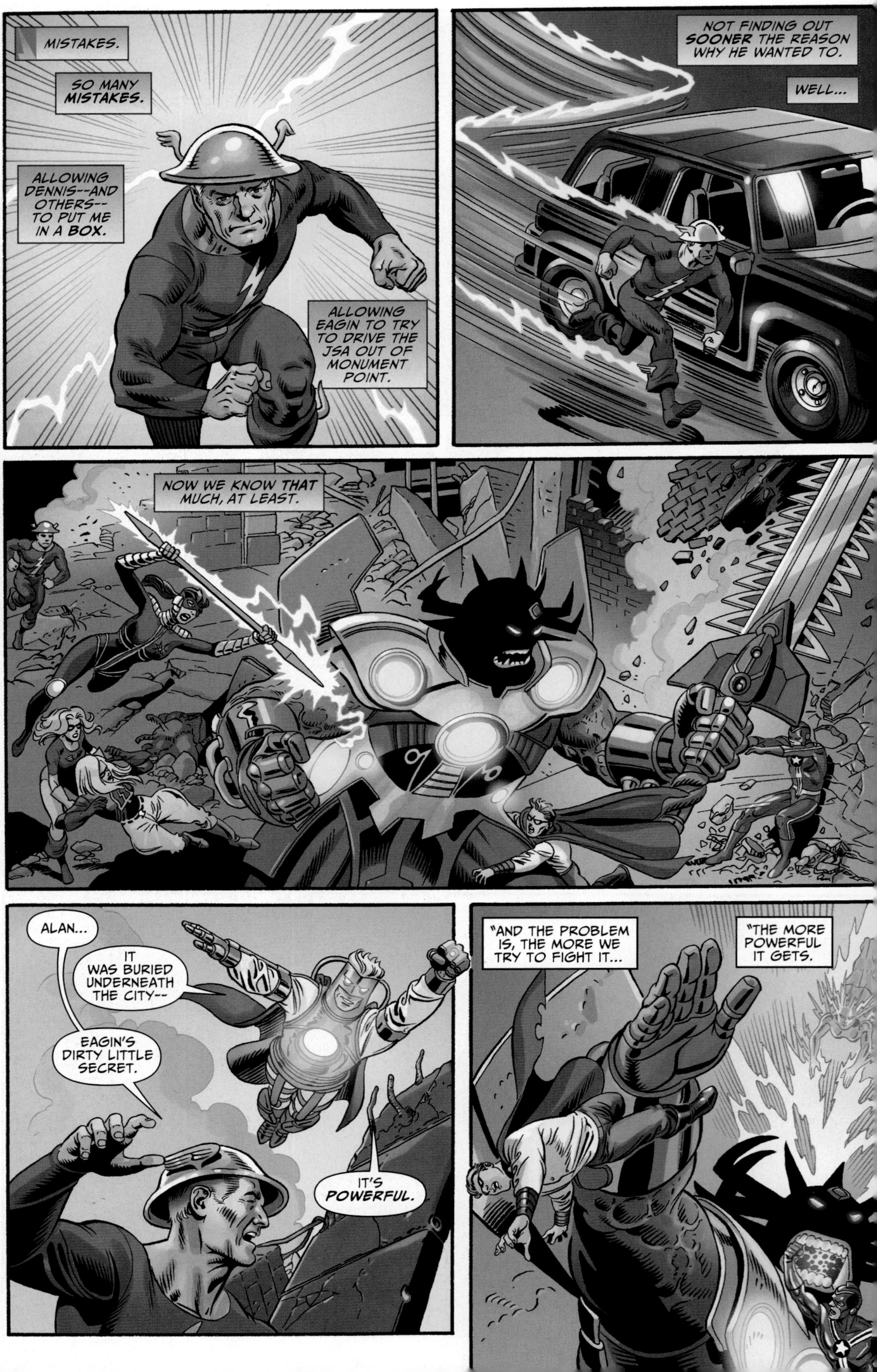
MISTAKES.
SO MANY MISTAKES.
ALLOWING DENNIS--AND OTHERS--TO PUT ME IN A BOX.
ALLOWING EAGIN TO TRY TO DRIVE THE JSA OUT OF MONUMENT POINT.
NOT FINDING OUT SOONER THE REASON WHY HE WANTED TO.
WELL...
NOW WE KNOW THAT MUCH, AT LEAST.
ALAN...
IT WAS BURIED UNDERNEATH THE CITY--
EAGIN'S DIRTY LITTLE SECRET.
IT'S POWERFUL.
"AND THE PROBLEM IS, THE MORE WE TRY TO FIGHT IT...
"THE MORE POWERFUL IT GETS.

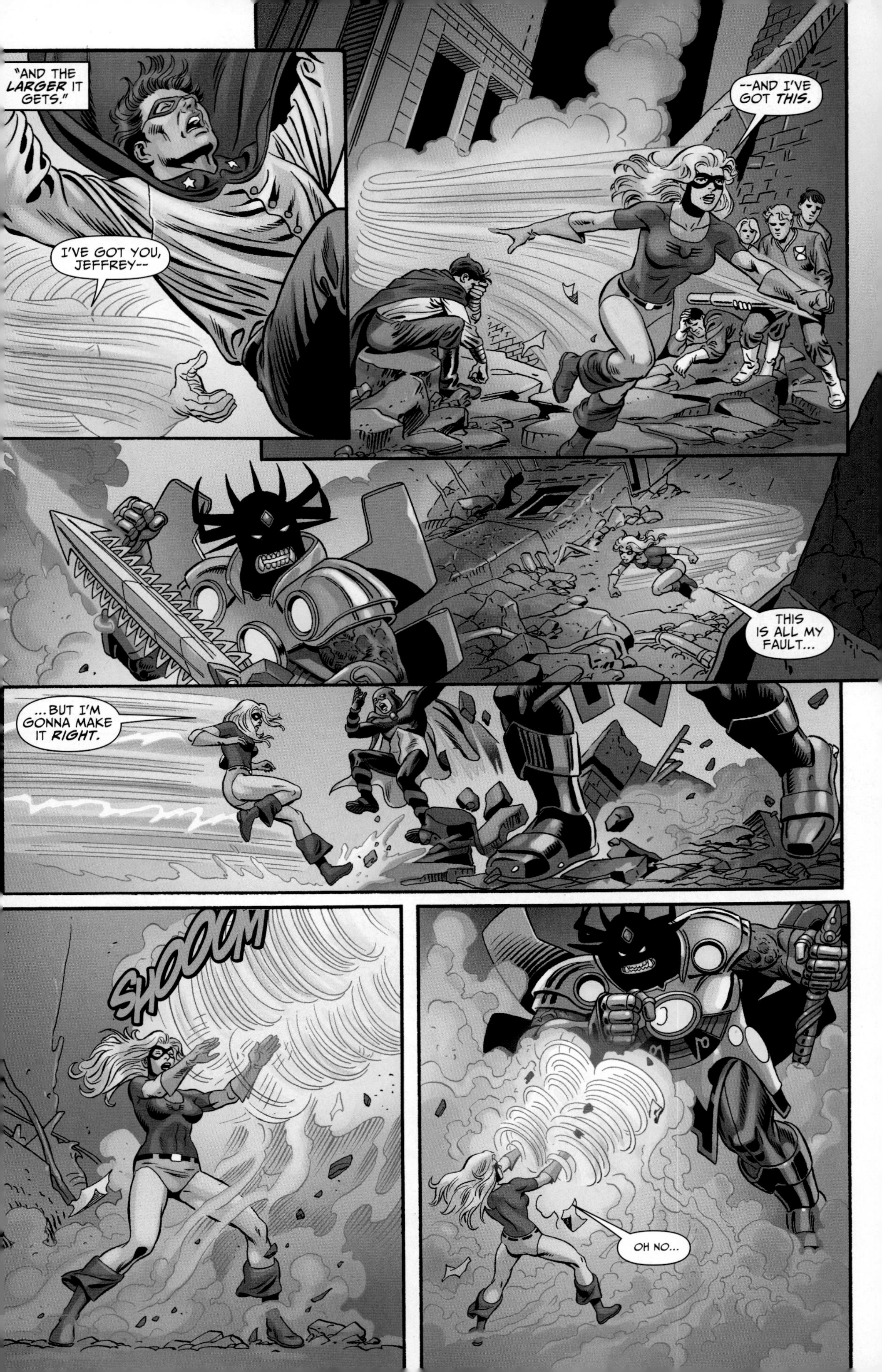
"AND THE LARGER IT GETS."
I'VE GOT YOU, JEFFREY--
--AND I'VE GOT THIS.
THIS IS ALL MY FAULT...
...BUT I'M GONNA MAKE IT RIGHT.
SHOOOM
OH NO...

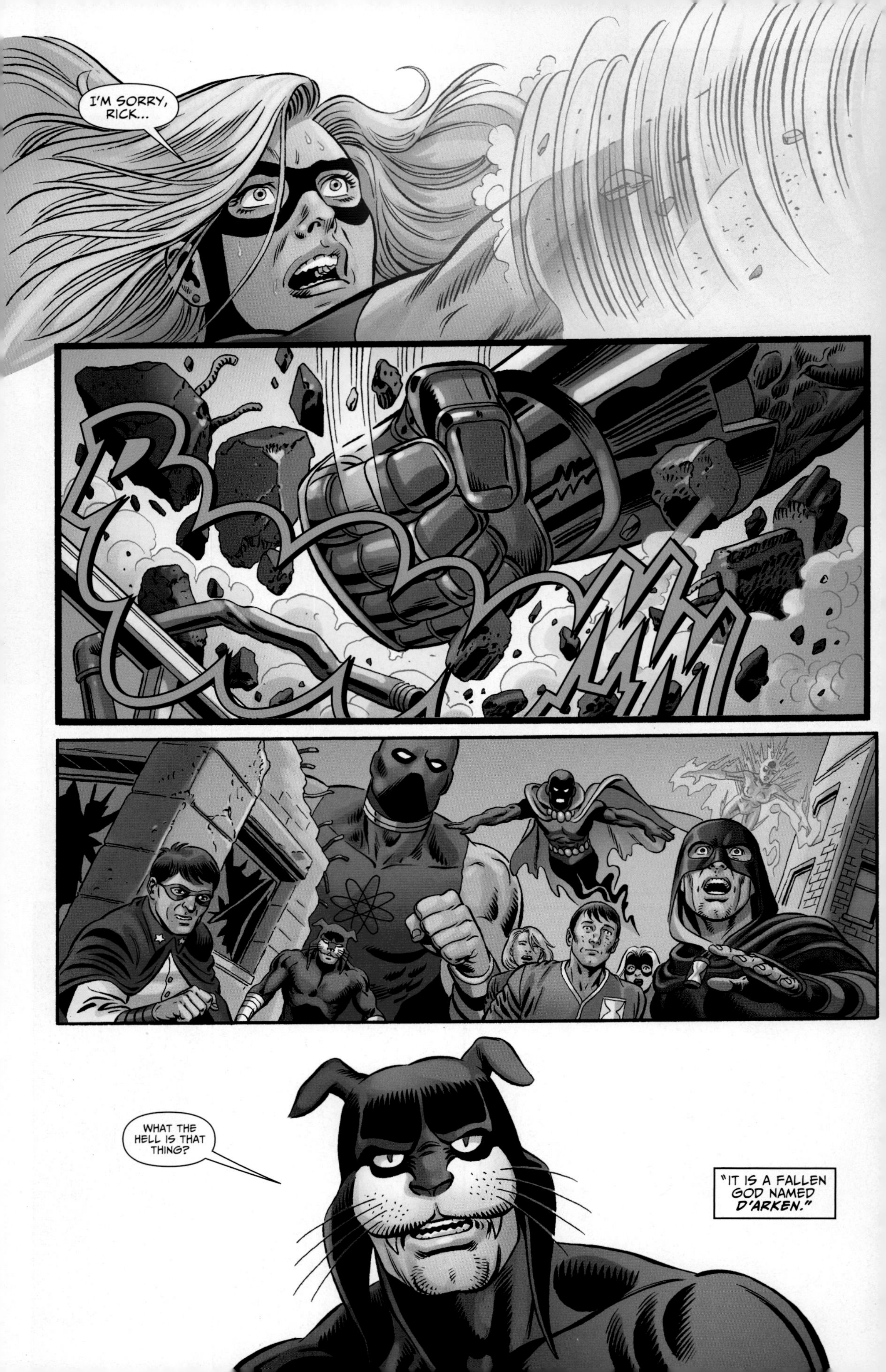
I'M SORRY, RICK...
BRRROOOMM
WHAT THE HELL IS THAT THING?
"IT IS A FALLEN GOD NAMED D'ARKEN."

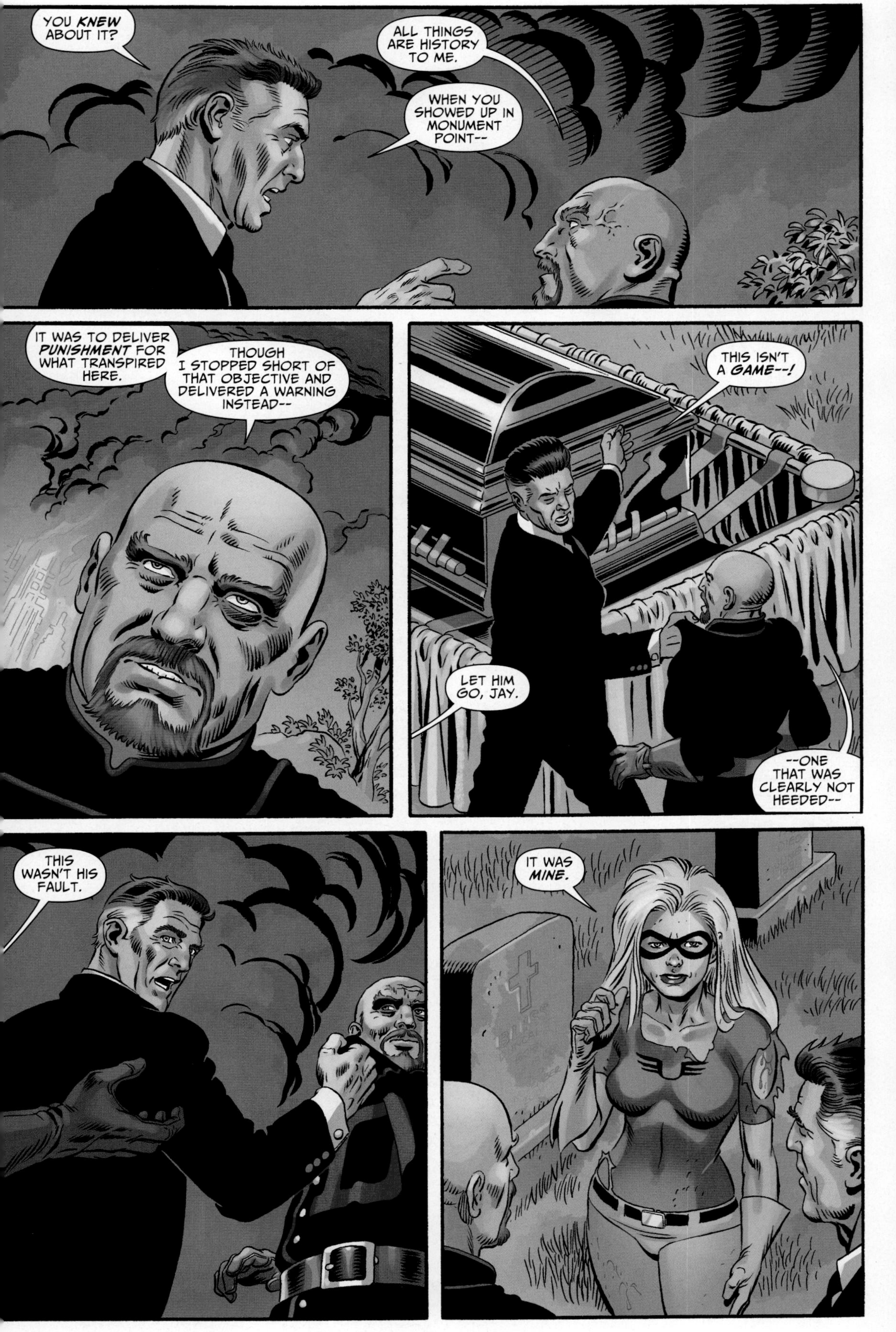

YOU KNEW ABOUT IT?
ALL THINGS ARE HISTORY TO ME.
WHEN YOU SHOWED UP IN MONUMENT POINT--
IT WAS TO DELIVER PUNISHMENT FOR WHAT TRANSPIRED HERE.
THOUGH I STOPPED SHORT OF THAT OBJECTIVE AND DELIVERED A WARNING INSTEAD--
THIS ISN'T A GAME--!
LET HIM GO, JAY.
--ONE THAT WAS CLEARLY NOT HEEDED--
THIS WASN'T HIS FAULT.
IT WAS MINE.

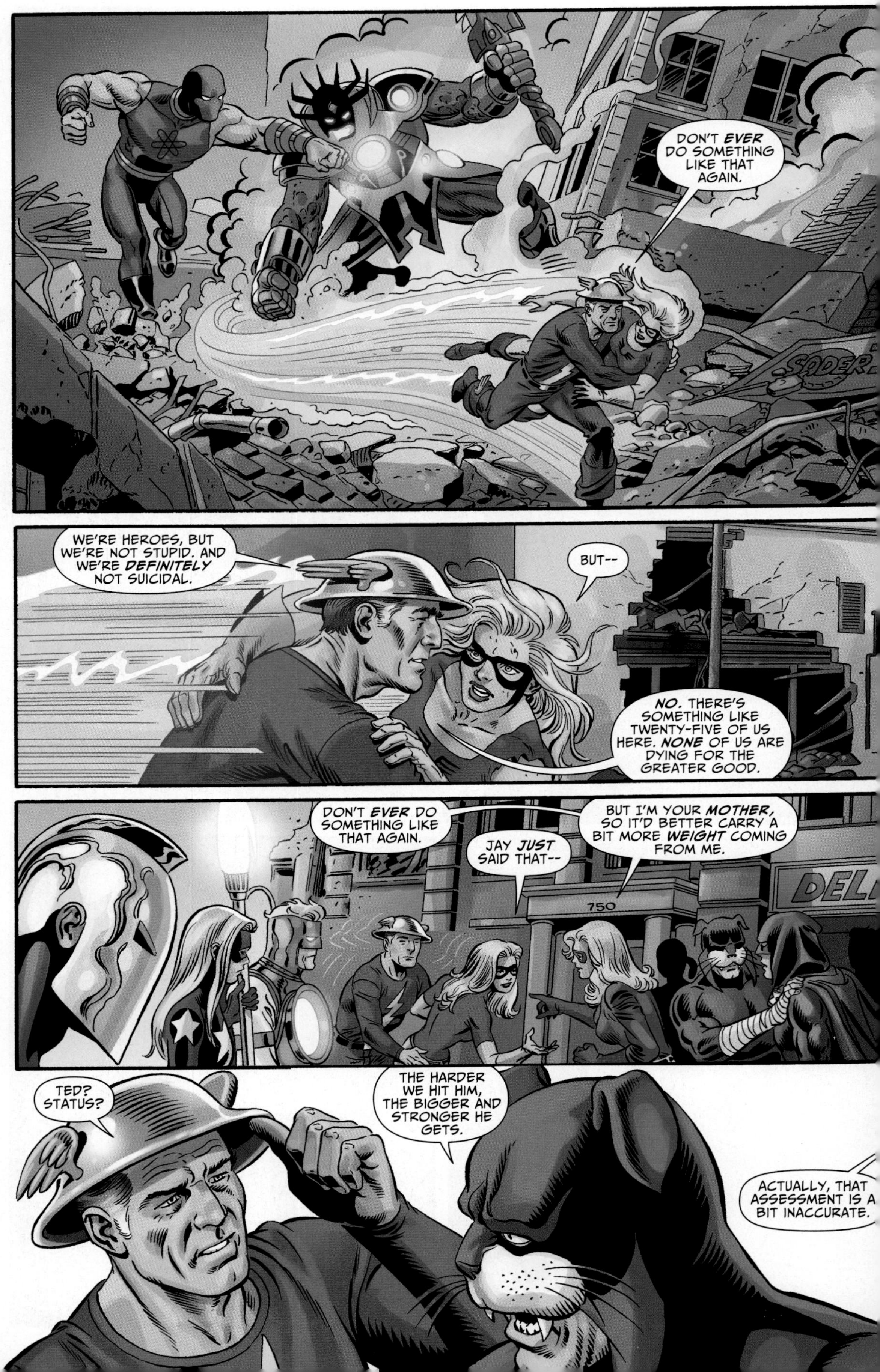
DON'T EVER DO SOMETHING LIKE THAT AGAIN.
SADER
WE'RE HEROES, BUT WE'RE NOT STUPID. AND WE'RE DEFINITELY NOT SUICIDAL.
BUT--
NO. THERE'S SOMETHING LIKE TWENTY-FIVE OF US HERE. NONE OF US ARE DYING FOR THE GREATER GOOD.
DON'T EVER DO SOMETHING LIKE THAT AGAIN.
JAY JUST SAID THAT--
BUT I'M YOUR MOTHER, SO IT'D BETTER CARRY A BIT MORE WEIGHT COMING FROM ME.
750
DELI
TED? STATUS?
THE HARDER WE HIT HIM, THE BIGGER AND STRONGER HE GETS.
ACTUALLY, THAT ASSESSMENT IS A BIT INACCURATE.

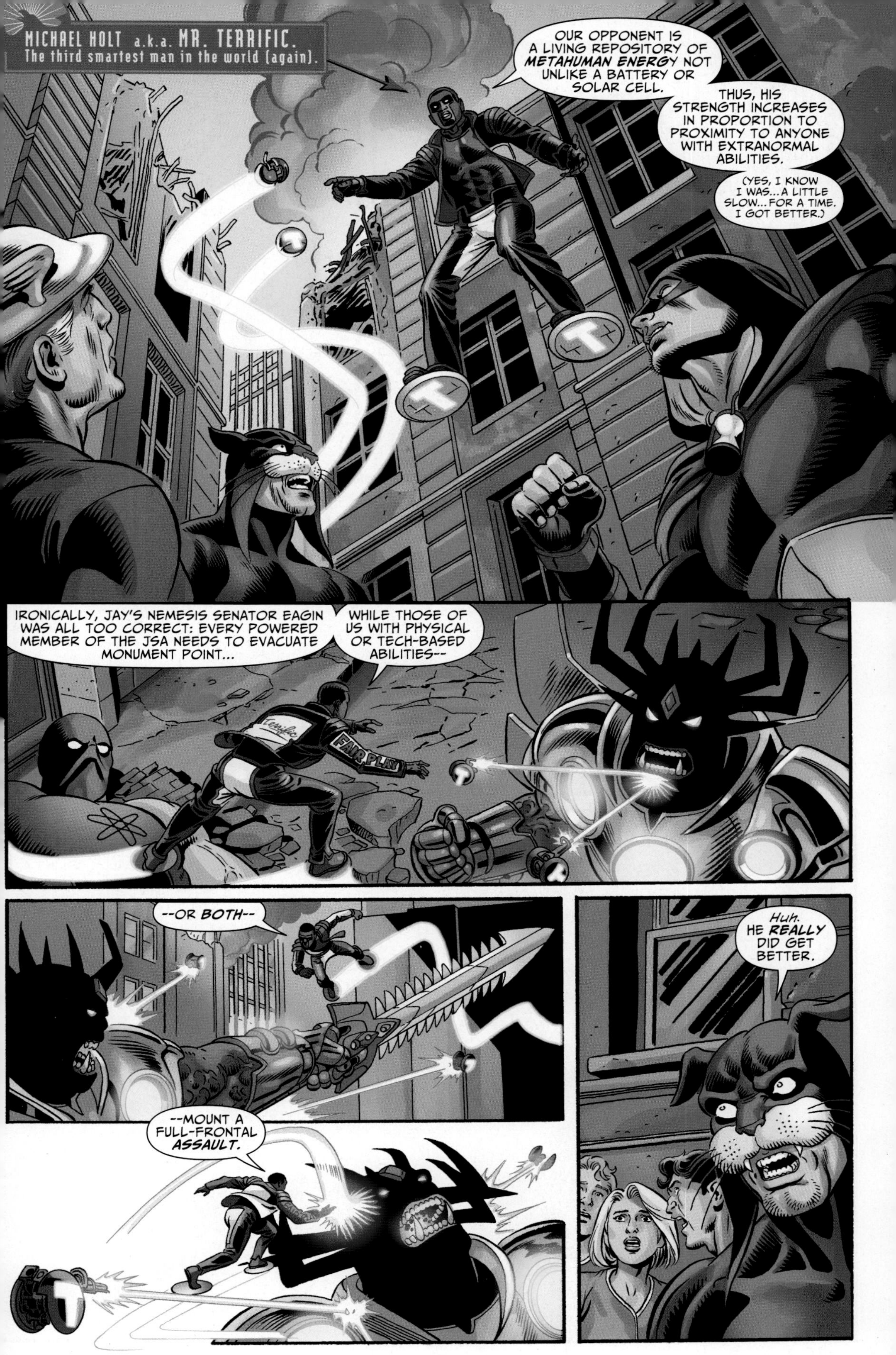
MICHAEL HOLT a.k.a. MR. TERRIFIC.
The third smartest man in the world (again).
OUR OPPONENT IS A LIVING REPOSITORY OF METAHUMAN ENERGY NOT UNLIKE A BATTERY OR SOLAR CELL.
THUS, HIS STRENGTH INCREASES IN PROPORTION TO PROXIMITY TO ANYONE WITH EXTRANORMAL ABILITIES.
(YES, I KNOW I WAS...A LITTLE SLOW...FOR A TIME. I GOT BETTER.)
IRONICALLY, JAY'S NEMESIS SENATOR EAGIN WAS ALL TOO CORRECT: EVERY POWERED MEMBER OF THE JSA NEEDS TO EVACUATE MONUMENT POINT...
WHILE THOSE OF US WITH PHYSICAL OR TECH-BASED ABILITIES--
Terrific
FAIR PLAY
--OR BOTH--
--MOUNT A FULL-FRONTAL ASSAULT.
Huh. HE REALLY DID GET BETTER.

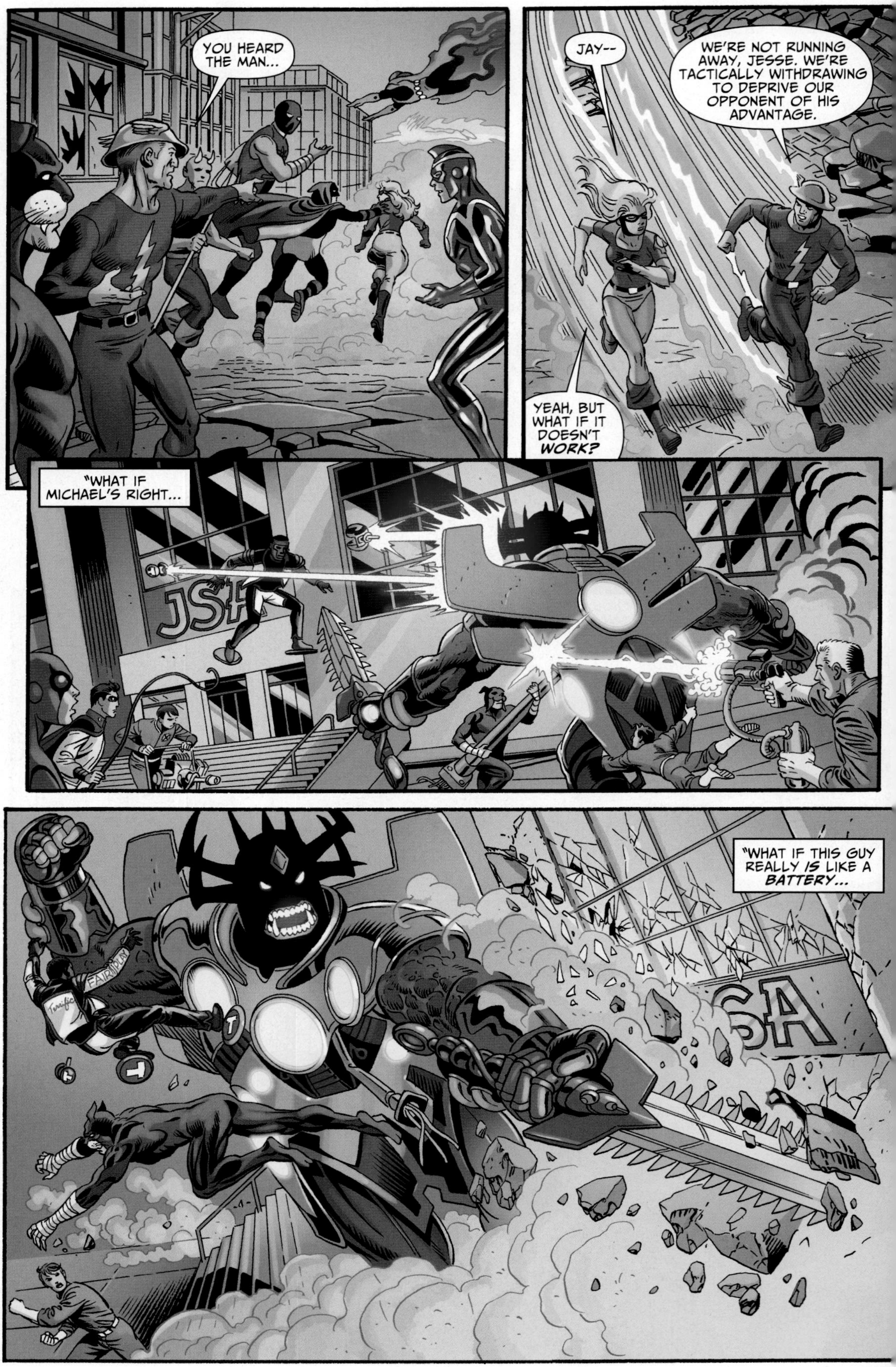
YOU HEARD THE MAN...
JAY--
WE'RE NOT RUNNING AWAY, JESSE. WE'RE TACTICALLY WITHDRAWING TO DEPRIVE OUR OPPONENT OF HIS ADVANTAGE.
YEAH, BUT WHAT IF IT DOESN'T *WORK?*
"WHAT IF MICHAEL'S RIGHT...
JSA
"WHAT IF THIS GUY REALLY *IS* LIKE A *BATTERY*...
SA

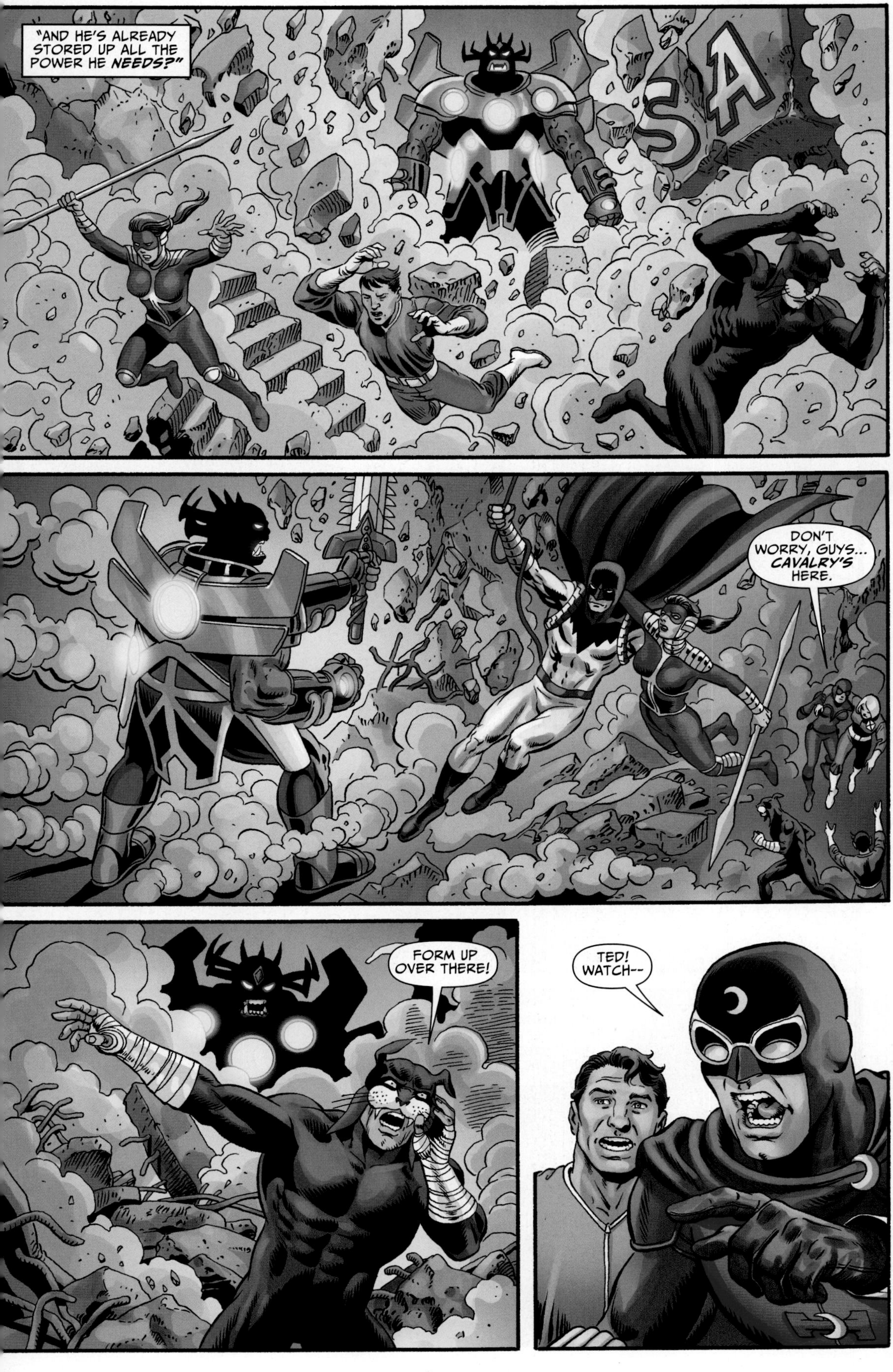
"AND HE'S ALREADY STORED UP ALL THE POWER HE NEEDS?"
DON'T WORRY, GUYS... CAVALRY'S HERE.
FORM UP OVER THERE!
TED! WATCH--

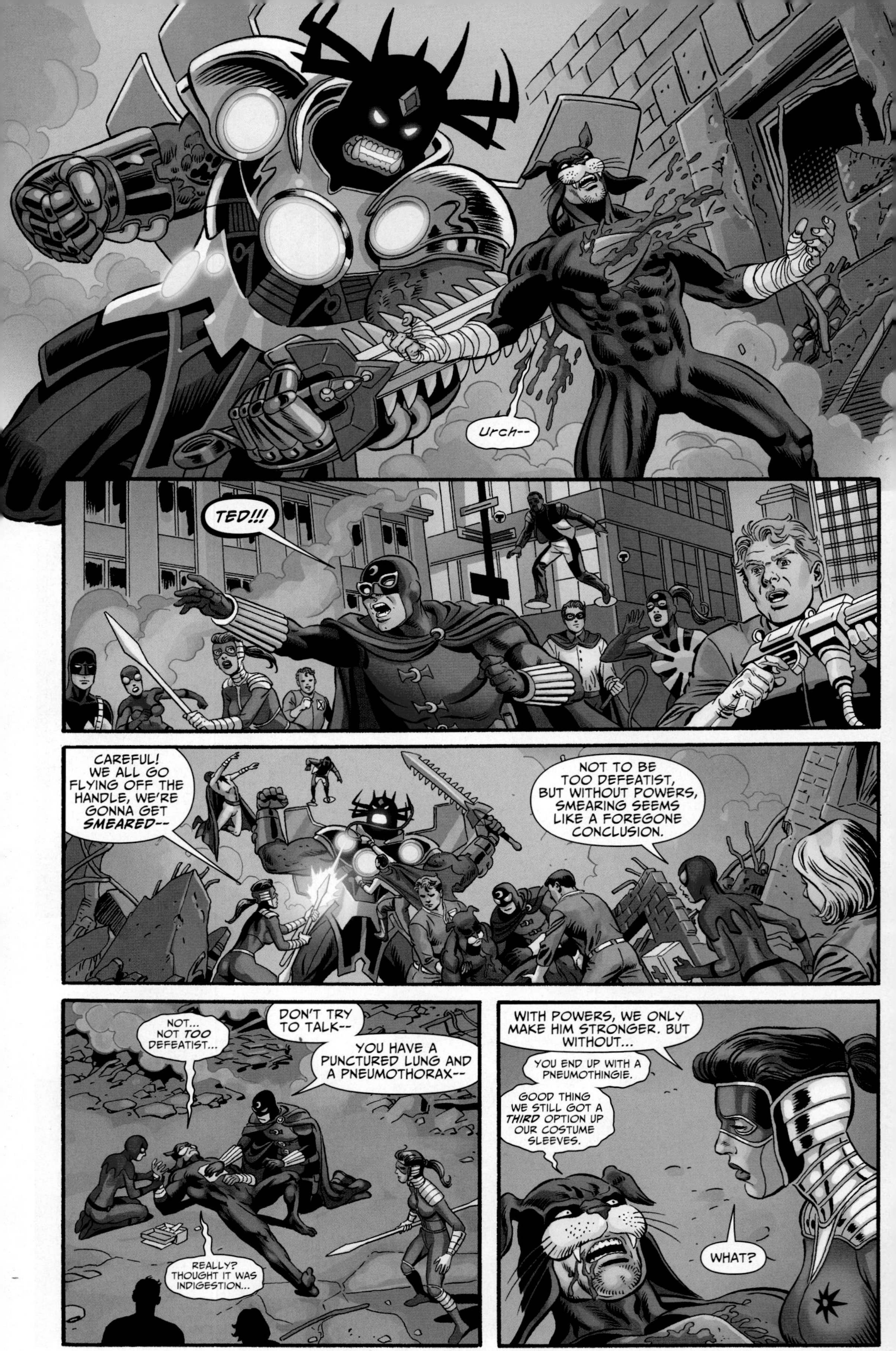
Urch--
TED!!!
CAREFUL! WE ALL GO FLYING OFF THE HANDLE, WE'RE GONNA GET SMEARED--
NOT TO BE TOO DEFEATIST, BUT WITHOUT POWERS, SMEARING SEEMS LIKE A FOREGONE CONCLUSION.
NOT... NOT TOO DEFEATIST...
DON'T TRY TO TALK--
YOU HAVE A PUNCTURED LUNG AND A PNEUMOTHORAX--
REALLY? THOUGHT IT WAS INDIGESTION...
WITH POWERS, WE ONLY MAKE HIM STRONGER. BUT WITHOUT...
YOU END UP WITH A PNEUMOTHINGIE.
GOOD THING WE STILL GOT A THIRD OPTION UP OUR COSTUME SLEEVES.
WHAT?

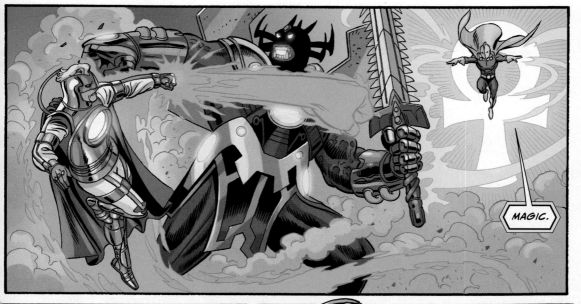

MAGIC.

WHAT TOOK YOU SO LONG?

WAITING FOR THE RIGHT MOMENT FOR A DRAMATIC ENTRANCE.

AND TO WORK UP THE PROPER ENCHANTMENTS.

KERCHAKASHHH

FOR ALL THE GOOD THEY DID.

ALAN--

I HAVE A PLAN.

"THIS WASN'T YOUR FAULT."

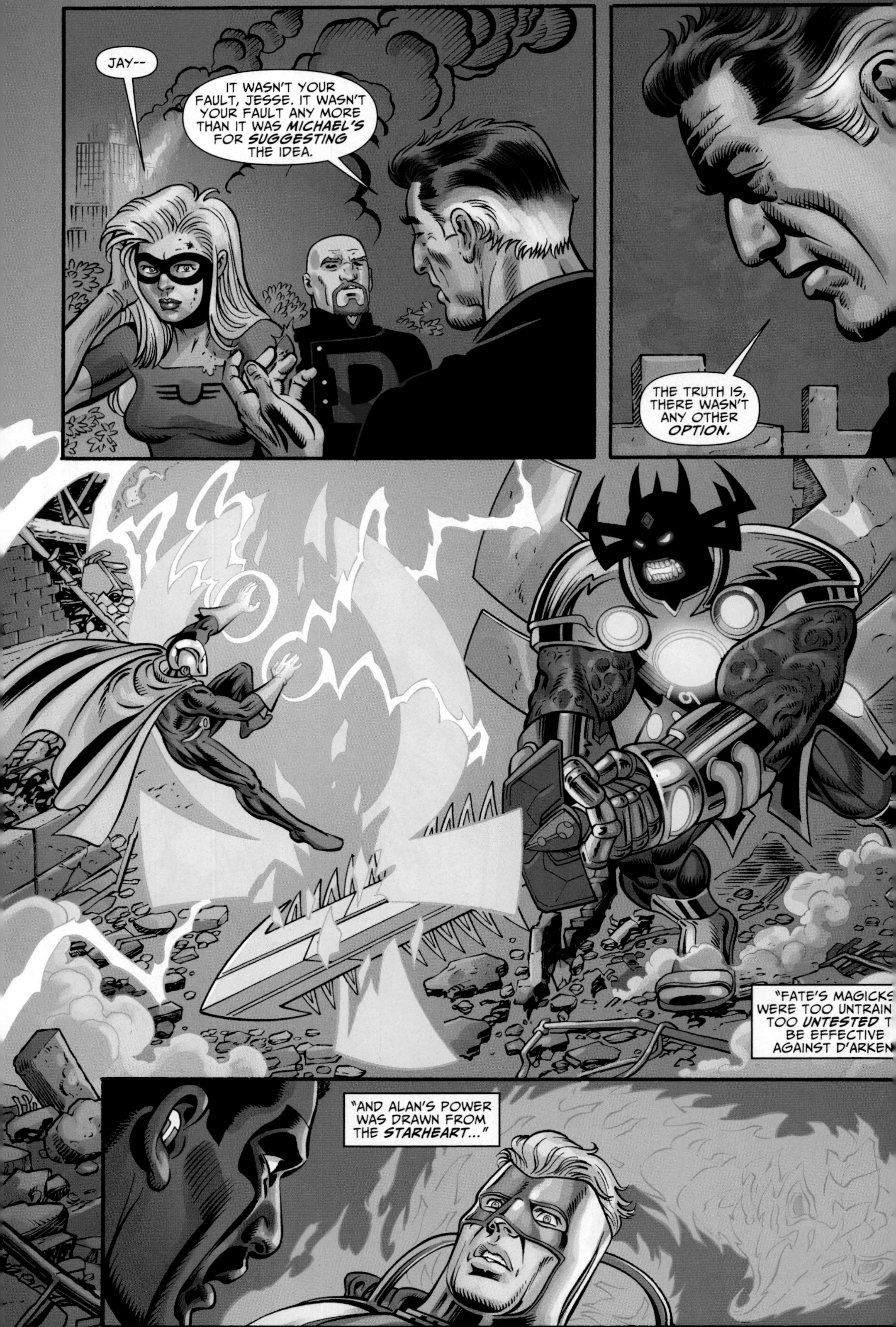

JAY--
IT WASN'T YOUR FAULT, JESSE. IT WASN'T YOUR FAULT ANY MORE THAN IT WAS MICHAEL'S FOR SUGGESTING THE IDEA.
THE TRUTH IS, THERE WASN'T ANY OTHER OPTION.
"FATE'S MAGICKS WERE TOO UNTRAIN TOO UNTESTED T BE EFFECTIVE AGAINST D'ARKEN
"AND ALAN'S POWER WAS DRAWN FROM THE STARHEART..."

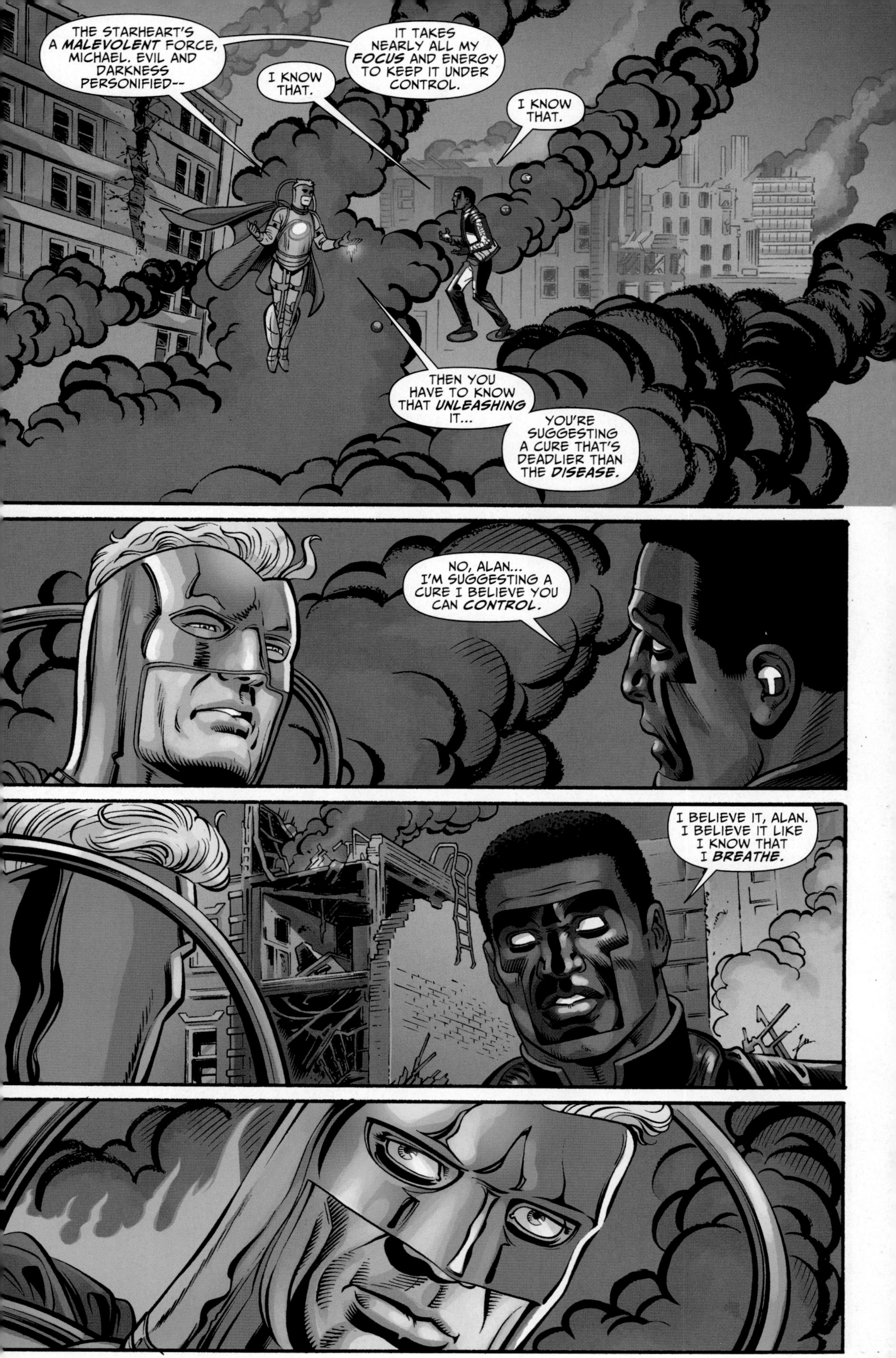

THE STARHEART'S A *MALEVOLENT* FORCE, MICHAEL. EVIL AND DARKNESS PERSONIFIED--
I KNOW THAT.
IT TAKES NEARLY ALL MY *FOCUS* AND ENERGY TO KEEP IT UNDER CONTROL.
I KNOW THAT.
THEN YOU HAVE TO KNOW THAT *UNLEASHING* IT...
YOU'RE SUGGESTING A CURE THAT'S DEADLIER THAN THE *DISEASE.*
NO, ALAN... I'M SUGGESTING A CURE I BELIEVE YOU CAN *CONTROL.*
I BELIEVE IT, ALAN. I BELIEVE IT LIKE I KNOW THAT I *BREATHE.*

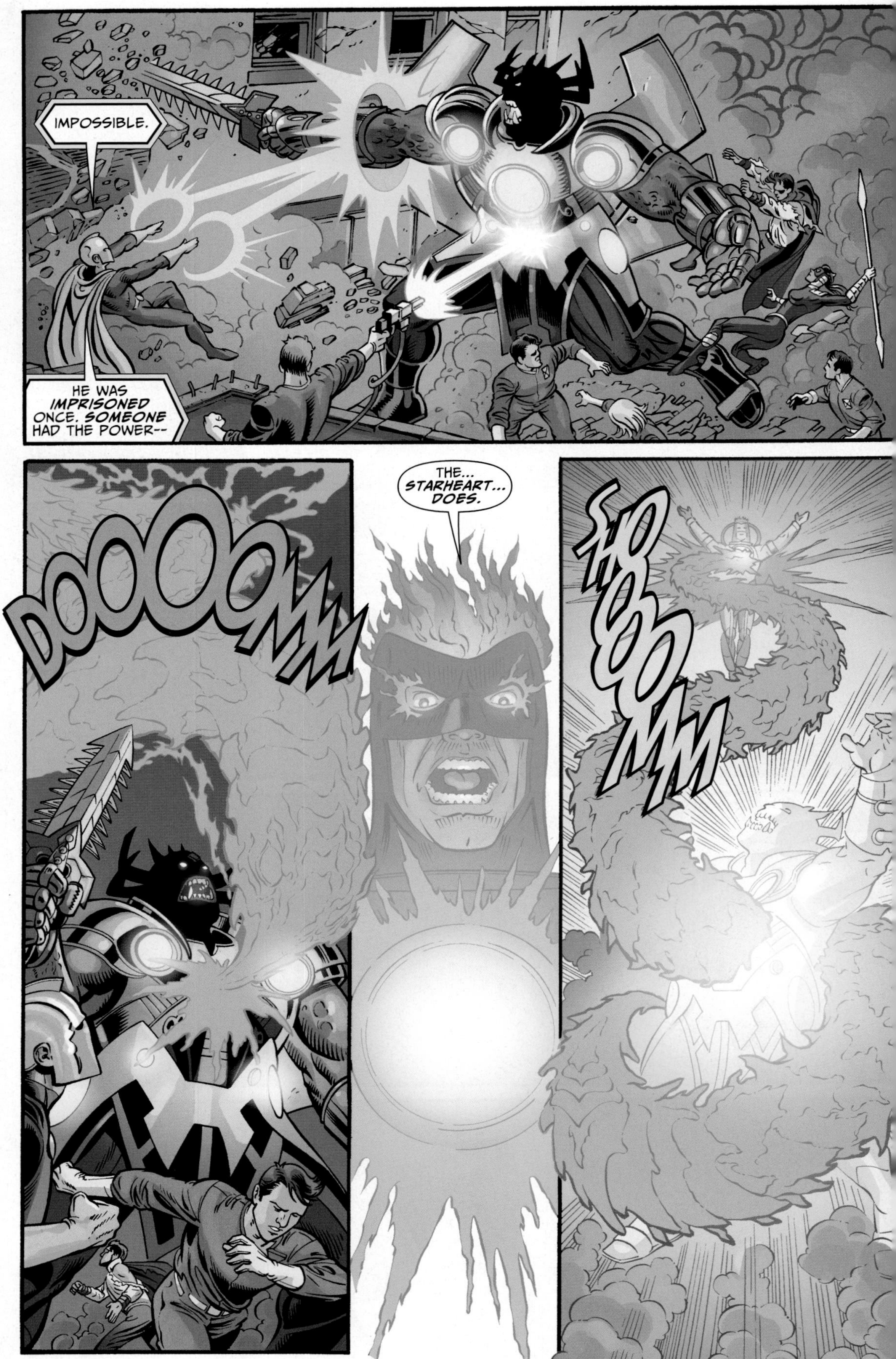
IMPOSSIBLE.
HE WAS IMPRISONED ONCE. SOMEONE HAD THE POWER--
DOOOOMM
THE... STARHEART... DOES.
FHOOOOMM

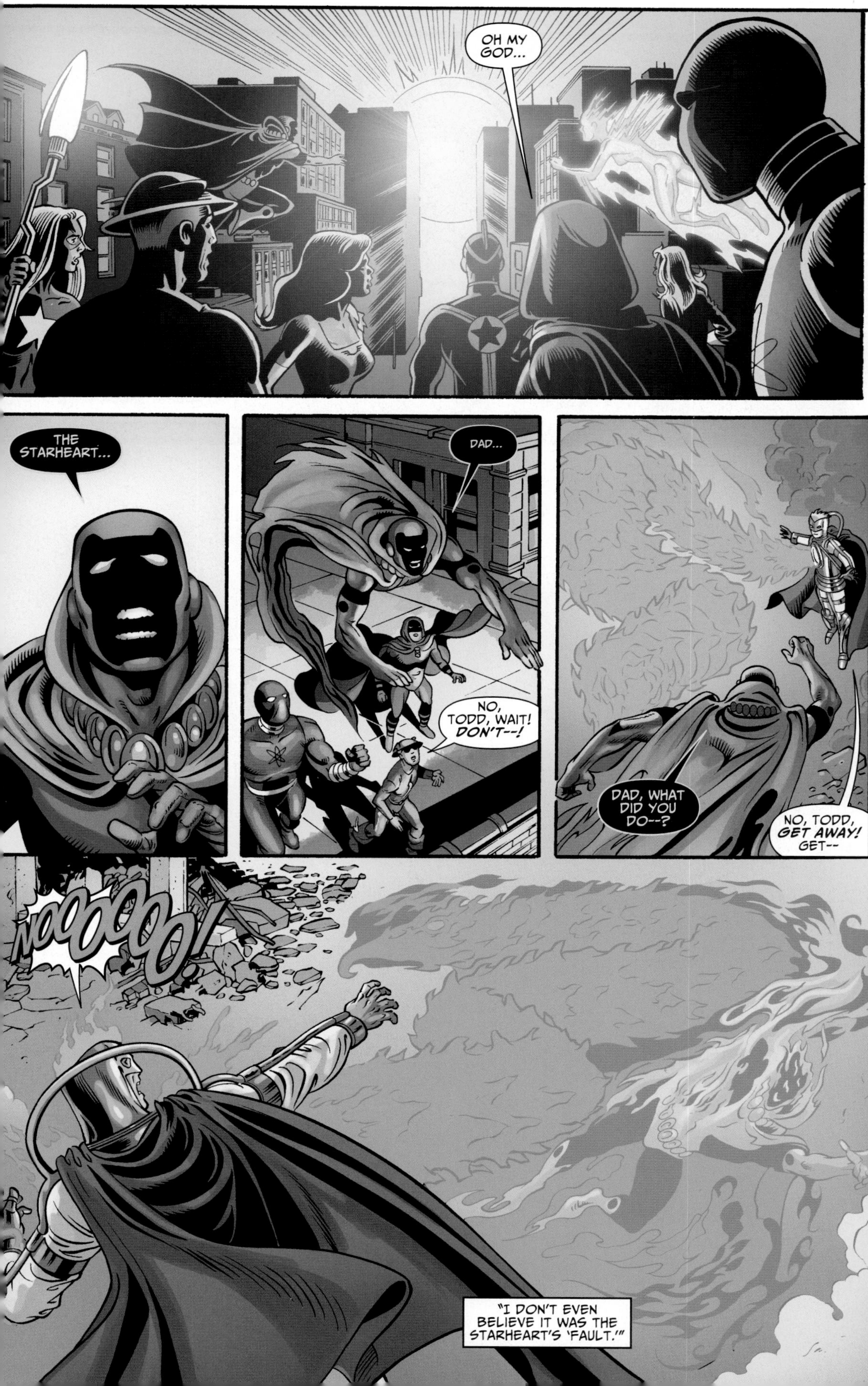
OH MY GOD...
THE STARHEART...
DAD...
NO, TODD, WAIT! DON'T--!
DAD, WHAT DID YOU DO--?
NO, TODD, GET AWAY! GET--
NOOOOOO!
"I DON'T EVEN BELIEVE IT WAS THE STARHEART'S 'FAULT.'"

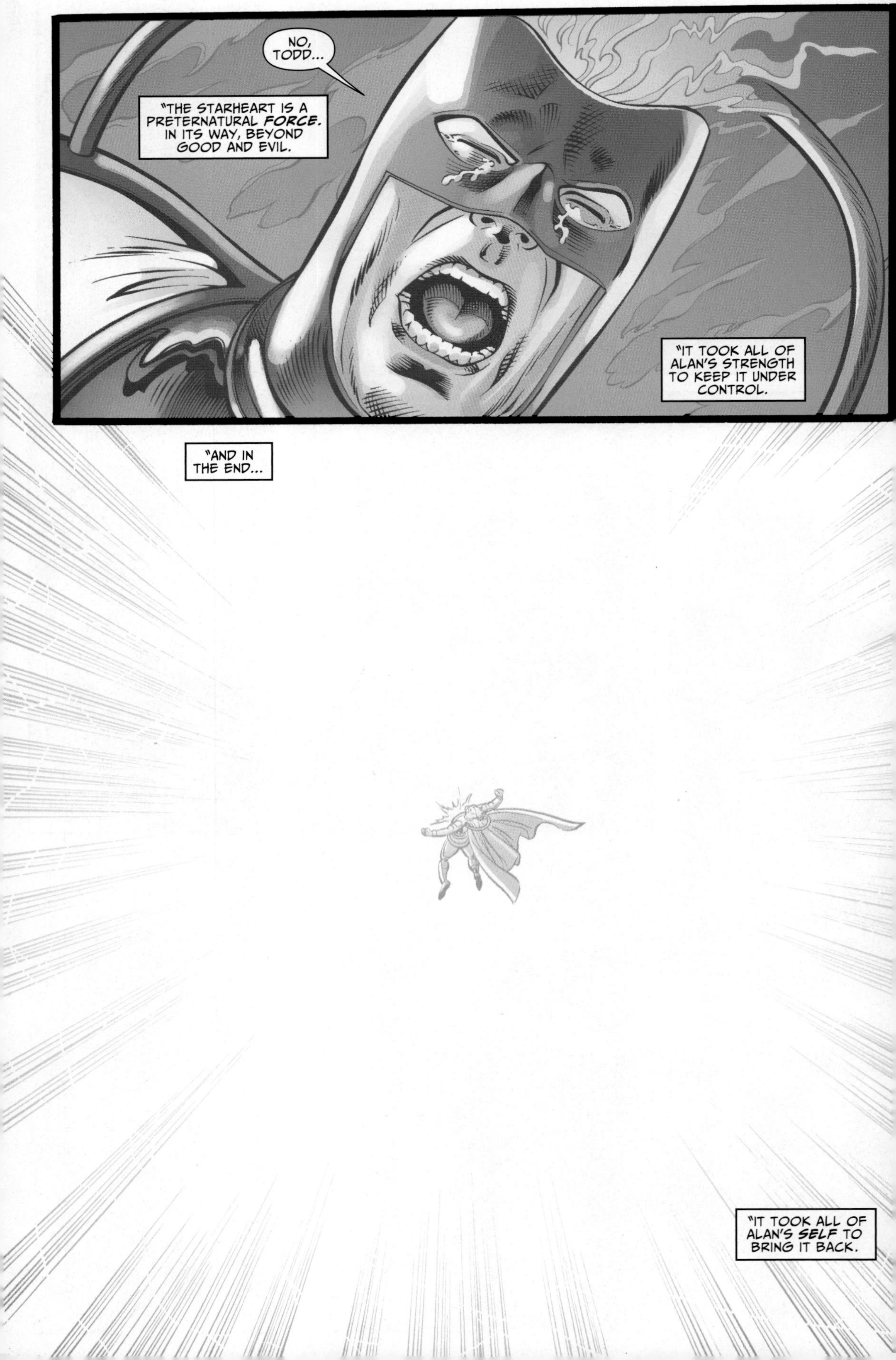
NO, TODD...
"THE STARHEART IS A PRETERNATURAL *FORCE.* IN ITS WAY, BEYOND GOOD AND EVIL.
"IT TOOK ALL OF ALAN'S STRENGTH TO KEEP IT UNDER CONTROL.
"AND IN THE END...
"IT TOOK ALL OF ALAN'S *SELF* TO BRING IT BACK.

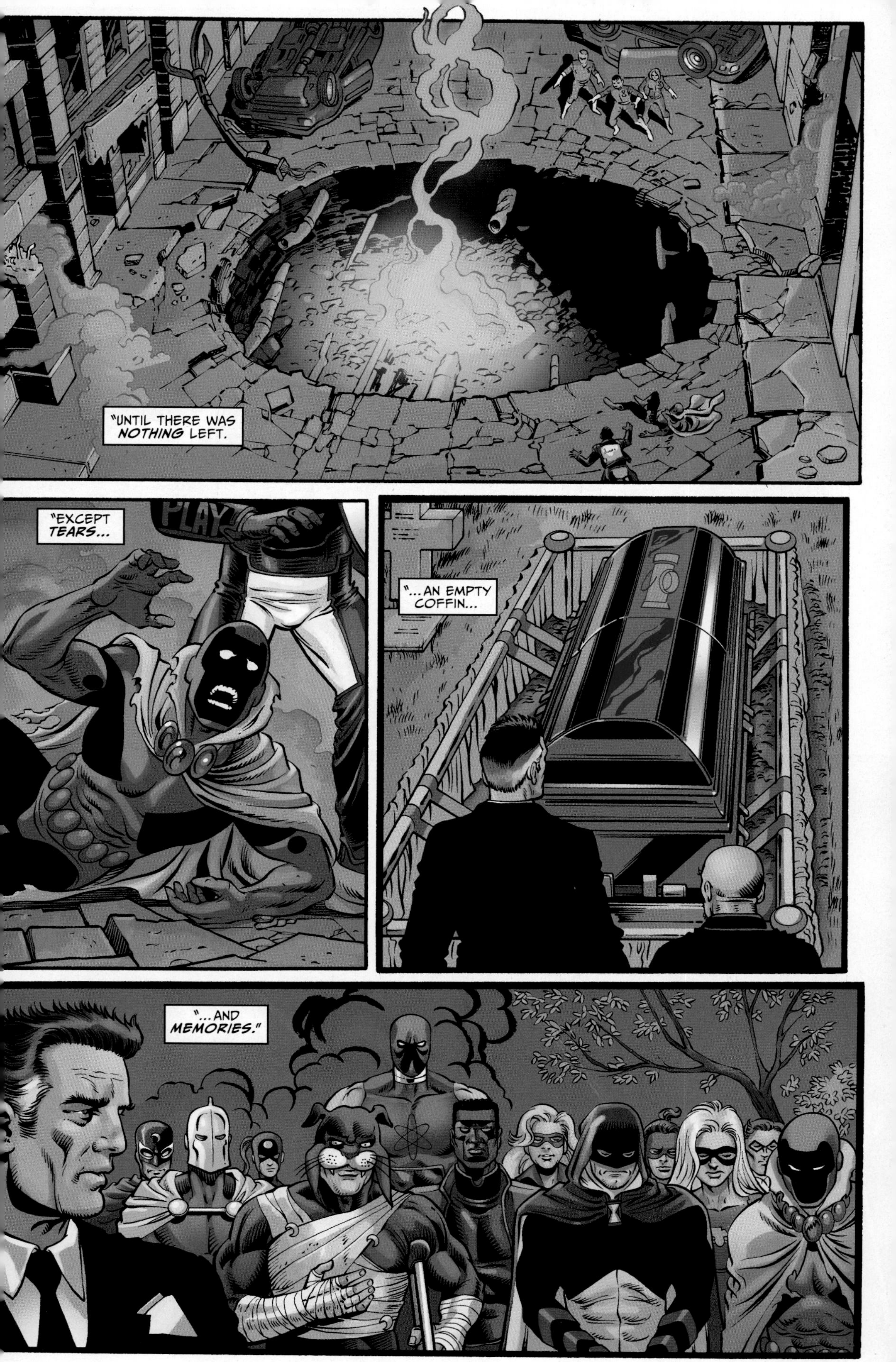
"UNTIL THERE WAS NOTHING LEFT.
PLAY
"EXCEPT TEARS...
"...AN EMPTY COFFIN...
"...AND MEMORIES."

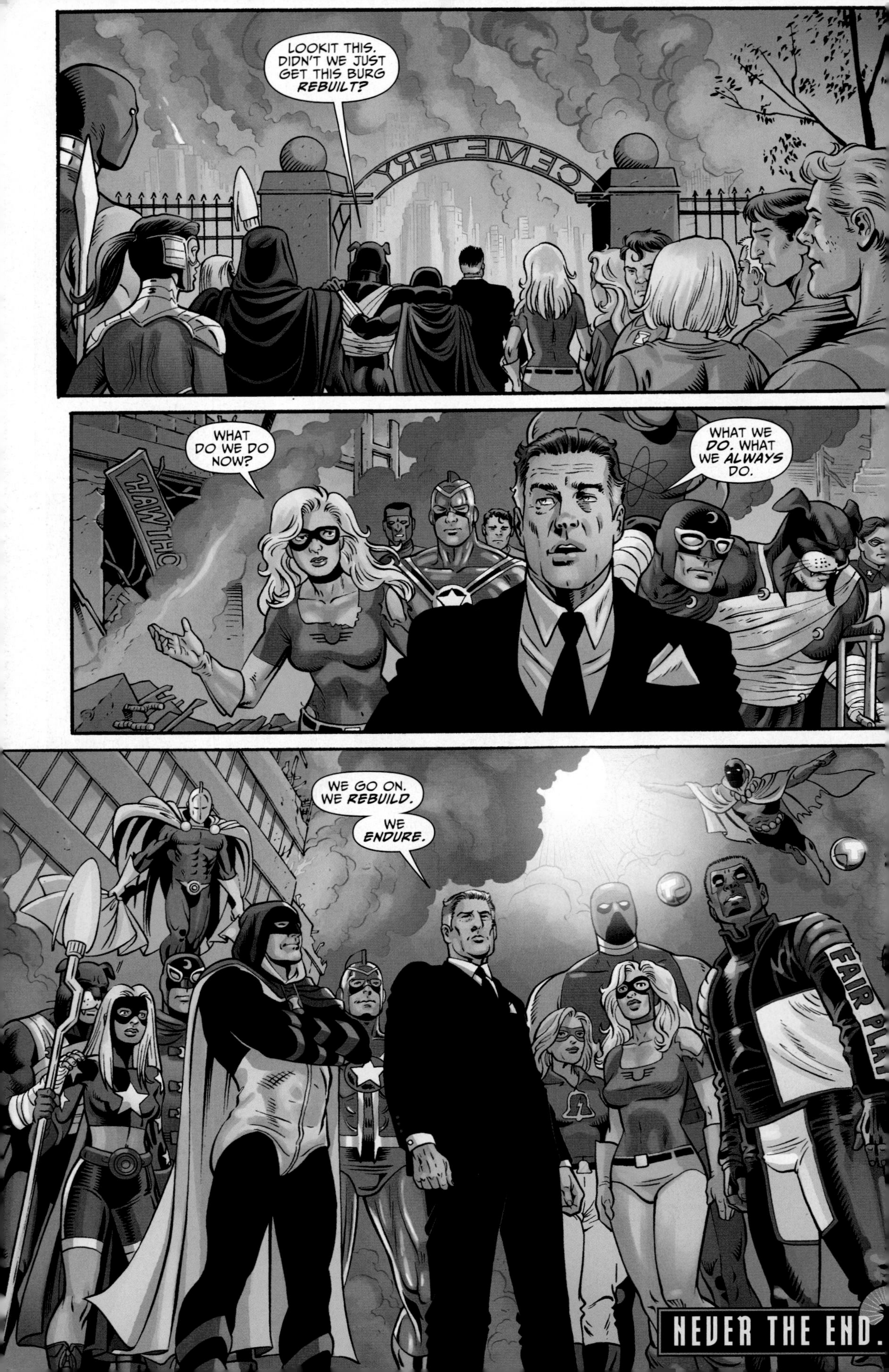
LOOKIT THIS. DIDN'T WE JUST GET THIS BURG REBUILT?
CEMETERY
WHAT DO WE DO NOW?
WHAT WE DO. WHAT WE ALWAYS DO.
HAWTHC
WE GO ON. WE REBUILD.
WE ENDURE.
FAIR PLAY
NEVER THE END.

Justice Society of America #50 Variant cover by DARWYN COOKE

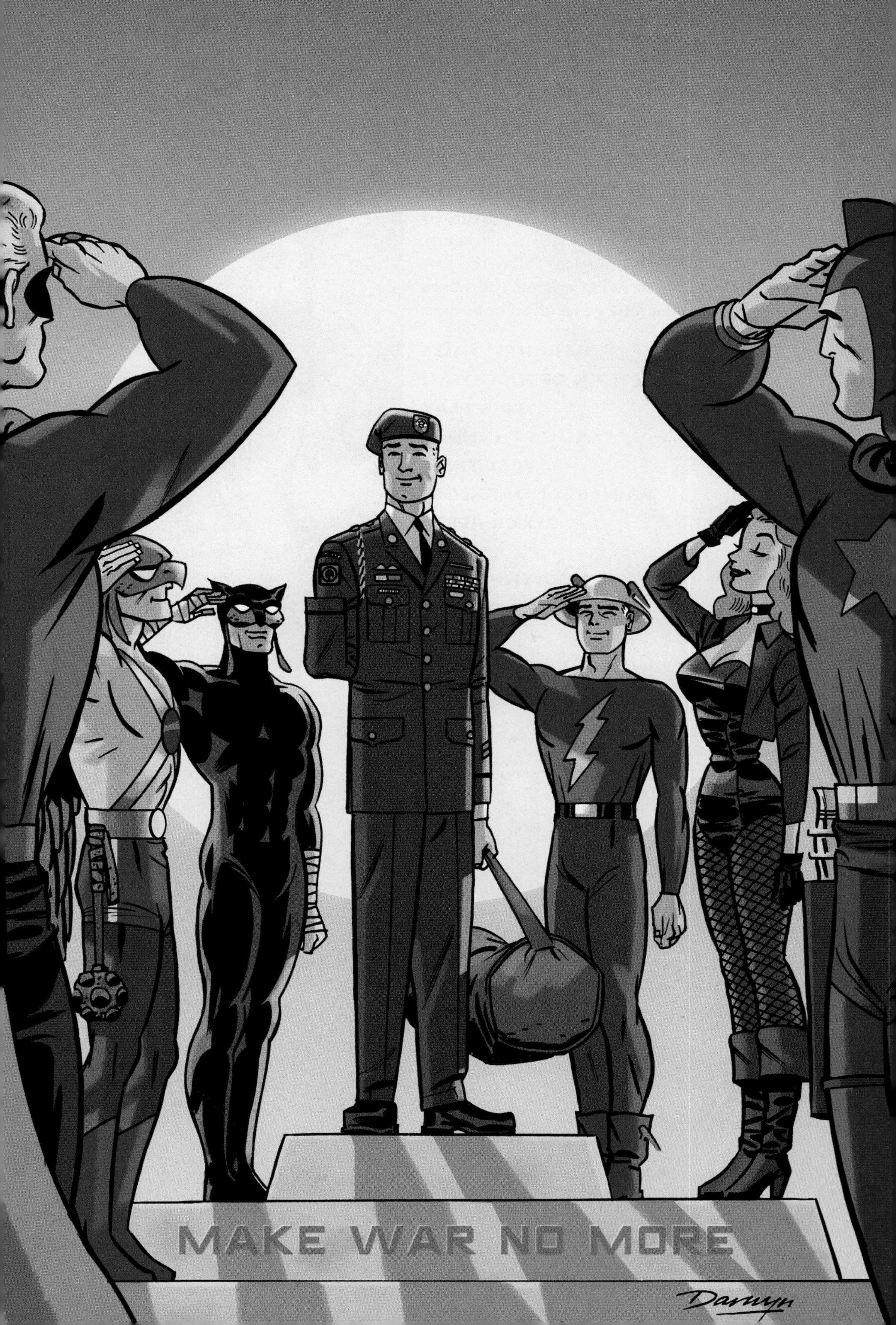
MAKE WAR NO MORE
Darwyn

DC
JSA
GEOFF JOHNS
BLACK VENGEANCE
DON KRAMER · KEITH CHAMPAGNE

JSA
THE RETURN OF HAWKMAN

JSA
BLACK REIGN
GEOFF JOHNS · RAGS MORALES
DON KRAMER · MICHAEL BAIR
KEITH CHAMPAGNE

JSA
GEOFF JOHNS
MIXED SIGNALS
KEITH CHAMPAGNE · DON KRAMER

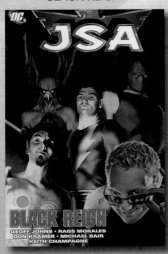

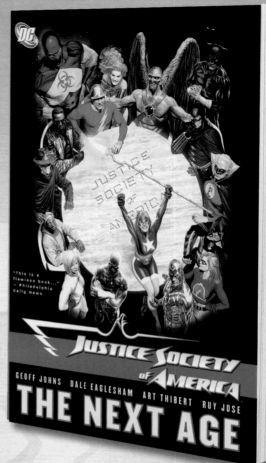
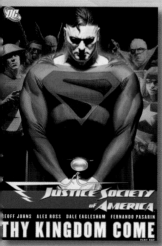

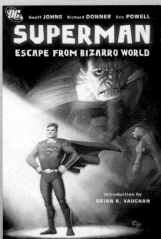